Faulkner:
An Annotated Checklist of Recent Criticism

Faulkner:

An Annotated Checklist of Recent Criticism

John Earl Bassett

The Kent State University Press

The Serif Series: Number 42
Bibliographies and Checklists

Dean H. Keller, General Editor
Kent State University

Library of Congress Cataloging in Publication Data

Bassett, John Earl, 1942–
    Faulkner, an annotated checklist of recent criticism.

    (The Serif series ; no. 42)
    Bibliography: p.
    Includes index.
    1. Faulkner, William 1897–1962—Bibliography.
I. Title. II. Series.
Z8288.B38 1983   [PS3511.A86]   016.813'52   83-11277
ISBN 0-87338-291-9

For

Laura and Gregory

Contents

Contents

Preface

More than a decade has elapsed since my first attempt to organize and annotate the scholarship and criticism on William Faulkner. During that period two other similar tools for Faulkner scholars, one compiled by Thomas McHaney and another by Beatrice Ricks, have also appeared. Commentary on Faulkner, however, proliferates faster than that on any other American novelist—each year a half dozen books, two dozen dissertations, a hundred or more articles. The publication of Joseph Blotner's biography in 1974, and subsequently Faulkner's letters and previously unprinted manuscripts, has raised new questions for scholars. The controversies in critical theory of the past decade have resulted in a number of books and articles using Faulkner's fiction as an example of modernism or of particular thematic patterns or technical devices. Such discussions are not always itemized in checklists on Faulkner. In any case it seems that the sheer quantity of criticism on Faulkner calls for a work complementary to the now somewhat dated *William Faulkner: An Annotated Checklist of Criticism* (New York: David Lewis, 1972). In this book, therefore, I have sought to make a reasonably comprehensive compilation of criticism and scholarship on Faulkner in English from about 1971 through 1982.

It has been compiled from a variety of sources—the periodic checklists provided by *PMLA*, *American Literature*, *Mississippi Quarterly*, and other journals; indexes to newspapers, magazines, and dissertations; earlier checklists on Faulkner, including the book-length ones by McHaney and Ricks; a personal review of books and general critical articles likely to have some discussion of Faulkner; and the miscellaneous tips and leads one depends on when doing such a project. Unlike the earlier volume, this one includes few journalistic reviews of Faulkner's works. One of the purposes of that checklist was to allow for a study of Faulkner's critical reception as his reputation grew. This checklist, however, covers a time period during all of which Faulkner has been considered a major writer. Consequently many references to Faulkner that might have had historical significance had they appeared in 1935 are simply perfunctory and predictable in discussions of modern fiction in 1975. They have generally been omitted. Similarly the many textbook and anthology introductions on Faulkner almost invariably do not warrant inclusion. At the same time I have preferred to err on the side of inclusiveness; comments on Faulkner, even if brief, by contemporary writers are included, as are a number of general critical articles with only a paragraph or two on Faulkner.

Most entries carry annotations. When the content of an article, particularly a short article, is clear from the title, however, there is no annotation. Annotations to collections of criticism list the code numbers of the articles included. The organization, coding, indexing, and cross-references remain similar to those in the first volume. There are five basic sections: books on Faulkner; studies of individual novels; studies of stories, poetry, and miscellaneous writings; more general critical, biographical, and bibliographical articles; and other materials—including brief comments on Faulkner in books and articles, reviews about Faulkner, and dissertations. At the end are a list of entries received too late for inclusion in the text, a checklist of criticism in other languages, a list of errors in the first volume, and an index of critics. Within each category items are listed chronologically, although books on Faulkner (A) and dissertations (LL, MM) are alphabetized within each year, and reviews of *Uncollected Stories of William Faulkner* (W) are alphabetized. The criticism in other languages is also alphabetized within each year.

No system of cross-reference can be complete, and indeed most of the books and the general articles on theme or technique cover several novels. There is a separate entry, however, for a book under each novel to which it devotes an entire chapter or section; and a cross-reference under "Further commentary" is added when a major part of an item is on a novel or story other than that under which the entry appears. There are no cross-references to Joseph Blotner's important biography or his edition of Faulkner's letters, or to David Minter's critical biography. All three have information on nearly all of Faulkner's works, but scattered throughout their pages. There are no cross-references to dissertations, but the volume and page number of the abstract in *Dissertation Abstracts International* are noted.

Among reviews of books about Faulkner, only those in scholarly and critical journals and a few substantial magazine and newspaper reviews are included. The list of articles in other languages does not pretend to be comprehensive. It is compiled from standard sources, and is included only to increase the usefulness of this checklist. I have chosen 1966, rather arbitrarily, as the cutoff date for that list; but earlier items in other languages are tabulated in other checklists (see section GG). The basic coding system remains the same as that used in the first volume. In each part the numbering begins with "1," but the subscript "2" has been added to distinguish entries from those in the earlier list ($A1_2$, $B1_2$). The categories "DD" and "FF," used in the first volume to indicate interviews with

Faulkner (DD) and obituaries and articles on Faulkner's death (FF), are omitted from this list.

I am grateful to George Masterton of the Wayne State University Library for his continual assistance and encouragement. James Hinkle, Joseph Blotner, James B. Meriwether, and William Boozer helpfully forwarded several additions and corrections. I wish to thank Linda W. Wagner for originally suggesting this updating of the Faulkner checklist. The English Department at Wayne State University provided support for completing the project, and Margaret Maday, Sue Coppa, and Deborah Currie helped in preparing the manuscript.

I. Books on Faulkner

A1₂   Peavy, Charles D. *Go Slow Now: Faulkner and the Race Question.* Eugene: Univ. of Oregon Books, 1971.

> Introduction by Patrick G. Hogan, Jr. Surveys Faulkner's fictional and nonfictional statements on this topic under such rubrics as slavery, miscegenation, racism, desegregation, the Howe interview, and states' rights.

A2₂   Barth, J. Robert, ed. *Religious Perspectives in Faulkner's Fiction: Yoknapatawpha and Beyond.* Notre Dame: Univ. of Notre Dame Press, 1972.

> Collection of articles by Barth (AA178), Douglas and Daniel (AA116), Brooks (AA161), Hunt (from A28), Wilder (AA123), Rule (F6₂), Waggoner (from A65), Perluck (N86), and King (R210). For this collection Barth writes an introduction, an epilogue, and commentary on each article.

A3₂   Bassett, John. *William Faulkner: An Annotated Checklist of Criticism.* New York: David Lewis, 1972.

> A fairly comprehensive list of reviews and criticism in English through 1970.

A4₂   Bedell, George C. *Kierkegaard and Faulkner: Modalities of Existence.* Baton Rouge: Louisiana State Univ. Press, 1972.

> A book about religion, literature, and the crisis of modernity that juxtaposes Kierkegaard's existential ideas—particularly the model of aesthetic, ethical, and religious modalities of existence—with Faulkner's fictional situations and themes.

A5₂   Early, James. *The Making of* Go Down, Moses: *William Faulkner's Creative Imagination at Work.* Dallas: Southern Methodist Univ. Press, 1972.

> Studies the genesis of the novel out of earlier typescripts and magazine stories.

A6₂   Langford, Gerald. *Faulkner's Revision of* Sanctuary: *A Collation of the Unrevised Galleys and the Published Book.* Austin: Univ. of Texas Press, 1972.

A7₂   Page, Sally R. *Faulkner's Women: Characterization and Meaning.* Deland, Fla.: Everett/Edwards, 1972.

> Introduction by Cleanth Brooks. Surveys the female characters, emphasizing their individuality, and denying that they are stereotypes. Describes a pattern of a life-nourishing female principle in opposition to a life-destroying male principle, and argues that selfless maternal love is presented as an ideal.

A8₂   Bleikasten, André. *Faulkner's* As I Lay Dying. Trans. Roger
       Little with the collaboration of the author. Bloomington:
       Indiana Univ. Press, 1973.

       Introduction by Michel Gresset. Revised edition of study published in
       French in 1970. A close reading of the text, including its stages of
       composition, and an analysis of both thematic and formal elements.
       Chapters cover genesis and sources, language and style, technique,
       characters, setting, themes, and critical reception.

A9₂   Boecker, Eberhard. *William Faulkner's Later Novels in
       German: A Study in the Theory and Practice of Translation.*
       Tübingen: Niemeyer, 1973.

A10₂   Collins, R. G., and Kenneth McRobbie, eds. *The Novels of
       William Faulkner.* Winnipeg: Univ. of Manitoba Press, 1973.

       Articles in the Fall 1973 issue of *Mosaic*, by Millgate (B2₂), Watson (D8₂),
       Longley (E22₂), Gold (F12₂), Brown (G7₂), Collins (H22₂), Brooks (J24₂),
       MacMillan (I2₂), and Norris (U7₂).

A11₂   Hunter, Edwin R. *William Faulkner: Narrative Practice and
       Prose Style.* Washington: Windhover Press, 1973.

       Studies rhetorical and narrative techniques and style.

A12₂   Leary, Lewis. *William Faulkner of Yoknapatawpha County.*
       New York: Crowell, 1973.

       General introduction to Faulkner's life and career.

A13₂   Pitavy, François. *Faulkner's* Light in August. Trans. Gillian E.
       Cook with the collaboration of the author. Bloomington:
       Indiana Univ. Press, 1973.

       Revised edition of a study published in French in 1970. A close reading of
       the novel and the process of its composition, with emphasis on Faulkner's
       development of "a new form—contrapuntal structure." Chapters cover
       structure and technique, characters, the landscape, themes, stylistic
       approaches, and critical reception.

A14₂   Reed, Joseph W., Jr. *Faulkner's Narrative.* New Haven: Yale
       Univ. Press, 1973.

       Studies strategies of narration in Faulkner's novels and stories, voice and
       point of view.

A15₂   Schmitter, Dean Morgan, ed. *William Faulkner.* New York:
       McGraw-Hill, 1973.

       Collection of earlier articles, by Cowley (from AA38), Brooks (from A5),
       Vickery (from A63), Aiken (from CC2), O'Connor (CC27), Warren (from
       A66), Hoffman (from A23), Millgate (from A44), Chase (from AA117),
       Longley (from A37), Thompson (from A59), and Backman (N93), and an
       introduction by Schmitter.

A16$_2$ Wagner, Linda W., ed. *William Faulkner: Four Decades of Criticism*. East Lansing: Michigan State Univ. Press, 1973.

Collection of earlier articles, by Adams (BB61), Garrett (X116), Gidley (BB115), Wheeler (U14), O'Donnell (AA24), Warren (W117), Bowling (AA176), Brooks (AA161), Aiken (CC2), Beck (CC3), Slatoff (CC26), Millgate (CC63), West (X33), Thompson (E52), Watkins (from A67), Kerr (F49), Hirshleifer (H75), Benson (H83), Lind (J111), Beauchamp (K99), Greet (M75), Gold (M83), Tick (N96), Straumann (R205), and Rossky (V205).

A17$_2$ Zyla, W. T., and W. M. Aycock, eds. *William Faulkner: Prevailing Verities and World Literature*. Lubbock: Texas Tech Univ., 1973.

Nine articles on Faulkner's reception in other countries, from Proceedings of the Comparative Literature Symposium. The articles are by P. G. Adams (AA50$_2$), Aytür (AA51$_2$), Brooks (GG14$_2$), Brown (E16$_2$), Cambon (GG15$_2$), Carlock (AA52$_2$), Langford (GG17$_2$), Stewart (AA53$_2$), and Collmer (KK27$_2$).

A18$_2$ Blotner, Joseph. *Faulkner: A Biography*. 2 vols. New York: Random House, 1974.

A thorough and authoritative biography.

A19$_2$ Broughton, Panthea Reid. *William Faulkner: The Abstract and the Actual*. Baton Rouge: Louisiana State Univ. Press, 1974.

Argues that Faulkner believed in an organic relationship between abstractions and experience, that although he emphasized human misuse of abstractions, he was continually concerned with them as "a means to a more complete truth" about experience. Chapters cover topics, not individual novels.

A20$_2$ Dabney, Lewis M. *The Indians of Yoknapatawpha: A Study in Literature and History*. Baton Rouge: Louisiana State Univ. Press, 1974.

Studies the significance and function of Indians in the stories and novels, with commentary on Faulkner's transformation of history, folklore, and personal experience into fiction.

A21$_2$ Meriwether, James B., ed. *A Faulkner Miscellany*. Jackson: Univ. Press of Mississippi, 1974.

The Summer 1973 issue of *Mississippi Quarterly*, with some additions and deletions. The articles are by Polk (X104$_2$, X110$_2$), McHaney (X105$_2$), Butterworth (X108$_2$), Millgate (X109$_2$), Meriwether (BB18$_2$, BB19$_2$, X111$_2$, X112$_2$, E17$_2$, R3$_2$), Samway (O8$_2$), and Gregory (S1$_2$).

A22$_2$ Weisgerber, Jean. *Faulkner and Dostoevsky: Influence and Confluence*. Trans. Dean McWilliams. Athens: Ohio Univ. Press, 1974.

Published in French in 1968. Studies not only influence but also similarities in themes, moral visions, and attitudes toward fiction. Among themes covered are pride and humility, honor, decorum, evil and suffering, and tradition and change. The second half surveys Dostoevskyan elements in specific Faulkner novels.

A23$_2$ Bassett, John, ed. *William Faulkner: The Critical Heritage.* London: Routledge and Kegan Paul, 1975.

Includes representative reviews and critical articles up to the 1950s, and an introduction studying Faulkner's critical reception.

A24$_2$ Fadiman, Regina K. *Faulkner's* Light in August: *A Description and Interpretation of the Revisions.* Charlottesville: Univ. Press of Virginia, 1975.

Detailed study of manuscript and typescript versions, and the process of revision.

A25$_2$ Irwin, John T. *Doubling and Incest / Repetition and Revenge: A Speculative Reading of Faulkner.* Baltimore: Johns Hopkins Univ. Press, 1975.

A psychoanalytic study, influenced by Lacan, structuralism, and Nietzsche, this emphasizes Quentin Compson in *Absalom, Absalom!* and *The Sound and the Fury.* It focuses on patterns of doubling and twinning, and father-son relationships.

A26$_2$ McHaney, Thomas L. *William Faulkner's* The Wild Palms: *A Study.* Jackson: Univ. Press of Mississippi, 1975.

A close reading of the novel section by section, with an examination of the stages of composition. Emphasizes the intricate structure and the method of counterpoint, and explains the purpose of allusions and the significance of sources.

A27$_2$ Petersen, Carl. *Each in Its Ordered Place: A Faulkner Collector's Notebook.* Ann Arbor: Ardis, 1975.

Catalogue of a large personal collection. Also see GG55$_2$.

A28$_2$ Wagner, Linda W. *Hemingway and Faulkner: Inventors / Masters.* Metuchen, N.J.: Scarecrow Press, 1975.

A study, at times comparative, of their experiments in technique and genre and of the works that resulted.

A29$_2$ Beck, Warren. *Faulkner: Essays.* Madison: Univ. of Wisconsin Press, 1976.

Five earlier articles plus seven new ones: a 250-page close reading of themes and methods in *Go Down, Moses*; an essay on *Requiem for a Nun*; "Faulkner after 1940," which analyzes the hostility and impercipience of early Faulkner critics and changes in both his fiction and reception after 1940; "Fictional Entities and the Artist's Oeuvre," which speculates on ways to see interrelations among Faulkner's works; "Good and Evil," covering his treatment of ethical issues; "Realist and Regionalist," a long essay on Faulkner as humanist fusing regional materials and realism; and "Short Stories into Novels," which studies the amalgamation of earlier stories into novels and the publication of sections of novels as stories.

A30₂ Bleikasten, André. *The Most Splendid Failure: Faulkner's* The Sound and the Fury. Bloomington: Indiana Univ. Press, 1976.

A close reading of the novel with a chapter on Faulkner's early development; one on the genesis of the book, "Caddy, or the Quest for Eurydice"; one on each section of the novel emphasizing both narrative techniques and psychological patterns; and one on time in the novel, mostly in relation to Quentin.

A31₂ Brown, Calvin S. *A Glossary of Faulkner's South.* New Haven: Yale Univ. Press, 1976.

Definition of terms and identification of places.

A32₂ Guerard, Albert J. *The Triumph of the Novel: Dickens, Dostoevsky, Faulkner.* New York: Oxford Univ. Press, 1976.

Emphasizes innovations in method; includes chapters on *Sanctuary* and *Absalom, Absalom!*

A33₂ Harrington, Evans, and Ann J. Abadie, eds. *Faulkner and Yoknapatawpha 1974: Selections.* University: Dept. of English, Univ. of Mississippi, 1976.

Papers from a 1974 conference, with an introduction by Harrington. The papers are by Sansing (BB26₂), Kerr (AA87₂), Blotner (AA88₂), Cowley (E46₂, N43₂), Flynn (AA89₂), Cowley et al. (AA90₂), and Blotner et al. (AA91₂, AA92₂).

A34₂ Jehlen, Myra. *Class and Character in Faulkner's South.* New York: Columbia Univ. Press, 1976.

Arguing that a sense of conflict between planter and yeoman classes is central in the novels, this book illustrates restrictions that Faulkner's racial and class assumptions impose on his imagination.

A35₂ Levins, Lynn Gartrell. *Faulkner's Heroic Design: The Yoknapatawpha Novels.* Athens: Univ. of Georgia Press, 1976.

Studies Faulkner's strategy of enlarging meaning of events by mythic allusion and by the context of Greek tragedy or chivalric romance or epic.

A36₂ McHaney, Thomas L. *William Faulkner: A Reference Guide.* Boston: G. K. Hall, 1976.

A chronologically arranged and annotated checklist of criticism through 1973.

A37₂ Wilde, Meta Carpenter, and Orin Borsten. *A Loving Gentleman: The Love Story of William Faulkner and Meta Carpenter.* New York: Simon & Schuster, 1976.

An autobiographical account of Meta Carpenter's intimate relationship with Faulkner in Hollywood.

A38$_2$ Wolfe, George H., ed. *Faulkner: Fifty Years After* The Marble Faun. University: Univ. of Alabama Press, 1976.

Papers from a 1974 Faulkner conference, by Blotner (AA93$_2$), Adams (AA94$_2$), Rubin (AA96$_2$), Simpson (AA99$_2$), Page (AA100$_2$), Watkins (AA101$_2$), Brooks (AA102$_2$), and Meriwether (X120$_2$).

A39$_2$ Blotner, Joseph, ed. *Selected Letters of William Faulkner.* New York: Random House, 1977.

A40$_2$ Capps, Jack L., ed. As I Lay Dying: *A Concordance to the Novel.* Ann Arbor: UMI, 1977.

Introduction by Cleanth Brooks.

A41$_2$ Creighton, Joanne V. *William Faulkner's Craft of Revision:* The Snopes Trilogy, The Unvanquished, *and* Go Down, Moses. Detroit: Wayne State Univ. Press, 1977.

Compares the magazine and the book versions, and assesses the significance of revisions.

A42$_2$ Franklin, Malcolm. *Bitterweeds: Life with William Faulkner at Rowan Oak.* Irving, Tex.: The Society for the Study of Traditional Culture, 1977.

A family memoir by Faulkner's stepson.

A43$_2$ Harrington, Evans, and Ann J. Abadie, eds. *The South and Faulkner's Yoknapatawpha: The Actual and the Apocryphal.* Jackson: Univ. Press of Mississippi, 1977.

Papers from a 1976 conference, with an introduction by Harrington. The papers are by Aaron (KK36$_2$), Millgate (AA117$_2$, AA126$_2$), S. Foote (AA118$_2$, AA125$_2$), D. Turner (AA119$_2$), Pilkington (AA122$_2$), Wagner (AA123$_2$), Rubin (J62$_2$), S. Foote et al. (AA120$_2$), and Wagner et al. (AA124$_2$).

A44$_2$ Kawin, Bruce F. *Faulkner and Film.* New York: Ungar, 1977.

Surveys adaptations of Faulkner's fiction to film, plus Faulkner's work in Hollywood.

A45$_2$ Schoenberg, Estella. *Old Tales and Talking: Quentin Compson in William Faulkner's* Absalom, Absalom! *and Related Works.* Jackson: Univ. Press of Mississippi, 1977.

Studies the genesis of Quentin as both a narrator and a protagonist in *Absalom, Absalom!*, often in relation to short stories in which he is a character and other stories similar to or anticipating situations in that novel.

A46$_2$ Skei, Hans H. *Bold and Tragical and Austere: William Faulkner's* These 13. Oslo, Norway: Dept. of Literature, Univ. of Oslo, 1977.

Offers critical readings and discusses the genesis of the stories and their arrangement in the book.

A47$_2$ Williams, David. *Faulkner's Women: The Myth and the Muse.* Montreal and London: McGill-Queen's Univ. Press, 1977.

Discusses the female characters in terms of Jungian archetypes and symbols, for example the "Great Goddess" figure. Argues that the anima instills Faulkner's work with its basic meaning, and that there is a development towards dominance of masculine over feminine in the later novels.

A48$_2$ Brooks, Cleanth. *William Faulkner: Toward Yoknapatawpha and Beyond.* New Haven: Yale Univ. Press, 1978.

Completes his earlier study of Faulkner with close readings of the five novels set outside Yoknapatawpha County, essays on the poetry and early prose, a study of *Flags in the Dust* and early Yoknapatawpha stories, and an article on "Faulkner on Time and History." Also reprints two articles on *Absalom, Absalom!* and one on Faulkner and Yeats.

A49$_2$ Capps, Jack L., ed. Go Down, Moses: *A Concordance to the Novel.* Ann Arbor: UMI, 1978.

Introduction by André Bleikasten.

A50$_2$ Cofield, Jack. *William Faulkner: The Cofield Collection.* Oxford, Miss.: Yoknapatawpha Press, 1978.

Collection of photographs, with an introduction by Carvel Collins.

A51$_2$ Fadiman, Regina K. *Faulkner's* Intruder in the Dust: *Novel Into Film.* Knoxville: Univ. of Tennessee Press, 1978.

Emphasizes script and production decisions, and offers critical readings.

A52$_2$ Harrington, Evans, and Ann J. Abadie, eds. *Faulkner and Yoknapatawpha 1975: Selections.* University: Dept. of English, Univ. of Mississippi, 1978.

Papers from a 1975 conference, with an introduction by Harrington. The papers are by Brooks (AA134$_2$, U15$_2$), Jackson (AA135$_2$, KK46$_2$), Kerr (J68$_2$, AA136$_2$), Godden (F36$_2$), Boozer (GG45$_2$), Collins (F37$_2$, L10$_2$), Duvall et al. (BB39$_2$), Black et al. (BB38$_2$), and Collins et al. (AA137$_2$).

A53$_2$ Harrington, Evans, and Ann J. Abadie, eds. *The Maker and the Myth: Faulkner and Yoknapatawpha.* Jackson: Univ. Press of Mississippi, 1978.

Papers from a 1977 conference, with an introduction by Abadie. The papers are by Brown (AA143$_2$, AA148$_2$), Guerard (AA144$_2$, CC11$_2$), Simpson (AA145$_2$, R11$_2$), Lind (AA146$_2$), and Alexander (AA147$_2$).

A54₂   Kinney, Arthur F. *Faulkner's Narrative Poetics: Style as Vision*. Amherst: Univ. of Massachusetts Press, 1978.

> Sets Faulkner in a modernist tradition of novelists of consciousness and examines their influence on him as well as his alteration of the tradition. Argues that Faulkner's fiction depends on a dynamic reading process in which the reader's "constitutive consciousness" assimilates all perspectives, juxtapositions, and language patterns.

A55₂   Capps, Jack L., ed. Light in August: *A Concordance to the Novel*. Ann Arbor: UMI, 1979.

> Introduction by Joseph Blotner.

A56₂   Capps, Jack L., ed. Requiem for a Nun: *A Concordance to the Novel*. Ann Arbor: UMI, 1979.

> Introduction by Noel Polk.

A57₂   Harrington, Evans, and Ann J. Abadie, eds. *Faulkner, Modernism, and Film: Faulkner and Yoknapatawpha*, 1978. Jackson: Univ. Press of Mississippi, 1979.

> Papers from a 1978 conference, with an introduction by Abadie. The papers are by Cowley (N60₂), Kenner (E79₂, AA173₂), Young (K11₂, J82₂), H. Foote (L12₂, P5₂), Lind (CC20₂, CC21₂), and Kawin (CC19₂, AA172₂).

A58₂   Kartiganer, Donald M. *The Fragile Thread: The Meaning of Form in Faulkner's Novels*. Amherst: Univ. of Massachusetts Press, 1979.

> Emphasizes Faulkner's place in literary modernism, and his use of fragmentation as a technique. Argues that each major novel is an open experiment, with the possibilities and limitations of literary form, and a "process work."

A59₂   Kerr, Elizabeth M. *William Faulkner's Gothic Domain*. Port Washington, N.Y.: Kennikat, 1979.

> Surveys Gothic elements in Faulkner's novels and the importance of the Gothic tradition as one of the major influences on Faulkner.

A60₂   Stonum, Gary Lee. *Faulkner's Career: An Internal Literary History*. Ithaca: Cornell Univ. Press, 1979.

> Traces a pattern of continuing self-criticism and a conscious sense of career, in which Faulkner writes new work out of his sense of his previous work. Seeing the concept of "arrested motion" as one constant paradigm, Stonum outlines four phases in Faulkner's career.

A61₂   Wittenberg, Judith B. *Faulkner: The Transfiguration of Biography*. Lincoln: Univ. of Nebraska Press, 1979.

> A biographical study making some use of psychoanalytic methods, this emphasizes influences of family situations on Faulkner's themes, his work as a redemptive factor, portraits of artist figures, and "love and other destructive forces."

A62$_2$ Bezzerides, A. I. *William Faulkner, a Life on Paper*. Jackson: Univ. Press of Mississippi, 1980.

> Transcript of a 1979 television show, with an introduction by Carvel Collins. Edited by Ann J. Abadie.

A63$_2$ Carey, Glenn O., ed. *Faulkner: The Unappeased Imagination, A Collection of Critical Essays*. Troy, N.Y.: Whitston, 1980.

> Consists mostly of new articles. The articles are by Campbell (BB54$_2$), Backman (F50$_2$), Cushman (L16$_2$), MacMillan (B12$_2$), Moses (S3$_2$), Volpe (X7$_2$), Samway (O13$_2$), Pinsker (E93$_2$), Sharma (AA107$_2$), Rankin (U19$_2$), Milum (AA181$_2$), Herndon (J98$_2$), Stroble (U20$_2$), Howell (AA182$_2$), Porter (CC22$_2$), and Carey (AA84$_2$).

A64$_2$ Fowler, Doreen, and Ann J. Abadie, eds. *Fifty Years of Yoknapatawpha*. Jackson: Univ. Press of Mississippi, 1980.

> Papers from a 1979 conference, with an introduction by Fowler. The papers are by Blotner (BB52$_2$, BB53$_2$), Millgate (AA189$_2$, D39$_2$), Polk (U18$_2$, AA191$_2$), Keiser (D38$_2$), Pilkington (K14$_2$), Watson (AA190$_2$, X99$_2$), and McHaney (AA192$_2$, AA193$_2$).

A65$_2$ Guttenberg, Barnett, ed. *Faulkner Studies 1: An Annual of Research, Criticism, and Reviews*. Miami: Univ. of Miami, 1980.

> A collection of new articles and reviews, by Baker (BB51$_2$), Kerr (G25$_2$), Hagopian (J95$_2$), Hunt (J96$_2$), Komar (F51$_2$), Kinney (X97$_2$), Watson (X98$_2$), Volpe (P6$_2$), Zender (N66$_2$), Polk (Q7$_2$), Lind (AA194$_2$), Strandberg (AA195$_2$), Reed (AA196$_2$), and the reviews numbered HH284$_2$ through HH295$_2$.

A66$_2$ Minter, David. *William Faulkner: His Life and Work*. Baltimore: Johns Hopkins Univ. Press, 1980.

> A critical biography illustrating the impact of Faulkner's personal life on his fiction, this emphasizes initiatory and shaping experiences; Faulkner's obsession with both privacy and carefully patterned personal relationships; and the double purpose of his fiction—deception and expression.

A67$_2$ Polk, Noel, and Kenneth L. Privratsky, eds. The Sound and the Fury: *A Concordance to the Novel*. Ann Arbor: UMI, 1980.

> Introduction by André Bleikasten.

A68$_2$ Powers, Lyall H. *Faulkner's Yoknapatawpha Comedy*. Ann Arbor: Univ. of Michigan Press, 1980.

> Argues that recurrent themes clarify Faulkner's overall comic vision and "optimistic attitude toward mankind": the self-destructive nature of evil, the second chance given man, and the "saving remnant" of humans such as Ratliff and Dilsey who oppose evil.

A69$_2$ Samway, Patrick H., S.J. *Faulkner's* Intruder in the Dust*: A Critical Study of the Typescripts.* Troy, N.Y.: Whitston, 1980.

A70$_2$ Dasher, Thomas E. *William Faulkner's Characters: An Index to the Published and Unpublished Fiction.* New York: Garland, 1981.

    A comprehensive index to characters with page references.

A71$_2$ Fowler, Doreen, and Ann J. Abadie, eds. *"A Cosmos of My Own": Faulkner and Yoknapatawpha.* Jackson: Univ. Press of Mississippi, 1981.

    Papers from a 1980 conference by Hamblin (AA205$_2$), Broughton (CC23$_2$, CC24$_2$), Carothers (V14$_2$, AA209$_2$), Brodsky (GG66$_2$), Douglas (AA206$_2$, AA210$_2$), Nilon (AA207$_2$, AA208$_2$), Pitavy (J105$_2$).

A72$_2$ Jenkins, Lee Clinton. *Faulkner and Black-White Relations: A Psychoanalytical Approach.* New York: Columbia Univ. Press, 1981.

    Focusing on the literary importance of Faulkner's probing exploration of racial themes but also on his limitations in handling black characters, Jenkins argues that the "mind divided against itself is Faulkner's great and recurring theme."

A73$_2$ Pilkington, John. *The Heart of Yoknapatawpha.* Jackson: Univ. Press of Mississippi, 1981.

    Critical interpretations of nine Faulkner novels with close explications of troublesome passages. Relates his themes to those of other writers of the 1920s and 1930s, and argues that the two major human faults Faulkner criticizes are man's "insatiable greed" and his failure to recognize the humanity of others.

A74$_2$ Polk, Noel. *Faulkner's* Requiem for a Nun*: A Critical Study.* Bloomington: Indiana Univ. Press, 1981.

    A comprehensive critical analysis, this emphasizes the centrality of Temple Drake to the novel and criticizes those studies identifying Faulkner's position too closely with Gavin Stevens and Nancy.

A75$_2$ Polk, Noel, and Kenneth Privratsky, eds. A Fable*: A Concordance to the Novel.* Ann Arbor: UMI, 1981.

    Introduction by Keen Butterworth.

A76$_2$ Ricks, Beatrice. *William Faulkner: A Bibliography of Secondary Works.* Metuchen, N.J.: Scarecrow, 1981.

    An extensive checklist of Faulkner scholarship through 1978, with many annotations.

A77$_2$ Strandberg, Victor H. *A Faulkner Overview: Six Perspectives.* Port Washington, N.Y.: Kennikat, 1981.

Discusses Faulkner's fiction "within successive frames of thought provided by various sources, influences, and affinities": biblical references and inversions, musical techniques, "biopsychology" ("Liebestod: The Lessons of Eros"), religion, Freudian and Marxist thought, and the ideas of William James.

A78₂   Turner, Dixie M. *A Jungian Psychoanalytic Interpretation of William Faulkner's* As I Lay Dying. Washington: University Press of America, 1981.

A monograph-length Jungian explication of the novel.

II. Studies of Individual Novels

B. *Soldiers' Pay*

B1$_2$ Miller, Wayne C. *An Armed America: Its Face in Fiction.*
New York: New York Univ. Press, 1970, pp. 119–22.

> The book surveys the portrayal in American fiction of characters in the
> armed forces.

B2$_2$ Millgate, Michael. "Starting Out in the Twenties: Reflections
on *Soldiers' Pay*." *Mosaic*, 7, No. 1 (Fall 1973), 1–14.

> Outlines the book's new techniques, and its combination of a common
> postwar theme with the abstract formalism of late romantic prose.

B3$_2$ Wallis, Donald des G. "*Soldiers' Pay*: Faulkner's First Myth."
*Bulletin of the West Virginia Association of College English
Teachers*, 1, No. 2 (Fall 1974), 15–21.

B4$_2$ Dalgarno, Emily. "*Soldiers' Pay* and Virginia Woolf."
Mississippi Quarterly, 29 (Summer 1976), 339–46.

> Influence of *Jacob's Room.*

B5$_2$ Mellard, James M. "*Soldiers' Pay* and the Growth of
Faulkner's Comedy." In *American Humor: Essays Presented to
John C. Gerber.* Ed. O. M. Brack, Jr. Scottsdale, Ariz.: Arete,
1977, pp. 99–117.

> The comic characters, incidents, devices, and structure anticipate more
> mature comedy in later fiction.

B6$_2$ Castille, Philip. "Women and Myth in Faulkner's First Novel."
Tulane Studies in English, 23 (1978), 175–86.

> The mythic method, along with ironic parallels, highlights a world of
> sexual frustration amid natural fertility.

—   Brooks, Cleanth. *William Faulkner* (A48$_2$; 1978), pp. 67–99,
366–74.

> Includes material in B44.

B7$_2$ Bosha, Francis J. "Faulkner's Early Editors: On Edith Brown,
Grace Hudson, and *Soldiers' Pay*." *American Notes and
Queries*, 17 (April 1979), 125–26.

> On the editors of his first novel.

—   Wittenberg, Judith B. *Faulkner* (A61$_2$; 1979), pp. 42–50.

B8$_2$ Dalgarno, Emily K. "Faulkner and Gibbon: A Note on
Soldiers' Pay." *Notes on Mississippi Writers*, 12 (Summer
1979), 36–39.

References to Gibbon's *History* in both the text and the title contribute to Faulkner's portrayal of a "postwar society blind to the causes of its corruption and decline."

B9$_2$ Folks, Jeffrey J. "A Source for the Title of *Soldiers' Pay*." *Notes on Modern American Literature*, 5 (Winter 1980), 7.
The title may come from debates over war bonuses for veterans.

B10$_2$ Yonce, Margaret J. "The Composition of *Soldiers' Pay*." *Mississippi Quarterly*, 33 (Summer 1980), 291–326.
A thorough study of the genesis of the novel and Faulkner's revisions.

B11$_2$ McHaney, Thomas L. "The Modernism of *Soldiers' Pay*." *William Faulkner: Materials, Studies, and Criticism*, 3, No. 1 (July 1980), 16–30.
Techniques and attitudes of modernism.

B12$_2$ MacMillan, Duane J. "'Carry on, Cadet': Mores and Morality in *Soldiers' Pay*." In A63$_2$ (1980), pp. 39–57.
Emphasizes Faulkner's examination of traditional social and moral conventions in a postwar context.

Further commentary: A7$_2$ (Page), A12$_2$ (Leary), A22$_2$ (Weisgerber), A47$_2$ (Williams), A54$_2$ (Kinney), A60$_2$ (Stonum), AA40$_2$ (Putzel), AA106$_2$ (Cowley), JJ22$_2$ (Mitgang).

C. *Mosquitoes*

C1$_2$ Carey, Glenn O. "Faulkner and *Mosquitoes*: Writing Himself and His Age." *Research Studies* [Washington State Univ.], 39 (December 1971), 271–83.
Relates the novel to attitudes of the 1920s and also to Faulkner's statements in the 1950s.

C2$_2$ Arnold, Edwin T. "Freedom and Stasis in Faulkner's *Mosquitoes*." *Mississippi Quarterly*, 28 (Summer 1975), 281–97.
Shows that the theme of freedom/bondage anticipates Faulkner's later theme of motion/stasis.

C3$_2$ Kreiswirth, Martin. "William Faulkner and Siegfried Sassoon: An Allusion in *Mosquitoes*." *Mississippi Quarterly*, 29 (Summer 1976), 433–34.

C4$_2$ Brooks, Cleanth. "Faulkner's *Mosquitoes*." *Georgia Review*, 31 (Spring 1977), 213–34. Included in *William Faulkner* (A48$_2$; 1978), pp. 129–51, 378–80.
Considers romantic influences on the novel, and Faulkner's ideas on art.

C5₂ Arnold, Edwin T. "Faulkner and Huxley: A Note on *Mosquitoes* and *Crome Yellow*." *Mississippi Quarterly*, 30 (Summer 1977), 433–36.

— Wittenberg, Judith B. *Faulkner* (A61₂; 1979), pp. 50–60.
   Considers satire, and relationships between sexual issues and the theme of art.

C6₂ Bassett, John Earl. "Faulkner's *Mosquitoes*: Towards a Self-Image of the Artist." *Southern Literary Journal*, 12, No. 2 (Spring 1980), 49–64.
   The major characters and their conflicts suggest Faulkner is working through problems related to his own career.

Further commentary: A7₂ (Page), A12₂ (Leary), A19₂ (Broughton), A28₂ (Wagner), A47₂ (Williams), A54₂ (Kinney), A60₂ (Stonum), AA61₂ (Ditsky), AA108₂ (Cowley), AA164₂ (Werner).

D. *Sartoris* and *Flags in the Dust*

D1₂ Corrington, John W. "Escape into Myth: The Long Dying of Bayard Sartoris." *Recherches Anglaises et Américaines*, 4 (1971), 31–47.
   Focuses on Bayard, explaining the novel as an analysis of order and chaos in the post–Civil War South, and of the alienation of twentieth-century Southerners from their past and Southern myths.

D2₂ McDonald, Walter R. "Sartoris: The Dauntless Hero in Modern American Fiction." In *Modern American Fiction: Insights and Foreign Lights*. Ed. W. T. Zyla and W. M. Aycock. Lubbock: Texas Tech Univ., 1972, pp. 107–20.
   Discusses the Sartorises in relation to a type in American fiction.

D3₂ Muehl, Lois. "Form as Seen in Two Early Works by Faulkner." *Library Chronicle* [Univ. of Pennsylvania], 38 (1972), 147–57.
   Devices in *Sartoris* and *Light in August*.

D4₂ Brown, Calvin S. "Faulkner's Idiot Boy: The Source of a Simile in *Sartoris*." *American Literature*, 44 (November 1972), 474–76.
   A novel by Harris Dickson.

D5₂ Spears, James E. "William Faulkner, Folklorist: A Note." *Tennessee Folklore Society Bulletin*, 38 (December 1972), 95–96.
   Faulkner uses "folk" character types from several social classes.

D6₂   Blotner, Joseph. "William Faulkner's Essay on the
        Composition of *Sartoris.*" *Yale University Library Gazette*, 47
        (January 1973), 121–24.
        Discusses a previously unpublished commentary by Faulkner on the novel.

D7₂   Walker, Ronald G. "Death in the Sound of Their Name:
        Character Motivation in Faulkner's *Sartoris.*" *Southern
        Humanities Review*, 7 (Summer 1973), 271–78.
        The Sartoris legend has a major impact on Narcissa, who is terrified by it,
        and Bayard, who is a victim of it.

D8₂   Day, Douglas. Introduction to *Flags in the Dust.* New York:
        Random House, 1973.

D9₂   Brooks, Cleanth. "The Birth of Yoknapatawpha—as Faulkner
        Himself Wanted It." *Chicago Tribune*, July 29, 1973, Sec. 7,
        p. 3.

D10₂   Yardley, Jonathan. "Where It First Happened." *New Republic*,
        September 8, 1973, pp. 32–33.

D11₂   Inge, M. Thomas. "Faulty Look at Faulkner Novel."
        Richmond Times-Dispatch, September 30, 1973, p. F3.

D12₂   Watson, James G. "'The Germ of My Apocrypha': *Sartoris*
        and the Search for Form." *Mosaic*, 7, No. 1 (Fall 1973), 15–33.
        Within Faulkner's career, this novel was seminal not only in setting and
        theme but also in its mythic method, a present set against a mythic or
        legendary past.

D13₂   Hirsch, Foster. Review. *America*, November 3, 1973, pp.
        336–37.

D14₂   Corwin, Phillip. "Call It 'Flags' or 'Sartoris,' It's a Fine Book."
        National Observer, November 10, 1973, p. 23.

D15₂   Boozer, William. "Footnotes on 'Flags,' 'Sartoris.'" *Memphis
        Commercial Appeal*, November 18, 1973, Sec. 6, p. 6.

D16₂   Adamowski, T. H. "Bayard Sartoris: Mourning and
        Melancholia." *Literature and Psychology*, 23, No. 4 (1973),
        149–58.
        In killing himself, Bayard, an ambivalently narcissistic melancholiac, kills
        the oppressive Sartoris myth.

D17₂   Broughton, Panthea. "Faulkner's Fancywork." *Saturday
        Review World*, January 26, 1974, pp. 43–45.

D18₂   McHaney, Tom. "The Start of the Cycle: What Is the True Version of *Sartoris*?" *Richmond Mercury*, March 27, 1974, Book Review, p. 10.

D19₂   Martin, Carter W. "Faulkner's *Sartoris*: The Tailor Re-Tailored." *South Carolina Review*, 6, No. 2 (April 1974), 56–59.
        The clothing imagery is related to Bayard's pessimism.

D20₂   Ditsky, John M. Review. *Southern Humanities Review*, 8 (Summer 1974), 404–05.

D21₂   McSweeney, Kerry. "Sexuality and Artistry." *Queen's Quarterly*, 81 (Summer 1974), 327–28.

D22₂   Adams, Richard P. "At Long Last, *Flags in the Dust*." *Southern Review*, 10 (October 1974), 878–88.

D23₂   Kane, Patricia. "The Narcissa Benbow of Faulkner's *Flags in the Dust*." *Notes on Contemporary Literature*, 4, No. 4 (September 1974), 2–3.

D24₂   Rogers, Douglas G. "Faulkner's Treatment of Negro Characters in *Sartoris* and *The Unvanquished*." *North Dakota Quarterly*, 43 (Spring 1975), 67–72.

D25₂   Hayhoe, George F. "William Faulkner's *Flags in the Dust*." *Mississippi Quarterly*, 28 (Summer 1975), 370–86.
        Criticizes Day's editing.

D26₂   Grover, D. C. Review. *Arizona Quarterly*, 32 (Spring 1976), 74–77.

D27₂   Miller, William. "Hardy, Falls, and Faulkner." *Mississippi Quarterly*, 29 (Summer 1976), 435–36.
        Influence of *The Mayor of Casterbridge*.

D28₂   Mulqueen, James E. "Horace Benbow: Avatar of Faulkner's Marbel Faun." *Notes on Mississippi Writers*, 9 (Fall 1976), 88–96.
        Studying *The Marble Faun* helps to clarify the role of Horace in the novel.

D29₂   Burelbach, Frederick M. "Two Family Names: Faulkner and Sartoris." *Literary Onomastic Studies*, 4 (1977), 81–95.

D30₂   McSweeney, Kerry. "The Subjective Intensities of Faulkner's *Flags in the Dust*." *Canadian Review of American Studies*, 8 (Fall 1977), 154–64.

Discusses relationships between two aspects of the novel—the recreation of "an authentic picture of a time and place" and the rhetorical and poetical embellishments that accompany "the impulse to self-expression." The "power of sexuality and the power of the past" are the principal "subjective intensities."

D31₂   Eitner, Walter H. "The Aristoi of Yoknapatawpha County." *Notes on Contemporary Literature*, 7, No. 4 (September 1977), 10–11.

The name "Sartoris" may be an anagram for "aristoi," a term once used to mean "aristocracy."

—   Brooks, Cleanth. *William Faulkner* (A48₂; 1978), pp. 165–77, 388–95.

Considers the contrast between generations, between tradition and modernism, between realism and romanticism.

—   Kinney, Arthur F. *Faulkner's Narrative Poetics* (A54₂; 1978), pp. 123–39.

Emphasizes the consciousness of young Bayard, and shows that "the burden of his unfolding consciousness . . . is to show how agonizing and unavoidable his death became."

D32₂   Hodgin, Katherine C. "Horace Benbow and Bayard Sartoris: Two Romantic Figures in Faulkner's *Flags in the Dust*." *American Literature*, 50 (January 1979), 647–52.

Horace embodies "a type of Keatsian romantic, while Bayard with his love for adventure embodies the Byronic hero."

—   Wittenberg, Judith B. *Faulkner* (A61₂; 1979), pp. 61–72.

D33₂   Folks, Jeffrey J. "A Problem with Internal Dating of *Flags in the Dust*." *Notes on Contemporary Literature*, 9, No. 3 (May 1979), 8–9.

—   Kerr, Elizabeth M. "*Sartoris*: The Haunted Hero, or, Come, Sweet Death." *William Faulkner's Gothic Domain* (A59₂; 1979), pp. 74–87.

D34₂   Cosgrove, William. The 'Soundless Moiling' of Bayard Sartoris." *Arizona Quarterly*, 35 (Summer 1979), 165–69.

On Bayard's inarticulateness.

D35₂   Harley, Marta P. "Faulkner's *Sartoris* and the Legend of Rinaldo and Bayard." *American Notes and Queries*, 18 (February 1980), 92–93.

Finds references to the stories of Rinaldo and Ganelon.

D36₂ McDaniel, Linda E. "Horace Benbow: Faulkner's Endymion."
      Mississippi Quarterly, 33 (Summer 1980), 363–70.
      Studies "Keats's idealistic Endymion as a source for Faulkner's futile
      Benbow." The contrasts between them "develop a rather sophisticated
      irony."

D37₂ Hayhoe, George F., ed. "The Rejected Manuscript Opening of
      Flags in the Dust." *Mississippi Quarterly*, 33 (Summer 1980),
      371–83.
      The first seven pages of the manuscript at the University of Virginia
      (printed here) relate the death of John Sartoris and help clarify Bayard's
      motives.

—   Powers, Lyall H. *Faulkner's Yoknapatawpha Comedy* (A68₂;
      1980), pp. 9–23.
      Compares Bayard and Horace, and discusses the novel as "the tragedy of
      the Second Chance refused."

D38₂ Keiser, Merle W. "*Flags in the Dust* and *Sartoris*." In A64₂
      (1980), pp. 44–70.
      Studies the genesis of the text and the main themes.

D39₂ Millgate, Michael. "Faulkner's First Trilogy: *Sartoris*,
      Sanctuary, and *Requiem for a Nun*." In A64₂ (1980), pp.
      90–109.
      Contrapuntal relationships among the three novels.

D40₂ Putzel, Max. "Faulkner's Trial Preface to *Sartoris*: An Eclectic
      Text." *Papers of the Bibliographical Society of America*, 74
      (October–December 1980), 361–78.
      Prints a preface Faulkner wrote for the novel and discusses its
      composition.

D41₂ Hayhoe, George F. "A Chronology of Events in Faulkner's
      Flags in the Dust." *Notes on Mississippi Writers*, 13, No. 1
      (1981), 1–6.

—   Pilkington, John. "The Poles of Historical Measurement:
      Sartoris." *The Heart of Yoknapatawpha* (A73₂; 1981), pp.
      3–33.
      Emphasizes Faulkner's handling of historical and biographical material,
      how the past can illuminate the present.

D42₂ Bassett, John Earl. "Faulkner, Sartoris, Benbow: Shifting
      Conflict in *Flags in the Dust*." *Southern Studies*, 20 (Spring
      1981), 39–54.
      Studies dynamic relationships between Faulkner and both Horace and
      Bayard, in tracing a shift in the novel from a tension between the Old and

the New (young Bayard) to an implicit thematic opposition between Bayard and Horace.

D43$_2$ McDaniel, Linda E. "Keats's Hyperion Myth: A Source for the Sartoris Myth." *Mississippi Quarterly*, 34 (Summer 1981), 325–33.

D44$_2$ Going, William T. "Faulkner's *Flags in the Dust*." *Explicator*, 39, No. 4 (Summer 1981), 37–39.

> The title may refer to a lyric from 1868, "The Conquered Banner."

Further commentary: A4$_2$ (Bedell), A7$_2$ (Page), A12$_2$ (Leary), A28$_2$ (Wagner), A34$_2$ (Jehlen), A35$_2$ (Levins), A47$_2$ (Williams), A60$_2$ (Stonum), H47$_2$ (McAlexander), V8$_2$ (Howe), AA40$_2$ (Putzel), AA54$_2$ (Carey), AA105$_2$ (Blotner), AA112$_2$ (McGinnis), AA127$_2$ (Gray), AA128$_2$ (Blotner), AA138$_2$ (Goldman), AA183$_2$ (Wyatt), AA201$_2$ (Messenger), GG22$_2$ (McHaney).

E.   *The Sound and the Fury*

E1$_2$ Burton, Dolores. "Intonation Patterns of Sermons in Seven Novels." *Language and Style*, 3 (Summer 1970), 205–20.

E2$_2$ Steege, M. Ted. "Dilsey's Negation of Nihilism: Meaning in *The Sound and the Fury*." *Research Studies* [Washington State Univ.], 38 (December 1970), 266–75.

E3$_2$ Luedtke, Carol. "*The Sound and the Fury* and *Lie Down in Darkness*: Some Comparisons." *Literatur in Wissenschaft und Unterricht*, 4 (1971), 45–51.

E4$_2$ Benson, Jackson J. "Quentin Compson: Self-portrait of a Young Artist's Emotions." *Twentieth Century Literature*, 17 (July 1971), 143–59.

> Faulkner "uses Quentin to expiate the emotional excesses of his own frustration and depression."

E5$_2$ Prasad, Thakur Guru. "Nihilism in *The Sound and the Fury*." *Punjab University Research Bulletin*, 3, No. 1 (April 1972), 35–43.

E6$_2$ Hutchens, E. N. "The Novel as Chronomorph." *Novel*, 5 (Spring 1972), 215–24.

> On the use of time to shape narratives.

E7₂   Davis, William V. "*The Sound and the Fury*: A Note on Benjy's Name." *Studies in the Novel*, 4 (Spring 1972), 60–61.
> The name suggests "Son of the South" and "Son of Sorrow."

E8₂   Ramsey, Roger. "Faulkner's *The Sound and the Fury*." *Explicator*, 30 (April 1972), 70.
> Benjy's memory of the smell of the corpse of Nancy the horse governs his later responses to death.

—   Page, Sally R. *Faulkner's Women* (A7₂; 1972), pp. 45–72.
> Emphasizes the sequence of good and bad mother figures, and the tendency of the male characters to confuse virginity or external beauty with moral qualities.

E9₂   Barrett, William. "Backward Toward the Earth." In *Time of Need: Forms of the Imagination in the Twentieth Century*. New York: Harper & Row, 1972, pp. 96–142.
> On Faulkner's sense of absurdity in the modern world, and sense of humor.

—   Bedell, George C. *Kierkegaard and Faulkner* (A4₂; 1972), pp. 195–206, 244–55.

E10₂   Brogunier, Joseph. "A Housman Source in *The Sound and the Fury*." *Modern Fiction Studies*, 18 (Summer 1972), 220–25.
> "The True Lover" from *A Shropshire Lad*.

E11₂   Millgate, Michael. "Faulkner and Lanier: A Note on the Name Jason." *Mississippi Quarterly*, 25 (Summer 1972), 349–50.

E12₂   Benson, Jackson J. "Quentin's Responsibility for Caddy's Downfall in Faulkner's *The Sound and the Fury*." *Notes on Mississippi Writers*, 5 (Fall 1972), 63–64.

E13₂   Meriwether, James B., ed. "An Introduction for *The Sound and the Fury*." *Southern Review*, 8 (Autumn 1972), 705–10.
> Includes an introduction Faulkner wrote in 1933 but never published. Discussed in Charlie East, "An Old, New Introduction to Him of 'Sound and Fury,'" *New Orleans Times-Picayune*, October 29, 1972, Sec. 1, p. 12. Also discussed in Eric Pace, "Creative Ecstasy: The Early Faulkner," *Washington Star and News*, November 1, 1972, p. C15.

E14₂   Grant, William E. "Benjy's Branch: Symbolic Method in Part I of *The Sound and the Fury*." *Texas Studies in Literature and Language*, 13 (Winter 1972), 705–10.
> On the use of Christian symbolism, and the perverse implications of Easter associations.

E15$_2$ Davis, William V. "Quentin's Death Ritual: Further Christian Allusions in *The Sound and the Fury*." *Notes on Mississippi Writers*, 6 (Spring 1973), 27–32.
    Considers "parallels between Quentin and Christ."

E16$_2$ Brown, Calvin S. "Dilsey: From Faulkner to Homer." In A17$_2$ (1973), pp. 57–75.
    Dilsey is a universal type, the dedicated nurse-figure.

E17$_2$ Meriwether, James B. "An Introduction to *The Sound and the Fury*." *Mississippi Quarterly*, 26 (Summer 1973), 410–15.
    Longer version than E13$_2$. Included in A21$_2$.

E18$_2$ Merton, Thomas. "Time and Unburdening and the Recollection of the Lamb: The Easter Service in Faulkner's *The Sound and the Fury*." *Katallagete Be Reconciled* [Journal of the Committee of Southern Churchmen], Summer 1973, pp. 7–15.

—   Hunter, Edwin R. *William Faulkner* (A11$_2$; 1973), pp. 29–47, 237–57.

E19$_2$ Peavy, Charles D. "'If I'd Just Had a Mother': Faulkner's Quentin Compson." *Literature and Psychology*, 23, No. 3 (1973), 114–21.
    An unloving mother and a cynical father warp the growth of Quentin, who develops an infantile attachment to his sister.

—   Leary, Lewis. *William Faulkner of Yoknapatawpha County* (A12$_2$; 1973), pp. 41–62.

E20$_2$ Welty, Eudora. "Some Notes on Time in Fiction." *Mississippi Quarterly*, 26 (Fall 1973), 488–92.

E21$_2$ Lilly, Paul R., Jr. "Caddy and Addie: Speakers of Faulkner's Impeccable Language." *Journal of Narrative Technique*, 3 (September 1973), 170–82.
    Covers Faulkner's ideas on poetic speech, limitations of language, and the relation between language and fictional space.

E22$_2$ Longley, John L., Jr. "'Who Never Had a Sister': A Reading of *The Sound and the Fury*." *Mosaic*, 7, No. 1 (Fall 1973), 35–53.
    Caddy is an obsession for each brother, in different ways.

E23$_2$ Baquira, Josephine Q. "Themes, Styles, and Symbolism in *The Sound and the Fury*." *St. Louis University Research Journal*, 4 (December 1973), 658–72.

E24₂   Messerli, Douglas. "The Problem of Time in *The Sound and the Fury*: A Critical Reassessment and Reinterpretation." *Southern Literary Journal*, 6, No. 2 (Spring 1974), 19–41.
> Studies the novel through the phenomenology of Eugene Minkowski, and closely examines both Dilsey and Caddy, who is the motivator of the action and an image of dynamism.

E25₂   Fridy, Will. "'Ichthus': An Exercise in Synthetic Suggestion." *South Atlantic Bulletin*, 39, No. 2 (May 1974), 95–101.
> On Quentin's scene with the three boys in Boston.

E26₂   Iser, Wolfgang. "Perception, Temporality, and Action as Modes of Subjectivity. W. Faulkner: *The Sound and the Fury*." In *The Implied Reader: Patterns of Communication in Prose Fiction from Bunyan to Beckett*. Baltimore: Johns Hopkins Univ. Press, 1974, pp. 136–52.
> The novel, by means of images of reduced subjectivity, illustrates basic features of subjectivity and the element of breakdown in any subjective comprehension. This phenomenological approach was published in German in 1972.

—   Weisgerber, Jean. *Faulkner and Dostoevsky* (A22₂; 1974), pp. 179–92.

E27₂   Weinstein, Arnold L. "Vision as Feeling: Bernanos and Faulkner." In *Vision and Response in Modern Fiction*. Ithaca: Cornell Univ. Press, 1974, pp. 91–153.
> On the affective power of Faulkner's narrative strategy, the book's associational structure, and tensions between images and perspectives.

E28₂   Naples, Diane C. "Eliot's 'Tradition' and *The Sound and the Fury*." *Modern Fiction Studies*, 20 (Summer 1974), 214–17.
> On mythic structure, mythical time, taboos, and rites.

E29₂   Cowan, James C. "Dream-Work in the Quentin Section of *The Sound and the Fury*." *Literature and Psychology*, 24, No. 3 (1974), 91–98.
> Five examples of Faulkner's use of dreams.

E30₂   Geffen, Arthur. "Profane Time, Sacred Time, and Confederate Time in *The Sound and the Fury*." *Studies in American Fiction*, 2 (Autumn 1974), 175–97.
> Uses Eliade's notion of sacred and profane time, and argues that only Benjy and Dilsey escape the meaninglessness of profane time.

E31₂   Murphy, Denis M. "*The Sound and the Fury* and Dante's *Inferno*: Fire and Ice." *Markham Review*, 4 (October 1974), 71–78.

E32₂   Auer, Michael J. "Caddy, Benjy, and the Acts of the Apostles: A Note on *The Sound and the Fury*." *Studies in the Novel*, 6 (Winter 1974), 475–76.

E33₂   Milliner, Gladys. "The Third Eve: Caddy Compson." *Midwest Quarterly*, 16 (April 1975), 268–75.
> Caddy is an independent woman doomed despite her curiosity, courage, and strength.

E34₂   Kellogg, Jean D. "William Faulkner and the Tyranny of Linear Consciousness." In *Dark Prophets of Hope: Dostoevsky, Sartre, Camus, Faulkner*. Chicago: Loyola Univ. Press, 1975, pp. 123–35.
> The novel progresses toward Dilsey as a higher type of humanity.

E35₂   Ruoff, Gene W. "Faulkner: The Way Out of the Waste Land." In *The Twenties: Fiction, Poetry, Drama*. Ed. W. French. Deland, Fla.: Everett/Edwards, 1975, pp. 235–48.
> This novel shows a development away from Faulkner's early war fiction, with its sense of futility, especially in the handling of evil.

E36₂   Gordon, Lois. "Meaning and Myth in *The Sound and the Fury* and *The Waste Land*." In *The Twenties: Fiction, Poetry, Drama*. Ed. W. French. Deland, Fla.: Everett/Edwards, 1975, pp. 269–302.
> Discusses not only similarities to Eliot's poem, but also Faulkner's psychological portrait of a family, especially negative effects of parents on the lives of children.

E37₂   Dickerson, Mary Jane. "'The Magician's Wand': Faulkner's Compson Appendix." *Mississippi Quarterly*, 28 (Summer 1975), 317–37.
> It "reveals the enduring role of the Compson family in shaping" Faulkner's work after 1929.

—   Irwin, John T. *Doubling and Incest/Repetition and Revenge* (A25₂; 1975).

E38₂   Ross, Stephen M. "The 'Loud World' of Quentin Compson." *Studies in the Novel*, 7 (Summer 1975), 245–57.
> Through modulated narration Faulkner creates a flexible voice for Quentin. Vocal imagery and remembered dialogue clearly define his relationships with others.

E39₂   Groden, Michael. "Criticism in New Composition: *Ulysses* and *The Sound and the Fury*." *Twentieth Century Literature*, 21 (October 1975), 265–77.
> On Faulkner's use of the interior monologue, and the influence of Joyce.

E40₂   Ramsey, Roger. "Light Imagery in *The Sound and the Fury*:
April 7, 1928." *Journal of Narrative Technique*, 6 (Winter
1976), 41–50.

> Considers literary and psychological meanings of light imagery in the past
> and present sequences.

E41₂   Hill, Douglas B., Jr. "Faulkner's Caddy." *Canadian Review of
American Studies*, 7 (Spring 1976), 26–38.

> Both a character and the pivot of three male fantasies, she moves the
> reader because of the importance of time not sexuality in her portrayal.

E42₂   Brannon, Lil. "Psychic Distance in the Quentin Section of *The
Sound and the Fury*." *Publications of the Arkansas
Philological Association*, 2, No. 2 (Spring 1976), 11–18.

E43₂   Sims, Barbara B. "Jaybirds as Portents of Hell in Percy and
Faulkner." *Notes on Mississippi Writers*, 9 (Spring 1976),
24–27.

> Compares *The Moviegoer*.

E44₂   Clark, Edward D., Sr. "Private Truth in *The Sound and the
Fury*." *College Language Association Journal*, 19 (June 1976),
513–23.

> Narrow commitments and obsessions of Quentin and Jason lead to
> spiritual deaths.

E45₂   Kopoor, Kapil. "Faulkner's *The Sound and the Fury*: A Note
on Form and Meaning." *Journal of the School of Languages*,
3, No. 2 (1976), 85–91.

—   Bleikasten, André. *The Most Splendid Failure* (A30₂; 1976).

E46₂   Cowley, Malcolm. "Dilsey and the Compsons." In A33₂ (1976),
pp. 79–88.

> Dilsey is a positive standard in the book, the good mother in contrast to
> Mrs. Compson.

E47₂   Handy, William J. "*The Sound and the Fury*: A Formalist
Approach." *North Dakota Quarterly*, 44, No. 3 (Summer
1976), 71–83.

> Closely studies the unity of Benjy's section, with references to the other
> sections.

E48₂   Fletcher, Mary Dell. "Jason Compson: Contemporary Villain."
Louisiana Studies, 15 (Fall 1976), 253–61.

> Although evil, Jason is a realistic and credible modern figure.

E49[2]   Ross, Stephen M "Jason Compson and Sut Lovingood:
         Southwestern Humor as Stream of Consciousness." *Studies in
         the Novel*, 8 (Fall 1976), 278–90.

> Jason's world and character resemble Sut's. He is the comic fool arrested in
> his development, but unlike Sut unable to laugh at himself.

E50[2]   Yamamoto, Masashi. "Faulkner's Use of Smell in *The Sound
         and the Fury.*" *Chu-Shikoku Studies in American Literature*,
         12 (1976), 19–31.

E51[2]   McGann, Mary E. "*The Waste Land* and *The Sound and the
         Fury*: To Apprehend the Human Process Moving in Time."
         Southern Literary Journal, 9, No. 1 (Fall 1976), 13–21.

> Similarities in the handling of time and imagery, and in the method of
> indirection.

E52[2]   Traschen, Isadore. "The Tragic Form of *The Sound and the
         Fury.*" *Southern Review*, 12 (October 1976), 798–813.

> Four-part tragic form: breakdown of order; conflict between tragic attitude
> and orthodox attitudes; discovery of tragic self; transformation of hero and
> his transcendence of his fate.

E53[2]   Davis, Thadious M. "The Other Family and Luster in *The
         Sound and the Fury.*" *College Language Association Journal*,
         20 (December 1976), 245–61.

> The black family provides a significant and symmetrical contrast to the
> Compsons.

E54[2]   Faber, M. D. "Faulkner's *The Sound and the Fury*: Object
         Relations and Narrative Structure." *American Imago*, 34
         (Winter 1977), 327–50.

> A psychoanalytic approach, using an object-relations model, to Quentin
> and his mother.

E55[2]   Slater, Judith. "Quentin's Tunnel Vision: Modes of Perception
         and Their Stylistic Realization in *The Sound and the Fury.*"
         Literature and Psychology, 27, No. 1 (1977), 4–15.

> A psychoanalytic study of the nature of the mental adjustments Quentin
> needs to make to space, time, and sex, this shows that his rigid and static
> view of life destroys him.

E56[2]   Bridges, Jean Bolen. "Similarities between 'The Waste Land'
         and *The Sound and the Fury.*" *Notes on Contemporary
         Literature*, 7, No. 1 (January 1977), 10–13.

E57[2]   Amano, Masafumi. "Faulkner's Narrative Technique in *The
         Sound and the Fury.*" *Chu-Shikoku Studies in American
         Literature*, 13 (1977), 24–35.

E58₂   Weinstein, Philip M. "Caddy *Disparue*: Exploring an Episode
       Common to Proust and Faulkner." *Comparative Literature
       Studies*, 14 (March 1977), 38–52.
       The "sister" episode in Boston.

E59₂   Aiken, David. "The 'Sojer Face' Defiance of Jason Compson."
       Thought, 52 (June 1977), 188–203.
       Jason exemplifies Kierkegaard's "despair of willing . . . to be oneself."

E60₂   Pratt, Mary Louise. *Toward a Speech Act Theory of Literary
       Discourse*. Bloomington: Indiana Univ. Press, 1977, pp.
       182–91.

E61₂   Mallard, William. "Faulkner's *The Sound and the Fury*." In
       *The Reflection of Theology in Literature: A Case Study in
       Theology and Culture*. San Antonio: Trinity Univ. Press, 1977,
       pp. 163–83.
       Emphasizes themes of time and order, and the character of Caddy, within a
       theological interpretation.

—   Williams, David. *Faulkner's Women* (A47₂; 1977), pp. 61–96.
       Considers archetypal associations of the major female characters that
       connect Mrs. Compson with the "terrible mother" type, Caddy with
       traditions of the "mother goddess," and Dilsey with the "sorrowful mother
       of death."

E62₂   Davis, Boyd. "Caddy Compson's Eden." *Mississippi Quarterly*,
       30 (Summer 1977), 381–94.
       An Edenic image of a girl in a tree becomes the book's "mythic center."

E63₂   Westbrook, Wayne W. "Jason Compson and the Costs of
       Speculation: A Second Look." *Mississippi Quarterly*, 30
       (Summer 1977), 437–40.
       Jason's cotton dealings.

E64₂   Idei, Yasuko. "Time as a Means of Conveying Nihilism in
       Faulkner's *The Sound and the Fury*." *Kyushu American
       Literature*, 18 (October 1977), 24–32.

E65₂   Rabkin, Eric S. "Spatial Form and Plot." *Critical Inquiry*, 4
       (Winter 1977), 253–70.
       Parataxis among the parts.

E66₂   Sterne, Richard C. "Why Jason Compson IV Hates Babe
       Ruth." *American Notes and Queries*, 16 (March 1978), 105–08.

E67₂   Chappell, Fred. "The Comic Structure of *The Sound and the
       Fury*." *Mississippi Quarterly*, 31 (Summer 1978), 381–86.

Describes the novel as "a comic novel with comic episodes, comic characters, humor, satire, and a symmetrical comic ending."

E68₂   Zender, Karl F. "Jason Compson and Death by Water." *Mississippi Quarterly*, 31 (Summer 1978), 421–22.
A sequence of associations at the beginning of Jason's reverie at the hardware store.

—   Kinney, Arthur F. *Faulkner's Narrative Poetics* (A54₂; 1978), pp. 139–61.
Emphasizes Benjy's consciousness, which "begins and closes the novel." The novel also depends on a set of circular patterns and images.

E69₂   Ford, Dan. "The Tragedy of 'Again' in *The Sound and the Fury*." *Publications of the Arkansas Philological Association*, 4, No. 3 (Fall 1978), 41–44.

E70₂   Cohn, Dorrit. *Transparent Minds: Narrative Modes of Presenting Consciousness in Fiction*. Princeton: Princeton Univ. Press, 1978, pp. 247–55.

E71₂   Hyman, Lawrence W. "Moral Attitudes and the Literary Experience." *Journal of Aesthetics and Art Criticism*, 38 (Winter 1979), 159–65.
A full literary response to a text requires the reader to bring his own moral attitudes, for example on incest, to the reading, not to suspend them.

E72₂   Davis, William V. "June 2, 1928: Further Thoughts on Time in *The Sound and the Fury*." *Notes on Mississippi Writers*, 11 (Winter 1979), 84–85.

E73₂   Telotte, J. P. "Butting Heads with Faulkner's Soldier." *Notes on Contemporary Literature*, 9, No. 3 (May 1979), 7–8.
Benjy at the statue.

E74₂   Bach, Peggy. "Melancholy Necessity: Evelyn Scott." *New Orleans Review*, 6, No. 4 (1979), 388–95.
Comments on Scott reading the manuscript.

—   Wittenberg, Judith B. *Faulkner* (A61₂; 1979), pp. 72–88.

E75₂   Fletcher, Mary Dell. "William Faulkner and Residual Calvinism." *Southern Studies*, 18 (Summer 1979), 199–216.
Examines both romantic and Calvinistic elements in Faulkner's characters, particularly Quentin Compson.

E76₂   Dukes, Thomas. "Christianity as Curse and Salvation in *The Sound and the Fury*." *Arizona Quarterly*, 35 (Summer 1979), 170–82.

Considering Faulkner's religious vision, this argues that Mrs. Compson is "the unresurrected soul," and Dilsey is saved "through Christian redemption."

—   Stonum, Gary Lee. *Faulkner's Career* (A60₂; 1979), pp. 61–93.

Faulkner juxtaposes the methods of visionary and realistic fiction, and the new method he consequently develops also self-reflexively objectifies and dramatizes the conflict between the two modes of fiction.

E77₂ Caserio, Robert L. *Plot, Story, and the Novel: From Dickens and Poe to the Modern Period.* Princeton: Princeton Univ. Press, 1979, pp. 235–36, 274–79.

—   Kerr, Elizabeth M. "*The Sound and the Fury*: The Freudian Dream, or, The Way to Dusty Death." In *William Faulkner's Gothic Domain* (A59₂; 1979), pp. 53–73.

E78₂ Suda, Minoru. "The Development of William Faulkner's Literature: With Special Emphasis on *The Sound and the Fury* and *Absalom, Absalom!*" *Essays and Studies in English Language and Literature* [Japan], 70 (1979), 23–30.

—   Kartiganer, Donald M. *The Fragile Thread* (A58₂; 1979), pp. 3–22.

Incorporates E155.

E79₂ Kenner, Hugh. "Faulkner and Joyce." In A57₂ (1979), pp. 20–33.

Studies influences, similarities, and differences.

E80₂ Morrow, Patrick D. "Mental Retardation in *The Sound and the Fury* and *The Last Picture Show*." *RE: Artes Liberales*, 6, No. 1 (Fall 1979), 1–9.

E81₂ Minter, David. "Faulkner, Childhood, and the Making of *The Sound and the Fury*." *American Literature*, 51 (November 1979), 376–93.

Traces the genesis of the novel back to disappointment over *Sartoris*, and its regressive themes back to childhood experiences. Incorporated into A66₂.

E82₂ Garlick, H. F. "Three Patterns of Imagery in Benjy's Section of *The Sound and the Fury*." *Journal of the Australasian Modern Language Association*, 52 (November 1979), 274–87.

E83₂ Simonton, Margaret. "Faulkner's Influence on Robbe-Grillet: The Quentin Section of *The Sound and the Fury* and *La Jalousie*." *International Fiction Review*, 7 (Winter 1980), 11–19.

E84₂   Burch, Beth. "Shades of Golden Fleece: Faulkner's Jason Once Again." *Notes on Mississippi Writers*, 12 (Winter 1980), 55–62.

E85₂   Fletcher, Mary Dell. "Edenic Images in *The Sound and the Fury*." *South Central Bulletin*, 40 (Winter 1980), 142–44.

E86₂   Brown, May Cameron. "The Language of Chaos: Quentin Compson in *The Sound and the Fury*." *American Literature*, 51 (January 1980), 544–53.

> The "blend of order and chaos" in his personality reflects a modern sensibility.

E87₂   Carter, Steve. "Caddy and Quentin: Anima and Animus Orbited Nice." *Hartford Studies in Literature*, 12, No. 2 (1980), 124–42.

> A Jungian interpretation of Caddy, Quentin, and their relationship.

E88₂   Grover, Frederic, and Harriet Mowshowitz. "Faulkner in French." *Canadian Review of Comparative Literature*, 7 (Spring 1980), 223–35.

> Critical examination of Coindreau's translation.

E89₂   Gervais, Ronald J. "The Trains of Their Youth: The Aesthetics of Homecoming in *The Great Gatsby*, *The Sun Also Rises*, and *The Sound and the Fury*." *Americana-Austriaca*, 6 (1980), 51–63.

E90₂   Glaze, Walter S. "The Protestant Work Ethic in Faulkner's *The Sound and the Fury*: Jason Compson as Southern Gentleman." *Publications of the Missouri Philological Association*, 5 (1980), 26–30.

E91₂   Fujihira, Ikuko. "Beyond Closed Doors: Quentin Compson and Isaac McCaslin." *William Faulkner: Materials, Studies, and Criticism*, 3, No. 1 (July 1980), 31–43.

> The significance of closed and open doors in three novels.

E92₂   Madden, David. "Time as Theme, Structure, Character and Symbol in Faulkner's *The Sound and the Fury*." In *A Primer of the Novel for Readers and Writers*. Metuchen, N.J.: Scarecrow Press, 1980, pp. 252–61.

—   Polk, Noel, and Kenneth L. Privratsky, eds. The Sound and the Fury: *A Concordance to the Novel* (A67₂; 1980).

E93₂   Pinsker, Sanford. "Squaring the Circle in *The Sound and the Fury*." In A63₂ (1980), pp. 115–21.

> Studies the novel as a Modernist text.

—   Powers, Lyall H. *Faulkner's Yoknapatawpha Comedy* (A68₂;
        1980), pp. 24–49.

        Considers the failure of love, the theme of time, the self-destructiveness of
        evil, and the relationship between Quentin and Jason.

E94₂   Mellard, James M. "Faulkner's *The Sound and the Fury*." In
        The Exploded Form: The Modernist Novel in America.
        Urbana: Univ. of Illinois Press, 1980, pp. 54–81.

        Modes of narration (dramatic, lyric, epic).

E95₂   Rollyson, Carl E., Jr. "Quentin Durward and Quentin
        Compson: The Romantic Standard-Bearers of Scott and
        Faulkner." *Massachusetts Studies in English*, 7, No. 3 (1980),
        34–39.

E96₂   Seymour, Thom. "Faulkner's *The Sound and the Fury*."
        Explicator, 39 (Fall 1980), 24–25.

        On Jason's comments about the New York Yankees.

E97₂   Moore, Andy J. "Luster's Ordered Role in *The Sound and the
        Fury*." In *American Bypaths: Essays in Honor of E. Hudson
        Long*. Ed. R. G. Collmer and J. W. Herring. Waco: Baylor
        Univ. Press, 1980, pp. 167–86.

E98₂   Wise, Gene. *American Historical Explanations: A Strategy for
        Grounded Inquiry*. 2nd ed. rev. Minneapolis: Univ. of
        Minnesota Press, 1980, pp. 3–56.

        Uses Benjy Compson's thoughts as examples to explore the problem of
        defining "ideas." The book is an attempt at a new historiographical model,
        using concepts of Thomas Kuhn and others. The first edition was published
        at Homewood, Ill.: Dorsey Press, 1973.

E99₂   Cheuse, Alan. "Candace." In *Candace & Other Stories*.
        Cambridge, Mass.: Apple-wood Books, 1980, pp. 57–100.

        Imagines a different kind of life for Caddy Compson.

E100₂   Tuck, Susan H. "House of Compson, House of Tyrone:
        Faulkner's Influence on O'Neill." *Eugene O'Neill Newsletter*, 5
        (Winter 1981), 10–16.

        Compares *Long Day's Journey into Night*.

E101₂   Mosely, Merrit. "Faulkner's Dickensian Humor in *The Sound
        and the Fury*." *Notes on Mississippi Writers*, 13, No. 1 (1981),
        7–13.

E102₂   Bassett, John Earl. "Family Conflict in *The Sound and the
        Fury*." *Studies in American Fiction*, 9 (Spring 1981), 1–20.

Studies sibling conflict and parental inadequacy in the novel in relation to
a dominant sense of loss, and considers the author's relationship to his
major characters.

— Jenkins, Lee Clinton. *Faulkner and Black-White Relations*
(A72$_2$; 1981), pp. 135–76.

A psychoanalytic study that considers narcissism, doubling, and the ways
in which blacks come to embody for whites those qualities whites repudiate
in themselves. Analyzes Dilsey's role in the novel, her self-perception, and
how others perceive her.

E103$_2$ Davis, Thadious. "Jason Compson's Place: A Reassessment."
Southern Studies, 20 (Summer 1981), 137–50.

Discusses Jason in relation to his acceptance of tradition.

E104$_2$ Kreiswirth, Martin. "Learning as He Wrote: Re-used Materials
in *The Sound and the Fury*." *Mississippi Quarterly*, 34
(Summer 1981), 281–98.

On the use of materials from earlier novels and other manuscripts.

E105$_2$ Stafford, William T. *Books Speaking to Books: A Contextual
Approach to American Fiction*. Chapel Hill: Univ. of North
Carolina Press, 1981.

Chapter 3 (pp. 27–50) is called "Benjy Compson, Jake Barnes, and Nick
Carraway: Replication in Three 'Innocent' American Narrators of the
1920s." Part of chapter 6 (pp. 119–26) is called "Faulkner's Revolt against
the 1920s: Parody and Transcendence, Continuation and Innovation." The
book also includes J24$_2$.

E106$_2$ Kauffman, Linda. "The Letter and the Spirit in *Hard Times*
and *The Sound and the Fury*." *Mississippi Quarterly*, 34
(Summer 1981) 299–313.

— Pilkington, John. "The Collapse of Family: *The Sound and the
Fury*." In *The Heart of Yoknapatawpha* (A73$_2$; 1981), pp.
35–85.

Emphasizes the pattern of family history portrayed in the novel, and
explicates troublesome passages in the monologues.

E107$_2$ Lanser, Susan S. *The Narrative Act: Point of View in Prose
Fiction*. Princeton: Princeton Univ. Press, 1981.

Includes several comments on the monologues in the novel.

E108$_2$ Wadlington, Warwick. "*The Sound and the Fury*: A Logic of
Tragedy." *American Literature*, 53 (November 1981), 409–23.

Locates the novel as tragedy within the debate over the possibility of a
modern tragedy. Two phases in the tragic process are "the decline of action
into passivity, and the attempt at reversal." Argues for "the dialectical
continuity between tragedy and pathos" in the novel.

E109₂   Ryan, Marie Laure. "The Pragmatics of Personal and
        Impersonal Fiction." *Poetics*, 10 (December 1981), 517–39.
        Uses this novel as an example in discussing unreliable narrators.

Further commentary: A19₂ (Broughton), A28₂ (Wagner), A34₂ (Jehlen),
A35₂ (Levins), A44₂ (Kawin), A45₂ (Schoenberg), F2₂ (Handy), G18₂
(Ford), X130₂ (Morrison), AA5₂ (Brumm), AA89₂ (Flynn), AA120₂
(Foote), AA133₂ (Milum), AA158₂ (Palumbo), AA171₂ (Ousby),
AA179₂ (Church), AA180₂ (King), AA203₂ (Porter), CC8₂ (Kantak),
CC23₂ (Broughton), CC24₂ (Broughton), II57₂ (Colson), KK9₂ (Hays).

F.   *As I Lay Dying*

F1₂   Woodbery, Potter. "Faulkner's Numismatics: A Note on *As I
      Lay Dying*." *Research Studies* [Washington State Univ.], 39
      (June 1971), 150–51.

F2₂   Handy, William J. *Modern Fiction: A Formalist Approach*.
      Carbondale: Southern Illinois Univ. Press, 1971, pp. 75–93.
      Incorporates F41.

F3₂   Clark, Eulalyn W. "Ironic Effects of Multiple Perspective in
      As I Lay Dying." *Notes on Mississippi Writers*, 5 (Spring
      1972), 15–28.
      Discrepancies and misconceptions, and Faulkner's use of them to develop
      character.

F4₂   Perlis, Alan D. "*As I Lay Dying* as a Study of Time." *South
      Dakota Review*, 10, No. 1 (Spring 1972), 103–10.
      Studying the characters' response to time reveals why Darl is an outsider.

—   Page, Sally R. *Faulkner's Women* (A7₂; 1972), pp. 111–22.
      A sympathetic study of Addie as "an admirable woman" whose flaw is an
      inability to adjust to "life on its own terms."

F5₂   Monaghan, David M. "The Single Narrator of *As I Lay
      Dying*." *Modern Fiction Studies*, 18 (Summer 1972), 213–20.
      Addie is the narrator, and the book's action is that of a wish fulfillment.

F6₂   Rule, Philip C. "The Old Testament Vision in *As I Lay
      Dying*." In A2₂ (1972), pp. 107–18.
      Considers Old Testament atmosphere, tone, themes, and rhythms in the
      novel.

F7[2]   May, John R. "Words and Deeds: Apocalyptic Judgment in Faulkner, West, and O'Connor." In *Toward a New Earth: Apocalypses in the American Novel*. Notre Dame: Univ. of Notre Dame Press, 1972, pp. 92–144.

   Apocalyptic symbolism and form.

F8[2]   Degenfelder, E. Pauline. "Yoknapatawphan Baroque: A Stylistic Analysis of *As I Lay Dying*." *Style*, 7 (Spring 1973), 121–56.

   Uses "recent developments in generative and transformational grammars" to analyze two basic styles—a baroque to dramatize alienation, a colloquial to depict solidarity of folk.

—   Bleikasten, André. *Faulkner's* As I Lay Dying (A8[2]; 1973).

F9[2]   Rosenman, John B. "A Note on William Faulkner's *As I Lay Dying*." *Studies in American Fiction*, 1 (Spring 1973), 104–05.

   Macbeth and Dewey Dell.

—   Hunter, Edwin R. *William Faulkner* (A11[2]; 1973), pp. 49–60.

F10[2]   Nadeau, Robert L. "The Morality of Act: A Study of Faulkner's *As I Lay Dying*." *Mosaic*, 6, No. 3 (Spring 1973), 23–25.

   Bergsonian patterns in Addie's section.

—   Leary, Lewis. *William Faulkner of Yoknapatawpha County* (A12[2]; 1973), pp. 63–77.

F11[2]   Leath, Helen Lang. "'Will the Circle Be Unbroken?' An Analysis of Structure in *As I Lay Dying*." *Southwestern American Literature*, 3 (1973), 61–68.

   Addie, Faulkner's spokesman, is the antithesis of Darl with his unreliable vision, and is the pivot of a unifying pattern of circle imagery.

—   Reed, Joseph W., Jr. *Faulkner's Narrative* (A14[2]; 1973), pp. 84–113.

   Considers reasons for the pattern in the alternation of voices, the questioning in the text of subject-object relationships, and the central theme of "Becoming." Also attends to patterns of imagery and metaphor.

F12[2]   Gold, Joseph. "'Sin, Salvation and Bananas': *As I Lay Dying*." *Mosaic*, 7, No. 1 (Fall 1973), 55–73.

   The novel deals with the old religious conflict between affirmation and denial of common human life.

F13[2]   Wagner, Linda W. "*As I Lay Dying*: Faulkner's 'All in the Family'" *College Literature*, 1 (Spring 1974), 73–82.

Addie is the sympathetic center of this novel, which provides a "tragic definition of the word *family*" and indicts such abstractions as *"fear, sin, salvation,* and *love."*

F14[2] Ross, Stephen M. "Shapes of Time and Consciousness in *As I Lay Dying.*" *Texas Studies in Literature and Language*, 16 (Winter 1974), 723–37.

Faulkner experiments with ways of representing time through grammar and narrative conventions. Guided by Bergson's "pure duration" he reworks fictive time into a flexible, shifting process.

F15[2] Rosenman, John. "Another *Othello* Echo in *As I Lay Dying.*" *Notes on Mississippi Writers*, 8 (Spring 1975), 19–21.

Darl's horse imagery.

F16[2] Brady, Ruth H. "Faulkner's *As I Lay Dying.*" *Explicator*, 33 (March 1975), 60.

Vardaman identifying mother with fish.

F17[2] Little, Matthew. "*As I Lay Dying* and 'Dementia Praecox' Humor." *Studies in American Humor*, 2 (April 1975), 61–70.

F18[2] Seltzer, Leon F. "Narrative Function Vs. Psychopathology: The Problem of Darl in *As I Lay Dying.*" *Literature and Psychology*, 25, No. 2 (1975), 49–64.

Six artistic double binds Faulkner created in the novel.

—   Wagner, Linda W. *Hemingway and Faulkner* (A28[2]; 1975), pp. 180–91.

F19[2] Stonum, Gary Lee. "Dilemma in *As I Lay Dying.*" *Renascence*, 28 (Winter 1976), 71–82. Expanded in A60[2] (1979), pp. 94–122.

The novel revolves around a series of dilemmas, situations in which no available choice is satisfactory. This is especially clear in the theme of "the self's relationship with the other."

F20[2] Annas, Pamela J. "The Carpenter of *As I Lay Dying.*" *Notes on Mississippi Writers*, 8 (Winter 1976), 84–99.

Study of Cash Bundren.

F21[2] Stich, K. P. "A Note on Ironic Word Formation in *As I Lay Dying.*" *Notes on Mississippi Writers*, 8 (Winter 1976), 100–103.

F22[2] White, Michael. "Inverse Mimesis in *As I Lay Dying.*" *Arizona Quarterly*, 32 (Spring 1976), 35–44.

Approaches the novel as a Greek drama, not in conventional narrative form.

F23₂   Garrison, Joseph M., Jr. "Perception, Language, and Reality in *As I Lay Dying.*" *Arizona Quarterly*, 32 (Spring 1976), 16–30.

> Focuses on Darl's language, his ontological considerations, his way of perceiving the world, and on the themes of human bondage and endurance.

F24₂   Richmond, Lee J. "The Education of Vardaman Bundren in Faulkner's *As I Lay Dying.*" In *Renaissance and Modern: Essays in Honor of Edwin M. Moseley.* Ed. M. J. Levith. Saratoga Springs, N.Y.: Skidmore College, 1976, pp. 133–42.

—   Levins, Lynn G. *Faulkner's Heroic Design* (A35₂; 1976), pp. 94–114.

> Considers heroic elements in the novel and in the major characters.

F25₂   Brumm, Anne-Marie. "The World as Madhouse: Motifs of Absurdity in Virginia Woolf's *Mrs. Dalloway*, William Faulkner's *As I Lay Dying*, and Jean-Paul Sartre's *Le Mur.*" *Neohelicon*, 4, Nos. 3–4 (1976), 295–330.

F26₂   Branch, Watson G. "Darl Bundren's 'Cubistic' Vision." *Texas Studies in Literature and Language*, 19 (Spring 1977), 42–59.

> Darl's "new way" of seeing reality reflects Faulkner's own experience.

F27₂   Rosenman, John B. "Physical-Spatial Symbolism in *As I Lay Dying.*" *College Literature*, 4 (Spring 1977), 176–77.

> On the opening scene at the cottonhouse.

F28₂   Middleton, David. "Faulkner's Folklore in *As I Lay Dying*: An Old Motif in a New Manner." *Studies in the Novel*, 9 (Spring 1977), 46–53.

> The novel is "a careful inversion of the 'grieving husband' conventions of the traditional 'mourning husband' story."

F29₂   DeSpain, LaRene, and Roderick A. Jacobs. "Syntax and Characterization in Faulkner's *As I Lay Dying.*" *Journal of English Linguistics*, 11 (March 1977), 1–8.

F30₂   Watkins, Floyd C. "*As I Lay Dying*: The Dignity of Earth." In *In Time and Place: Some Origins of American Fiction.* Athens: Univ. of Georgia Press, 1977, pp. 173–89.

> Discusses local realism, poverty in the Bundrens' world, and conventions in that world.

—   Capps, Jack L., ed. As I Lay Dying: *A Concordance to the Novel* (A40₂; 1977).

F31₂   Devlin, Albert J. "The Complex Pastoralism of *As I Lay
        Dying.*" *Publications of the Missouri Philological Association,*
        2 (1977), 46–52.

—   Williams, David. *Faulkner's Women* (A47₂; 1977), pp. 97–126.
        Analyzes Addie's relationship to her family in archetypal terms. Addie is
        the "mother of death, . . . who must die herself in order to bring new life
        into the world."

F32₂   Kehler, Joel R. "Faulkner, Melville, and a Tale of Two
        Carpenters." *Notes on Modern American Literature,* 1
        (Summer 1977), 22.

F33₂   Seib, Kenneth. "Midrashic legend in *As I Lay Dying.*" *Notes
        on Modern American Literature,* 2 (Winter 1977), 5.

F34₂   Palliser, Charles. "Fate and Madness: The Determinist Vision
        of Darl Bundren." *American Literature,* 49 (January 1978),
        619–33.
        Sees Darl's determinist nature as a central theme, and studies the
        relationship between his madness, clairvoyance, and determinism.

F35₂   Idei, Yasuko. "A Quest for Identity & the Meaning of the Be-
        Verb in *As I Lay Dying.*" *Kyushu American Literature,* 19
        (May 1978), 32–44.

—   Kinney, Arthur F. *Faulkner's Narrative Poetics* (A54₂; 1978),
        pp. 161–77.
        The book is "Darl's autobiography of consciousness." All the narrative
        consciousnesses "radiate from the core linkage of Addie and Darl."

F36₂   Godden, Richard. "William Faulkner, Addie Bundren, and
        Language." In A52₂ (1978), pp. 101–23.
        Analyzes the theory of language implicit in Addie's statements and
        Faulkner's attitude toward it.

F37₂   Collins, Carvel. "Faulkner and Mississippi." In A52₂ (1978),
        pp. 139–59.
        On Faulkner's real attitude toward Mississippi, with special reference to
        this novel.

F38₂   Alldredge, Betty. "Spatial Form in Faulkner's *As I Lay
        Dying.*" *Southern Literary Journal,* 11, No. 1 (Fall 1978),
        3–19.
        The novel requires "reflexive" reading to comprehend the centrality of
        Addie and the irony achieved through multiple viewpoints.

F39₂   Seltzer, Leon F., and Jan Viscomi. "Natural Rhythms and
        Rebellion: Anse's Role in *As I Lay Dying.*" *Modern Fiction
        Studies*, 24 (Winter 1978), 556–64.

> A sympathetic study of Anse, describing him as a man with qualities to
> endure the hardships of the journey. He does "what is best for his family,
> and possibly he is even the instrument of God's will."

F40₂   D'Avanzo, Mario L. "Reason and Madness: Darl's Farewell
        Scene in *As I Lay Dying.*" *Notes on Contemporary Literature*,
        9, No. 1 (January 1979), 9–10.

F41₂   Ross, Stephen M. "Voice in Narrative Texts: The Example of
        As I Lay Dying." *PMLA*, 94 (March 1979), 300–310.

> *Mimetic* voice, discourse that derives from verbal imitation and
> representation, and *textual* voice, which is the paralinguistic context of
> discourse.

F42₂   DeSpain, LaRene. "The Shape and Echo of Their Word:
        Narration and Character in *As I Lay Dying.*" *Massachusetts
        Studies in English*, 6, Nos. 1–2 (1979), 49–59.

F43₂   Shoemaker, Alice. "A Wheel within a Wheel: Fusion of Form
        and Content in Faulkner's *As I Lay Dying.*" *Arizona
        Quarterly*, 35 (Summer 1979), 101–13.

> Contrasting the perspectives of Bundrens and non-Bundrens, this argues
> that Faulkner uses "the architectonic structure of the wheel within the
> wheel" and blends it with the quest pattern.

F44₂   Brooks, George. "Vardaman's Journey in *As I Lay Dying.*"
        Arizona Quarterly, 35 (Summer 1979), 114–28.

> The deterioration of Vardaman.

—   Wittenberg, Judith. *Faulkner* (A61₂; 1979), pp. 103–17.

> Emphasizes psychological relationships among the three older brothers, but
> focuses more on Cash than most studies do.

—   Stonum, Gary Lee. *Faulkner's Career* (A60₂; 1979), pp. 61–93.

> This book is Faulkner's "purest and most extreme representation of the
> world as motion." It also deals with "the divergence of consciousness and
> knowledge."

F45₂   Kahane, Claire. "Comic Vibrations and Self-Construction in
        Grotesque Literature." *Literature and Psychology*, 29, No. 3
        (1979), 114–19.

—   Kartiganer, Donald M. *The Fragile Thread* (A58₂; 1979), pp.
        23–33.

> Emphasizes ambiguity in the novel, and the "basic differences between Darl
> and Cash."

F46₂   Goodman, Charlotte. "The Bundren Wagon: Narrative
         Strategy in Faulkner's *As I Lay Dying.*" *Studies in American
         Fiction*, 7 (Autumn 1979), 234–42.
         > The wagon is "a symbolic means of objectifying the death of Addie, the
         > disintegration of Darl, and the transformation of Jewel." It allows the
         > reader to become an active interpreter of events.

F47₂   Sitter, Deborah Ayer. "Self and Object Representations in *As I
         Lay Dying.*" *Hartford Studies in Literature*, 12, No. 1 (1980),
         143–55.
         > A psychoanalytic study.

F48₂   Lyday, Lance. "Jewel Bundren: Faulkner's Achilles." *Notes on
         Contemporary Literature*, 10 (March 1980), 2.

F49₂   Adamowski, T. H. "Meet Mrs. Bundren: *As I Lay Dying*—
         gentility, tact, and psychoanalysis." *University of Toronto
         Quarterly*, 69 (Spring 1980), 205–27.
         > Oedipal concerns, castration anxiety, oral patterns, and
         > closeness/separation in mother-child relationships.

—   Powers, Lyall H. *Faulkner's Yoknapatawpha Comedy* (A68₂;
         1980), pp. 50–72.
         > Emphasizes the family's difficulty in facing death, and the "Second
         > Chance" implied at the end of the novel.

F50₂   Backman, Melvin. "Addie Bundren and William Faulkner." In
         A63₂ (1980), pp. 7–23.
         > The creation of Addie comes out of Faulkner's need to combat the
         > Quentin-Darl element in himself.

F51₂   Komar, Kathleen. "A Structural Study of *As I Lay Dying.*" In
         A65₂ (1980), pp. 48–57.
         > The arrangement of the parts is related to the central themes.

F52₂   Robinson, Fred M. "Faulkner's *As I Lay Dying.*" In *The
         Comedy of Language: Studies in Modern Comic Literature.*
         Amherst: Univ. of Massachusetts Press, 1980, pp. 51–88.
         > Discusses comic structure in terms of dissolving and creating form, and the
         > function of Cash.

F53₂   Pierce, Constance. "Being, Knowing, and Saying in the 'Addie'
         Section of Faulkner's *As I Lay Dying.*" *Twentieth Century
         Literature*, 26 (Fall 1980), 294–305.
         > The relation between Being and the attempt to verbalize consciousness.

F54₂ Bakker, J. "Faulkner's World as the Extension of Reality: *As I Lay Dying* Reconsidered." In *From Cooper to Philip Roth.* Ed. J. Bakker and D. R. M. Wilkinson. Amsterdam: Rodopi, 1980, pp. 57-70.

> A close study of irony in the novel clarifies the relationships between comic, tragic, and epic elements as well as Faulkner's attitude toward heroism.

F55₂ Kaelin, E. F. "Language as a Medium for Art." *Journal of Aesthetics and Art Criticism*, 40 (Winter 1981), 121-30.

> Uses *As I Lay Dying* as an example in discussing literary works as "intentional" objects.

— Pilkington, John. "The Way of Naturalism: *As I Lay Dying.*" In *The Heart of Yoknapatawpha* (A73₂; 1981), pp. 87-110.

> Explains the novel as a Lost Generation fiction of "the human futility that results from the absence of love or brotherhood." Emphasizes the roles of Anse, Darl, and Cash.

F56₂ Bassett, John Earl. "*As I Lay Dying*: Family Conflict and Verbal Fiction." *Journal of Narrative Technique*, 11 (Spring 1981), 125-34.

> Relates sibling conflict and maternal betrayal to the self-reflexive themes of communication and verbal fictions.

— Turner, Dixie M. *A Jungian Psychoanalytic Interpretation of William Faulkner's* As I Lay Dying (A78₂; 1981).

F57₂ Kloss, Robert J. "Addie Bundren's Eyes and the Difference They Make." *South Carolina Review*, 14 (Fall 1981), 85-95.

> Uses theories of Erik Erikson and Margaret Mahler to analyze "the functioning of eyes in mirroring and the establishment of identity" in the novel. "There is a demonstrable *emotional* vision (or blindness) prevalent in each of the novel's main characters that Faulkner explicitly conveys through eyes and their functions."

Further commentary: A19₂ (Broughton), A22₂ (Weisgerber), E21₂ (Lilly), E70₂ (Cohn), E104₂ (Stafford), J12₂ (Garzilli), AA13₂ (Hauck), AA30₂ (Skaggs), AA86₂ (Rosenman), AA104₂ (Cook), AA112₂ (McGinnis), AA127₂ (Gray), AA158₂ (Palumbo), AA164₂ (Werner), AA171₂ (Ousby), AA203₂ (Porter), CC24₂ (Broughton).

G. *Sanctuary*

$G1_2$ Pavese, Cesar. "Faulkner, a Bad Pupil of Anderson." In
          American Literature: Essays & Opinions. Trans. E. Fussell.
          Berkeley: Univ. of California Press, 1970, pp. 142–45.
          A 1934 article.

—   Langford, Gerald. *Faulkner's Revision of* Sanctuary ($A6_2$;
          1972).

$G2_2$ Morell, Giliane. "The Last Scene of *Sanctuary.*" *Mississippi
          Quarterly*, 25 (Summer 1972), 351–55.
          Images emphasize the impotence of the law in the face of evil.

—   Page, Sally R. *Faulkner's Women* ($A7_2$; 1972), pp. 71–90.
          Emphasizes the theme of motherhood as it is related to moral order or
          chaos in society, and argues that the contrast between Ruby and Narcissa
          is central to the novel.

$G3_2$ Creighton, Joanne V. "Self-Destructive Evil in *Sanctuary.*"
          Twentieth Century Literature, 18 (October 1972), 259–70.
          Explores the theme of self-destructive evil, and the nature of the allegory in
          the book.

—   Bedell, George C. *Kierkegaard and Faulkner* ($A4_2$; 1972), pp.
          115–37.

$G4_2$ Esslinger, Pat M., et al. "No Spinach in *Sanctuary.*" *Modern
          Fiction Studies*, 18 (Winter 1973), 555–58.
          Ironic use of comicstrip Popeye.

$G5_2$ Phillips, Gene. "Faulkner and the Film: Two Versions of
          Sanctuary." *Literature/Film Quarterly*, 1 (July 1973), 263–73.

—   Reed, Joseph W., Jr. *Faulkner's Narrative* ($A14_2$; 1973), pp.
          58–73.
          Emphasizes a set of contrasts in imagery, setting, and character, and
          suggests that the book's weakness is a lack of possibility for empathy, a
          lack of some balance for the bleak coldness.

$G6_2$ Perry, J. Douglas, Jr. "Gothic as Vortex: The Form of Horror
          in Capote, Faulkner, and Styron." *Modern Fiction Studies*, 19
          (Summer 1973), 153–67.
          Faulkner turns the Gothic, as narrative form, inside out.

$G7_2$ Brown, Calvin S. "*Sanctuary*: From Confrontation to Peaceful
          Void." *Mosaic*, 7, No. 1 (Fall 1973), 75–95.

The novel is developed by a strategy of confrontations, first between individuals and then between groups and attitudes. It ends in the acceptance of meaninglessness.

G8₂ Schmuhl, Robert. "Faulkner's *Sanctuary*: The Last Laugh of Innocence." *Notes on Mississippi Writers*, 6 (Winter 1974), 73–80.

Tommy's role in the novel.

G9₂ Malraux, André. "Preface to William Faulkner's *Sanctuary*." Trans. V. M. Horvath. *Southern Review*, 10 (October 1974), 889–91.

A translation of Malraux's 1934 preface.

G10₂ Miller, James E., Jr. "*Sanctuary*: Yoknapatawpha's Waste Land." In *Individual and Community: Variations on a Theme in American Fiction*. Durham: Duke Univ. Press, 1975, pp. 137–59.

Most of this is also included in *The Twenties* (See E35₂; 1975), pp. 249–67. Discusses comedy and humor, and their relation to themes of horror and emptiness.

G11₂ Chapple, Richard L. "Character Parallels in *Crime and Punishment* and *Sanctuary*." *Germano-Slavica*, 2 (Spring 1976), 5–14.

G12₂ Guerard, Albert J. "The Misogynous Vision as High Art: Faulkner's *Sanctuary*." *Southern Review*, 12 (April 1976), 215–31.

Included in A32₂ (1976), pp. 109–35. Faulkner converts his misogyny into great art and a meaningful vision of evil.

G13₂ Tallack, Douglas G. "William Faulkner and the Tradition of Tough-Guy Fiction." In *Dimensions of Detective Fiction*. Ed. L. N. Landrum et al. [Bowling Green, Ohio]: Popular Press, 1976, pp. 247–64.

Relation of Faulkner's fiction to the popular genre.

G14₂ Yonce, Margaret. "'His True Penelope Was Flaubert': *Madame Bovary* and *Sanctuary*." *Mississippi Quarterly*, 29 (Summer 1976), 439–42.

Parallel passages, images, themes.

G15₂ Degenfelder, E. Pauline. "The Four Faces of Temple Drake: Faulkner's *Sanctuary*, *Requiem for a Nun*, and the Two Film Adaptations." *American Quarterly*, 28 (Winter 1976), 544–60.

Examined as indices to woman's social position, as demonstrations of the shift in woman's film images over time, and as evidence of Faulkner's arrival at artistic maturity in portraying women.

G16₂ Angelius, Judith W. "Temple's Provocative Quest: Or, What Really Happened at the Old Frenchman Place." *Notes on Mississippi Writers*, 10 (Winter 1977), 74–79.

G17₂ Adamowski, T. H. "Faulkner's Popeye: The 'Other' as Self." *Canadian Review of American Studies*, 8 (Spring 1977), 36–51.

It is not sufficient to see Popeye as a symbol of mechanical man or a modern wasteland. He is an "object" nonetheless "possessed of an inner life," a theatrical man of gestures. A reader's response to Popeye is important: "we experience him as both fascinating and indifferent."

G18₂ Ford, Daniel G. "Comments on William Faulkner's Temporal Vision in *Sanctuary, The Sound and the Fury, Light in August, Absalom, Absalom!*" *Southern Quarterly*, 15 (April 1977), 283–90.

The theme of time as a vehicle of change against a recurring sense of eternity.

G19₂ Kinney, Arthur F. "Faulkner and Flaubert." *Journal of Modern Literature*, 6 (April 1977), 222–47.

Affinities and influences, with emphasis on *Sanctuary* and *Requiem for a Nun*.

— Williams, David. *Faulkner's Women* (A47₂; 1977), pp. 127–56.

Studies archetypal female images, especially in relation to Faulkner's revisions.

G20₂ Kauffman, Linda. "The Madam and the Midwife: Reba Rivers and Sairy Gamp." *Mississippi Quarterly*, 30 (Summer 1977), 395–401.

Both represent human endurance and survival in a corrupt world.

— Kinney, Arthur F. *Faulkner's Narrative Poetics* (A54₂; 1978), pp. 177–94.

Temple "is the core character"; but Horace's "narrative consciousness" is important.

G21₂ Petesch, Donald A. "Temple Drake: Faulkner's Mirror for the Social Order." *Studies in American Fiction*, 7 (Spring 1979), 37–48.

She reflects corruption in the middle-class social order. The article emphasizes merging of identities in the book.

— Wittenberg, Judith B. *Faulkner* (A61₂; 1979), pp. 89–102.

Explores the novel's unusual bleakness in terms of symbolic patterns and the author's relationship to several main characters.

G22₂   Hardt, John S. "And Faulkner Nodded: Calvin Coolidge in *Sanctuary*." *Notes on Mississippi Writers*, 12 (Summer 1979), 30–31.

—   Kerr, Elizabeth M. "*Sanctuary*: The Persecuted Maiden, or Vice Triumphant." In *William Faulkner's Gothic Domain* (A59₂; 1979), pp. 88–106.

G23₂   Toles, George. "The Space Between: A Study of Faulkner's *Sanctuary*." *Texas Studies in Literature and Language*, 22 (Spring 1980), 22–47.

Analyzes the prose style of *Sanctuary* in comparison with that of *The Sound and the Fury* and *As I Lay Dying*, and studies Faulkner's personal conflicts as implied by the pattern of revisions of the manuscript. Pays special attention to the opening scene—the importance of Popeye's rigidity to the plot, and the contradictory impulses of moving the reader in on the scene and holding him away from it.

—   Powers, Lyall H. *Faulkner's Yoknapatawpha Comedy* (A68₂; 1980), pp. 73–88.

It is Faulkner's "most blatant presentation of the raw horror of evil," mitigated only by the self-destructiveness of evil.

G24₂   Hurd, Myles. "Faulkner's Horace Benbow: The Burden of Characterization and the Confusion of Meaning in *Sanctuary*." *College Language Association Journal*, 23 (June 1980), 416–30.

Revisions led to confusion in character portrayal.

G25₂   Kerr, Elizabeth M. "The Creative Evolution of *Sanctuary*." In A65₂ (1980), pp. 14–28.

Genesis of the novel.

G26₂   Polk, Noel, ed. *Sanctuary: The Original Text*. New York: Random House, 1981.

Polk has edited the original version of *Sanctuary*, submitted for publication in 1929 but not published. An afterword discusses textual history.

G27₂   Cowley, Malcolm. "Faulkner Was Wrong About 'Sanctuary.'" *New York Times Book Review*, February 22, 1981, pp. 9, 25.

Reviews Polk's edition, and also Minter's biography.

G28₂   Day, Douglas. "'The Most Horrific Tale I Could Imagine.'" *Washington Post*, March 8, 1981, Books, pp. 8–9.

G29₂   Boozer, William. "Faulkner On Faulkner A Fascinating Study." *Nashville Banner*, March 14, 1981, p. A5.

Reviews Polk's edition. A second review by Boozer appears in the
Memphis Commercial Appeal, April 5, 1981, p. G6.

G30₂   Mackinnon, Lachlan. "Transplanting the Art." *Times Literary
       Supplement*, August 21, 1981, p. 951.

G31₂   Morrison, Gail M., ed. "A Manuscript Fragment." *Mississippi
       Quarterly*, 34 (Summer 1981), 340–41.
       Possibly from a draft of *Sanctuary*.

—   Pilkington, John. "Spring's Futility: *Sanctuary*." In *The Heart
       of Yoknapatawpha* (A73₂; 1981), pp. 111–34.
       Places the novel against the background of gangsterism in the 1920s, and
       crime in Mississippi, and emphasizes the role of women in this
       "pessimistic" novel.

G32₂   Bassett, John E. "*Sanctuary*: Personal Fantasies and Social
       Fictions." *South Carolina Review*, 14 (Fall 1981), 73–82.
       Considers family patterns and conflicts in the novel and relates them to
       social themes.

Further commentary: A12₂ (Leary), A19₂ (Broughton), A22₂
(Weisgerber), A28₂ (Wagner), A44₂ (Kawin), D28₂ (Mulqueen), D39₂
(Millgate), Q9₂ (Samway), W25₂ (Hardwick), X29₂ (Morell), AA61₂
(Ditsky), AA69₂ (Cook), AA81₂ (Grossman), AA104₂ (Cook), AA133₂
(Milum), AA171₂ (Ousby), GG17₂ (Langford), HH326₂ (Boozer),
KK22₂ (Robinson).

H.   *Light in August*

H1₂   Wilson, Robert R. "The Pattern of Thought in *Light in
       August*." *Bulletin of the Rocky Mountain Modern Language
       Association*, 24 (December 1970), 155–61.

H2₂   Schatt, Stanley. "Faulkner's Thematic Use of Time in *Light in
       August*." *Proceedings of the Conference of College Teachers of
       English of Texas*, 36 (1971), 28–32.

H3₂   Krieger, Murray. "The Light-ening of the 'Burden' of History:
       Light in August." In *The Classic Vision: The Retreat from
       Extremity in Modern Literature*. Baltimore: Johns Hopkins
       Univ. Press, 1971, pp. 313–36.
       Puritanism, racism, fanaticism, tension between tragic and classical visions,
       and the burden of history.

H4₂ Porat, Tsfira. "Sawdust Dolls: Tragic Fate and Comic Freedom in Faulkner's *Light in August*." *Hasifrut*, 2 (1971), 767–82.
> In Hebrew with English summary.

H5₂ Griffith, Benjamin W. "Faulkner's Archaic Titles and the *Second Shepherds' Play*." *Notes on Mississippi Writers*, 4 (Fall 1971), 62–63.

H6₂ Peterson, Richard F. "Faulkner's *Light in August*." *Explicator*, 30 (December 1971), 35.
> Toothpaste episode.

H7₂ Campbell, J. H. "Polarity and Paradox: Faulkner's *Light in August*." *CEA Critic*, 34 (January 1972), 26–31.
> Hightower helps resolve some of the ambiguities in the novel.

H8₂ Inge, M. Thomas. "Faulknerian Light." *Notes on Mississippi Writers*, 5 (Spring 1972), 29.
> Response to H5₂.

H9₂ Sequeira, Isaac. "*Light in August*: The Initiation of Joe Christmas." *Indian Journal of American Studies*, 2, No. 1 (May 1972), 45–55.

H10₂ Borden, Caroline. "Characterization in Faulkner's *Light in August*." *Literature and Ideology* [Montreal], No. 13 (1972), pp. 41–50.
> Emphasis on the grotesque.

— Bedell, George C. *Kierkegaard and Faulkner* (A4₂; 1972), pp. 45–63, 127–30, 215–21.

H11₂ Tanaka, Hisao. "The Significance of the Past for Gail Hightower: One Aspect of *Light in August*." *Studies in American Literature* [Japan], 8 (1972), 24–38.

— Page, Sally R. *Faulkner's Women* (A7₂; 1972), pp. 139–53.
> Considers Lena as a moral norm in the novel, in opposition to Joe, Joanna, and Hightower.

H12₂ Blair, Walter. "'A Man's Voice, Speaking': A Continuum in American Humor." In *Veins of Humor*. Ed. H. Levin. Cambridge: Harvard Univ. Press, 1972, pp. 185–204.
> Covers use of narrators in chs. 15 and 21.

H13$_2$ Ficken, Carl. "The Opening Scene of William Faulkner's *Light in August.*" *Proof*, 2 (1972), 175–84.
An early draft.

H14$_2$ Carey, Glenn O. "*Light in August* and Religious Fanaticism." *Studies in the Twentieth Century*, 10 (Fall 1972), 101–13.
The novel makes a strong attack on religious fanaticism and bigotry.

H15$_2$ Kobler, J. F. "Lena Grove: Faulkner's 'Still Unravished Bride of Quietness.'" *Arizona Quarterly*, 28 (Winter 1972), 339–54.
Relates Lena, a central unifying image, to Keats's description of the urn.

H16$_2$ Heimer, Jackson W. "Faulkner's Misogynous Novel: *Light in August.*" *Ball State University Forum*, 14 No. 3 (Summer 1973), 11–15.

—   Leary, Lewis. *William Faulkner of Yoknapatawpha County* (A12$_2$; 1973), pp. 78–95.

H17$_2$ Schlepper, Wolfgang. "Knowledge and Experience in Faulkner's *Light in August.*" *Jahrbuch für Amerikastudien*, 18 (1973), 182–94.
Focuses on "Memory believes before knowing remembers" to show Faulkner's "choice of verbs to describe awareness."

—   Pitavy, François. *Faulkner's* Light in August (A13$_2$; 1973).

H18$_2$ Burroughs, Franklin G., Jr. "God the Father and Motherless Children: *Light in August.*" *Twentieth Century Literature*, 19 (July 1973), 189–202.
Repressive religion, racism, misogyny all reflect human failures to cope with change.

—   Reed, Joseph W., Jr. *Faulkner's Narrative* (A14$_2$; 1973), pp. 112–44.
Emphasizes dominance of "character" in the novel, the "multiple functions of time" and the temporal disjunctions, the importance of consciousness, and the nature of the reader's involvement.

H19$_2$ Brumm, Anne-Marie. "Authoritarianism in William Faulkner's *Light in August* and Alberto Moravia's *Il Conformista.*" *Rivista di Letterature Moderne e Comparate* [Firenze], 26 (September 1973), 197–220.

H20$_2$ Brooks, Cleanth. "When Did Joanna Burden Die? A Note." *Southern Literary Journal*, 6, No. 1 (Fall 1973), 43–46.
Included in A48$_2$ (1978), pp. 426–29.

H21₂   Wheeler, Sally P. "Chronology in *Light in August.*" *Southern
        Literary Journal*, 6, No. 1 (Fall 1973), 20–42.

H22₂   Collins, R. G. "*Light in August*: Faulkner's Stained Glass
        Triptych." *Mosaic*, 7, No. 1 (Fall 1973), 97–157.
        In this book Faulkner abandoned his progressive saga for a total mythic-
        symbolic analysis of his subject. He utilized a three-part division of social
        and psychological elements developed through Hightower, Joe and Joanna,
        Lena and Byron.

H23₂   Johnston, Walter E. "The Shepherdess in the City."
        Comparative Literature, 26 (Spring 1974), 124–41.
        Defines Lena's role in terms of the pastoral tradition. Also covers Musil
        and Joyce.

H24₂   Palmer, William J. "Abelard's Fate: Sexual Politics in
        Stendhal, Faulkner, and Camus." *Mosaic*, 7, No. 3 (Spring
        1974), 29–41.
        Faulkner uses sexual imagery to suggest repression and frustration of the
        individual in society.

—   Weisgerber, Jean. *Faulkner and Dostoevsky* (A22₂; 1974), pp.
        203–17.

H25₂   Graham, Don B., and Barbara Shaw. "Faulkner's Small Debt
        to Dos Passos: A Source for the Percy Grimm Episode."
        Mississippi Quarterly, 27 (Summer 1974), 327–31.

H26₂   James, David L. "Hightower's Name: A Possible Source."
        American Notes and Queries, 13 (September 1974), 4–5. Psalm
        18.

H27₂   Porter, Carolyn. "The Problem of Time in *Light in August.*"
        Rice University Studies, 61 (Winter 1975), 107–25.
        On the significance of language in relation to time.

H28₂   Young, Glenn. "Struggle and Triumph in *Light in August.*"
        Studies in the Twentieth Century, No. 15 (Spring 1975), pp.
        33–50.
        A story of the struggle against fate, and of the walls collapsing around each
        character.

H29₂   Kellogg, Jean D. "Alienated Man and the Faculty of
        Categorization." In *Dark Prophets of Hope* (See E34₂; 1975),
        pp. 136–56.
        On the allegorical significance of a healthy figure such as Lena and figures
        such as Joe, Joanna, and Grimm.

—   Fadiman, Regina K. *Faulkner's* Light in August (A24₂; 1975).

H30₂   Hays, Peter L. "More Light on *Light in August.*" *Papers on Language and Literature*, 11 (1975), 417–19.
       On the title.

H31₂   Lind, Ilse Dusoir. "Apocalyptic Vision as Key to *Light in August.*" *Studies in American Fiction*, 3 (Autumn 1975), 131–41.

H32₂   D'Avanzo, Mario L. "Allusion in the Percy Grimm Episode of *Light in August.*" *Notes on Mississippi Writers*, 8 (Fall 1975), 63–68.

H33₂   D'Avanzo, Mario L. "Bobbie Allen and the Ballad Tradition in *Light in August.*" *South Carolina Review*, 8, No. 1 (November 1975), 22–29.

H34₂   Rice, Julian C. "Orpheus and the Hellish Unity in *Light in August.*" *Centennial Review*, 19 (Winter 1975), 380–96.
       Violence is connected with self-assertion, self-definition, and man's need for separateness (masculine forces). The other need, for unity, is a feminine impulse toward bonding.

H35₂   Mulqueen, James E. "*Light in August*: Motion, Eros, and Death." *Notes on Mississippi Writers*, 8 (Winter 1975), 91–98.
       Patterns of motion, and conflict between Eros and Death.

H36₂   Davis, Charles E. "William Faulkner's Joe Christmas: A Rage for Order." *Arizona Quarterly*, 32 (Spring 1976), 61–73.
       Joe's futile but steady search for ordering principles reflects a larger tragedy in the South.

—   Jehlen, Myra. *Class and Character in Faulkner's South* (A34₂; 1976), pp. 78–96.

H37₂   Sternberg, Meir. "Temporal Ordering, Modes of Expositional Distribution, and Three Models of Rhetorical Control in the Narrative Text: Faulkner, Balzac and Austen." *PTL: A Journal for Descriptive Poetics and Theory*, 1 (April 1976), 295–316.
       Incorporated into *Expositional Modes and Temporal Ordering in Fiction.* Baltimore: Johns Hopkins Univ. Press, 1978. Uses the development of Joe Christmas as an example of a "primary effect," a fictional effect produced and then overturned "by subsequently revealed expositional materials."

H38₂   Fowler, Doreen F. "Faith as a Unifying Principle in Faulkner's *Light in August.*" *Tennessee Studies in Literature*, 21 (1976), 49–57.
       "The effects and capacities of belief."

H39₂   Anderson, Dianne Luce. "Faulkner's Grimms: His Use of the
        Name before *Light in August*." *Mississippi Quarterly*, 29
        (Summer 1976), 443.

H40₂   Poresky, Louise A. "Joe Christmas: His Tragedy as Victim."
        Hartford Studies in Literature, 8, No. 3 (1976), 209-22.
            His Past victimizes him, and he repeats his past experiences up to his
            death.

H41₂   D'Avanzo, Mario L. "Doc Hines and *Euphues* in *Light in
        August*." *Notes on Mississippi Writers*, 9 (Fall 1976), 101-06.

H42₂   D'Avanzo, Mario L. "Love's Labors: Byron Bunch and His
        Shakespeare." *Notes on Mississippi Writers*, 10 (Winter 1977),
        80-86.

H43₂   Donovan, Josephine. "Feminism and Aesthetics." *Critical
        Inquiry*, 3 (Spring 1977), 605-08.
            On stereotypes.

H44₂   Ruppersburg, Hugh M. "Byron Bunch and Percy Grimm:
        Strange Twins of *Light in August*." *Mississippi Quarterly*, 30
        (Summer 1977), 441-43.

H45₂   James, Stuart. "'I Lay My Hand on My Mouth': Religion in
        Yoknapatawpha County." *Illinois Quarterly*, 40, No. 1 (Fall
        1977), 38-53.
            Faulkner's world is naturalistic but with religious overtones.

—   Williams, David. *Faulkner's Women* (A47₂; 1977), pp. 157-84.
            Studies the novel in relation to a "Lena-Joanna nexus, through the
            psychologies of Sex and Calvinism" and the myth of the Great Mother.
            Argues that the novel allowed Faulkner to "come to terms with" his own
            anima.

H46₂   McDowell, Alfred. "Attitudes toward 'Time' in *Light in
        August*." *Itinerary 3: Criticism*. Bowling Green, Ohio: Bowling
        Green Univ. Press, 1977, pp. 149-58.

H47₂   McAlexander, Hubert, Jr. "General Earl Van Dorn and
        Faulkner's Use of History." *Journal of Mississippi History*, 39
        (November 1977), 357-61.
            His use of the Van Dorn legends.

H48₂   Griffith, Benjamin W., III. "Calvinism in Faulkner's *Light in
        August*." *Bulletin of the Center for the Study of Southern
        Culture and Religion*, 2 (Winter 1978), 8-10.

H49[2]   Cooke, Michael G. "Naming, Being, and Black Experience."
          Yale Review, 67 (Winter 1978), 167–86.
          Compares Faulkner's novel with several by black authors.

H50[2]   Bogel, Frederic V. "Fables of Knowing: Melodrama and
          Related Forms." *Genre*, 11 (Spring 1978), 83–108.
          Uses Faulkner's novel as an example of the modern novelist's "concern
          with problems of knowledge" and use of melodramatic strategies to present
          them.

H51[2]   Sugiura, Etsko. "Seeking for a *Light in August*." *Hiroshima
          Studies in English Language and Literature*, 23 (1978), 45–58.
          In Japanese but with an English abstract.

H52[2]   Um, Mee-sook. "Joe Christmas: A Modern Tragic Hero."
          Yonsei Review (Seoul), 5 (1978), 113–24.

—   Kinney, Arthur F. *Faulkner's Narrative Poetics* (A54[2]; 1978),
          pp. 15–30, 112–18.
          Emphasizes the importance of perception, visual thinking, and conscious-
          ness: "*Light in August* is explicitly concerned with the problems of
          narrative and constitutive consciousness."

H53[2]   Morrisseu, Thomas J. "Food Imagery in Faulkner's *Light in
          August*." *Nassau Review*, 3, No. 4 (1978), 41–49.

H54[2]   Bledsoe, Audrey. "Faulkner's Chiaroscuro: Comedy in *Light in
          August*." *Notes on Mississippi Writers*, 11 (Winter 1979),
          55–63.

H55[2]   Sichi, Edward. "Faulkner's Joe Christmas: 'Memory Believes
          Before Knowing Remembers.'" *Cithara*, 18 (May 1979), 70–78.
          As an Everyman figure, Joe is at the center of the journey pattern in the
          novel, which metaphorically presents the search for meaning and purpose
          in life.

—   Kerr, Elizabeth M. "*Light in August*: Diana in Dixie, or, The
          Way of the Cross." In *William Faulkner's Gothic Domain*
          (A59[2]; 1979), pp. 107–36.

H56[2]   Thompson, Deborah, ed. "*Light in August*: A Manuscript
          Fragment." *Mississippi Quarterly*, 32 (Summer 1979), 477–80.

H57[2]   Hoggard, James. "A Meditation on Comedy." *Southwest
          Review*, 64 (Summer 1979), 265–79.
          Examples from this novel.

—   Kartiganer, Donald M. *The Fragile Thread* (A58[2]; 1979), pp.
          37–68.

Explicates the novel with Christmas as the key, a shadowy figure but a Christ figure of sorts. Argues that the novel deals with "the violent collisions between illusion and reality."

H58₂   Pryse, Marjorie. "*Light in August*: Violence and Excommunity." In *The Mark and the Knowledge: Social Stigma in Classic American Fiction.* Columbus: Ohio State Univ. Press, 1979, pp. 108–42.

On social stigmas and Joe's search for identity, and Joe's threat to the community's identity.

—   Capps, Jack L., ed. Light in August: *A Concordance to the Novel* (A55₂; 1979).

H59₂   Holman, C. Hugh. "Faulkner's August Avatars." In *Windows on the World: Essays on American Social Fiction.* Knoxville: Univ. of Tennessee Press, 1979, pp. 129–43.

Discusses the book as a modernist novel, and describes the characters as avatars.

—   Wittenberg, Judith B. *Faulkner* (A61₂; 1979), pp. 117–29.

Connects the novel to *As I Lay Dying* through patterns of decay and regeneration.

H60₂   Ditsky, John. "Lena's Way: Shared Principles of Structure in Faulkner and Proust." *Journal of English* (Sana'a Univ.), 6 (September 1979), 41–53.

H61₂   Corey, Stephen. "The Avengers in *Light in August* and *Native Son.*" *College Language Association Journal*, 23 (December 1979), 200–212.

Compares Grimm and Buckley.

H62₂   Stuckey, Charles F. "Bill de Kooning and Joe Christmas." *Art in America*, March 1980, pp. 66–79.

Similarities between the novel and de Kooning's early abstract painting.

H63₂   Hlavsa, Virginia V. "St. John and Frazer in *Light in August*: Biblical Form and Mythic Function." *Bulletin of Research in the Humanities*, 83 (Spring 1980), 9–26.

On Faulkner's use of the Gospel and *The Golden Bough.*

H64₂   Martin, Timothy P. "The Art and Rhetoric Chronology in Faulkner's *Light in August.*" *College Literature*, 7 (Spring 1980), 125–35.

Purposes of an underlying "antichronology."

H65₂   Rosenzweig, Paul. "Faulkner's Motif of Food in *Light in August.*" *American Imago*, 37 (Spring 1980), 93–112.

A reading based on oedipal fears, oral patterns, the rejection of food, and the confusion of excrement and food.

H66₂   Taylor, Carole Anne. "*Light in August*: The Epistemology of Tragic Paradox." *Texas Studies in Literature and Language*, 22 (Spring 1980), 48–68.

Interrelated paradoxes of mind, including that of tragic consciousness, and their implications for Faulknerian tragedy.

H67₂   Tanner, Stephen L. "*Light in August*: The Varieties of Religious Fanaticism." *Essays in Literature*, 7 (Spring 1980), 79–90.

The novel is not antireligious but affirms a "humane religious impulse" against narrow concepts.

—   Powers, Lyall H. *Faulkner's Yoknapatawpha Comedy* (A68₂; 1980), pp. 89–105.

Joe's education "develops the theme of the self-destructiveness of Evil." Byron and Hightower are the "Saving Remnant."

H68₂   Godden, Richard. "'Call Me Nigger!': Race and Speech in Faulkner's *Light in August*." *Journal of American Studies*, 14 (August 1980), 235–48.

The meaning of words such as "community" and "nigger" is at the center of the novel.

H69₂   Shaw, Patrick W. "Joe Christmas and the Burden of Despair." *Texas Review*, 1 (Fall 1980), 89–97.

On the pairing of characters psychologically, and the role of Joe as a "vagabond of despair."

H70₂   Billy, Ted. "Faulkner's Feverish Buddha." *American Notes and Queries*, 19 (October 1980), 24–26.

On the ironic use of an image from *Heart of Darkness*.

H71₂   Shurr, William H. *Rappaccini's Children: American Writers in a Calvinist World*. Lexington: Univ. Press of Kentucky, 1981, pp. 112–19.

Faulkner's human allegory is "similar to the vision of John Calvin," and he may be "the deepest explorer of our national religion."

—   Pilkington, John. "Life as a Journey: *Light in August*." *The Heart of Yoknapatawpha* (A73₂; 1981), pp. 135–56.

H72₂   Pascal, Richard. "Faulkner's Debt to Keats in *Light in August*." *Southern Review* (Australia), 14 (July 1981), 161–67.

Criticizes conventional views of parallels between the novel and "Ode on a Grecian Urn."

—   Jenkins, Lee Clinton. *Faulkner and Black-White Relations* (A72₂; 1981), pp. 61–105.

> Studies Joe Christmas' character in relation to racial designations, his failure to establish an identity for himself, and his confrontation with "womanshenegro."

H73₂   Hays, Peter. "Hemingway, Faulkner, and a Bicycle for Death." *Notes on Modern American Literature*, 5 (Fall 1981), 28.

> Compares an image in "The Snows of Kilimanjaro" with one in this novel.

H74₂   D'Avanzo, Mario L. "Hightower and Tennyson in *Light in August.*" *South Carolina Review*, 14 (Fall 1981), 66–71.

> Literary sources in *Maud* and *The Lady of Shalott* clarify the purpose of Hightower's character and the novel's moral vision.

H75₂   Torgovnick, Marianna. "Story-telling as Affirmation at the End of *Light in August.*" In *Closure in the Novel*. Princeton: Princeton Univ. Press, 1981, pp. 157–75.

> Discusses "the pressure toward story-telling, toward the power of narrative to cope with experience" in the three-part ending of the novel.

Further commentary: A11₂ (Hunter), A19₂ (Broughton), A28₂ (Wagner), A35₂ (Levins), A60₂ (Stonum), D3₂ (Muehl), E104₂ (Stafford), G13₂ (Tallack), G18₂ (Ford), X28₂ (Pitavy), AA5₂ (Brumm), AA15₂ (Brooks), AA81₂ (Grossman), AA103₂ (Rose), AA112₂ (McGinnis), AA133₂ (Milum), AA138₂ (Goldman), AA141₂ (Berzon), AA158₂ (Palumbo), AA179₂ (Church), AA183₂ (Wyatt), AA203₂ (Porter), CC8₂ (Kantak), CC20₂ (Lind), GG17₂ (Langford), II18₂ (Boring), II29₂ (Anderson), KK9₂ (Hays).

I. *Pylon*

I1₂   Pearce, Richard. "'Pylon,' 'Awake and Sing!' and the Apocalpytic Imagination of the 30's." *Criticism*, 13 (Spring 1971), 131–41.

> Discusses works from the 1930s with a literary vision of apocalypse.

I2₂   MacMillan, Duane. "*Pylon*: From Short Stories to Major Work." *Mosaic*, 7, No. 1 (Fall 1973), 185–212.

> On the development of five themes from earlier stories of flyers to this novel.

I3₂   McElrath, Joseph R., Jr. "*Pylon*: The Portrait of a Lady." *Mississippi Quarterly*, 27 (Summer 1974), 277–90.

> Laverne is the center of the novel, the story of a complex, unhappy woman seen clearly by neither the reporter nor Roger.

I4$_2$	Lyons, Richard. *Faulkner on Love: A Letter to Marjorie Lyons.* Fargo, N.D.: Merrykit, [1974].
	Letter from Faulkner about the reporter.

I5$_2$	Degenfelder, Pauline. "Sirk's *The Tarnished Angels*: *Pylon* Recreated." *Literature/Film Quarterly*, 5 (Summer 1977), 242–51.

—	Brooks, Cleanth. *William Faulkner* (A48$_2$; 1978), pp. 178–204, 395–405.

I6$_2$	Stern, Michael. "*Pylon* (1935), William Faulkner." In *The Modern American Novel and the Movies.* Ed. G. Peary and R. Shatzkin. New York: F. Ungar, 1978, pp. 40–52.

—	Wittenberg, Judith B. *Faulkner* (A61$_2$; 1979), pp. 130–40.

I7$_2$	Jordan, Peter. "April Fool!" *Notes on Mississippi Writers*, 12 (Summer 1979), 17–22.
	On the reporter.

Further commentary: A4$_2$ (Bedell), A12$_2$ (Leary), A22$_2$ (Weisgerber), A28$_2$ (Wagner), A44$_2$ (Kawin), A54$_2$ (Kinney), AA54$_2$ (Carey).

J. *Absalom, Absalom!*

J1$_2$	Brick, Allen. "*Absalom* Reconsidered." *University of Toronto Quarterly*, 1 (October 1960), 45–57.
	The central theme of the novel is the South.

J2$_2$	Narain, S. K. "*Absalom, Absalom!* by William Faulkner." *Literary Criterion* (India), 6 (Summer 1964), 116–22.

J3$_2$	Loughrey, Thomas F. "Aborted Sacrament in *Absalom, Absalom!*" *Four Quarters*, 14, No. 1 (November 1964), 13–21.

J4$_2$	Yu, Beong-Cheon. "Quentin's Troubled Vision." *English Language and Literature*, 18 (Summer 1966), 112–19.

J5$_2$	Allen, Walter. *The Urgent West: The American Dream and the Modern Man.* New York: Dutton, 1969, pp. 88–90.

J6$_2$	Otomo, Yoshiro. "Young Thomas Sutpen in *Absalom, Absalom!*" *Bulletin, Collection of General Education* (Sendai, Japan), 12, No. 2 (1971), 90–104.

J7$_2$	Randel, Fred V. "Parentheses in Faulkner's *Absalom, Absalom!*" *Style*, 5 (Winter 1971), 70–87.

J8₂   Raper, J. R. "Meaning Called to Life: Alogical Structure in *Absalom, Absalom!" Southern Humanities Review*, 5 (Winter 1971), 9–23.

> Cinematic techniques, especially the use of montage in ch. 5.

J9₂   Tanaka, Hisao. "Quentin Doomed as a Southerner: A Study of *Absalom, Absalom!" Studies in American Literature* (Japan), 7 (1971), 1–14.

J10₂   Rome, Joy L. "Love and Wealth in *Absalom, Absalom!" Unisa English Studies*, 9, No. 1 (1971), 3–10.

> Emphasis on Sutpen.

J11₂   Kartiganer, Donald M. "Process and Product: A Study of Modern Literary Form." *Massachusetts Review*, 12 (Autumn 1971), 801–16.

> Faulkner is concerned with the processes of the imagination encountering experience. Here "the quest for meaning becomes the most vital type of human activity."

J12₂   Garzilli, Enrico. "Myth, Story, and Self." In *Circles Without Center: Paths to Discovery and Creation of Self in Modern Literature*. Cambridge: Harvard Univ. Press, 1972, pp. 52–65.

> The search for self in relation to the novel's mythic structures.

J13₂   Giordano, Frank R., Jr. "*Absalom, Absalom!* as a Portrait of the Artist." In *From Irving to Steinbeck: Studies of American Literature in Honor of Harry R. Warfel*. Ed. M. Deakin and P. Lisca. Gainesville: Univ. of Florida Press, 1972, pp. 97–107.

> In this *Künstlerroman* Quentin is an artist-hero.

J14₂   Wigley, Joseph A. "Imagery and the Interpreter." In *Studies in Interpretation*. Ed. E. M. Doyle and V. H. Floyd. Amsterdam: Rodopi N. V., 1972, pp. 171–90.

> Patterns of imagery.

J15₂   Wad, Søren: "I: William Faulkner; II: *Absalom, Absalom!*" In *Six American Novels: From New Deal to New Frontier*. Ed. J. Bøgh and S. Skovmand. Aarhus: Akademisk Boghandel, 1972, pp. 85–118.

J16₂   Muhlenfeld, Elisabeth S. "Shadows with Substance and Ghosts Exhumed: The Women in *Absalom, Absalom!" Mississippi Quarterly*, 25 (Summer 1972), 289–304.

> The female characters are not stereotypes, but varied and credible; they are abused by the men in the novel.

J17₂ Haury, Beth B. "The Influence of Robinson Jeffers' 'Tamar' on *Absalom, Absalom!*" *Mississippi Quarterly*, 25 (Summer 1972), 356–58.

J18₂ Adamowski, T. H. "Dombey and Son and Sutpen and Son." *Studies in the Novel*, 4 (Fall 1972), 378–89.
    Both novels criticize extreme individualism and the autonomous personality, against the backdrop of the family.

J19₂ Monaghan, David M. "Faulkner's *Absalom, Absalom!*" *Explicator*, 31 (December 1972), 28.
    Compared with *Oedipus Rex*.

J20₂ Tobin, Patricia. "The Time of Myth and History in *Absalom, Absalom!*" *American Literature*, 45 (May 1973), 252–70.
    The conflicting but complementary pulls to synchronic (mythic) or diachronic (historical) interpretations of Sutpen's story establish tension in the novel.

—   Leary, Lewis. *William Faulkner of Yoknapatawpha County* (A12₂; 1973), pp. 96–113.

J21₂ Sachs, Viola. "*Absalom, Absalom!*" In *The Myth of America: Essays in the Structure of Literary Imagination*. The Hague: Mouton, 1973, pp. 103–24.
    Sutpen's story represents a larger American pattern. Bon is the ascendant figure who might have been a redeemer. The alternative becomes Jim Bond.

—   Reed, Joseph, W., Jr. *Faulkner's Narrative* (A14₂; 1973), pp. 145–75.
    Considers telling and hearing, the metaphors each character uses to make sense of Sutpen's story, and the relationship between narrative and myth.

J22₂ Hagopian, John V. "*Absalom, Absalom!* and the Negro Question." *Modern Fiction Studies*, 19 (Summer 1973), 207–11.
    The novel criticizes Southern racism by showing its tragic consequences.

J23₂ Gray, Richard. "The Meanings of History: William Faulkner's *Absalom, Absalom!*" *Dutch Quarterly Review of Anglo-American Letters*, 3, No. 3 (1973), 97–110.
    The novel is a study of the meaning of history and historical re-creation. Included in AA127₂.

J24₂ Brooks, Cleanth. "On *Absalom, Absalom!*" *Mosaic*, 7, No. 1 (Fall 1973), 159–83.

Criticizes Langford's study of textual revisions; also discusses Sutpen as
bourgeois parvenu rather than Southern aristocrat, as another version of
innocence and the American Dream.

J25₂   Stark, John. "The Implications for Stylistics of Strawson's 'On
Referring,' with *Absalom, Absalom!* as an Example."
Language and Style, 6 (Fall 1973), 273–80.

> Response by William R. Brown, "Mr. Stark on Mr. Strawson on
> Referring." *Language and Style*, 7 (Summer 1974), 219–24. Strawson's
> article helps explain the novel's capacity "to compel thought by the reader
> and to involve him inextricably in the experiences Faulkner describes."

J26₂   Lasater, Alice E. "The Breakdown in Communication in the
Twentieth-Century Novel." *Southern Quarterly*, 12 (October
1973), 1–14.

> On the theme of alienation.

J27₂   Behrens, Ralph. "Collapse of Dynasty: The Thematic Center of
Absalom, Absalom!" *PMLA*, 89 (January 1974), 24–33.

> The novel analyzes the concept of family dynasty.

J28₂   Hagopian, John V. "The Biblical Background of Faulkner's
Absalom, Absalom!" *CEA Critic*, 36, No. 2 (January 1974),
22–24.

J29₂   Middleton, John. "Shreve McCannon and Sutpen's Legacy."
Southern Review, 10 (January 1974), 115–24.

> Shreve is not only necessary to Quentin, but also becomes the assenting
> heir to the Sutpen legacy, one who is able to bear the consequences of the
> story.

J30₂   Stafford, William T. "A Whale, an Heiress, and a Southern
Demigod: Three Symbolic Americas." *College Literature*, 1
(Spring 1974), 100–112.

> Compares *Moby Dick* and *The Wings of the Dove*.

J31₂   Ohki, Masako. "The Technique of Handling Time in *Absalom,
Absalom!*" *Kyushu American Literature*, 15 (May 1974),
89–94.

J32₂   Henderson, Harry B., III. *Versions of the Past: The Historical
Imagination in American Fiction*. New York: Oxford Univ.
Press, 1974, pp. 253–69.

> Faulkner's "holist" social and historical imagination.

—   Weisgerber, Jean. *Faulkner and Dostoevsky* (A22₂; 1974), pp.
236–48.

J33₂   Parker, Hershel. "What Quentin Saw 'Out There.'" *Mississippi Quarterly*, 27 (Summer 1974), 323–26.
> On Quentin's recognition of "three Sutpen faces" at the house.

J34₂   Ross, Stephen M. "Conrad's Influence on Faulkner's *Absalom, Absalom!*" *Studies in American Fiction*, 2 (Autumn 1974), 199–209.
> On the use of conjecture and subjective impressions, plus rhetorical strategies.

J35₂   Hartman, Geoffrey. "The Aesthetics of Complicity." *Georgia Review*, 28 (Fall 1974), 384–403.

J36₂   Kellner, R. Scott. "A Reconsideration of Character: Relationships in *Absalom, Absalom!*" *Notes on Mississippi Writers*, 7 (Fall 1974), 39–43.

J37₂   Hlavsa, Virginia V. "The Vision of the Advocate in *Absalom, Absalom!*" *Novel*, 8 (Fall 1974), 51–70.
> Patterns of legalisms, evidence, conjectures, and proof unify the novel, but are also ironically undercut.

J38₂   Wilson, Mary Ann. "Search for an Eternal Present: *Absalom, Absalom!* and *All the King's Men.*" *Connecticut Review*, 8, No. 1 (October 1974), 95–100.

—   Weinstein, Arnold L. *Vision and Response in Modern Fiction* (E27₂; 1974), pp. 136–53.
> Emphasizing the "affective power" of Faulkner's narrative, this argues the novel is "about the effort to open up the closed past, closed doors, and closed minds."

J39₂   Rubin, Louis D., Jr. "Looking Backward." *New Republic*, October 19, 1974, pp. 20–22.

J40₂   Doody, Terrence. "Shreve McCannon and the Confessions of *Absalom, Absalom!*" *Studies in the Novel*, 6 (Winter 1974), 454–69.
> Using the confessional form, with Shreve as model confessor, the novel affirms that freedom and identity can be found only in the individual's experience of community.

J41₂   Schrank, Bernice. "Patterns of Reversal in *Absalom, Absalom!*" *Dalhousie Review*, 54 (Winter 1975), 648–66.
> Interlocking patterns of reversal, especially reversal of cause and effect, join the subjective and social themes.

J42₂   Cleopatra, Sr. "*Absalom, Absalom!* The Failure of the Sutpen Design." *Literary Half-Yearly*, 16, No. 1 (January 1975), 74–93.

J43₂   Shirley, William. "The Question of Sutpen's 'Innocence.'" *Southern Literary Messenger*, 1 (Spring 1975), 31–37.

J44₂   Rodewald, F. A. "Faulkner's Possible Use of *The Great Gatsby*." *Fitzgerald/Hemingway Annual*, 1975, pp. 97–101.

J45₂   Lenson, David. "Classical Analogy: Giraudoux versus Faulkner." In *Achilles' Choice: Examples of Modern Tragedy*. Princeton: Princeton Univ. Press, 1975, pp. 98–116.
> The novel is a Nietzschean tragedy.

—   Irwin, John T. *Doubling and Incest/Repetition and Revenge* (A25₂; 1975).

J46₂   Brooks, Cleanth. "The Narrative Structure of *Absalom, Absalom!*" *Georgia Review*, 29 (Summer 1975), 366–94.
> Clarifies parts that have seemed inconsistent or contradictory to critics.

J47₂   Sabiston, Elizabeth. "Women, Blacks, and Thomas Sutpen's Mythopoeic Drive in *Absalom, Absalom!*" *Modernist Studies*, 1, No. 3 (1975), 15–26.
> Sutpen's attitude toward women and blacks.

J48₂   Lensing, George S. "The Metaphor of Family in *Absalom, Absalom!*" *Southern Review*, 11 (Winter 1975), 99–117.
> The family functions on several levels in the novel, and in several manifestations (ideal, perverted, pseudo).

J49₂   Watson, James G. "'If *Was* Existed': Faulkner's Prophets and the Patterns of History." *Modern Fiction Studies*, 21 (Winter 1975), 499–507.
> To Faulkner the past is not only immanent in the present, but has prophetic value in regard to the future.

J50₂   Korenman, Joan S. "Faulkner and 'That Undying Mark.'" *Studies in American Fiction*, 4 (Spring 1976), 81–91.
> His concern with time and change becomes, in this novel, a concern with immortality and transcendence through art.

J51₂   Polek, Fran J. "The Fourteenth Blackbird: Reflective
Deflection in *Absalom, Absalom!*" *University of Portland
Review*, Spring 1976, pp. 23–34.
  Multiple perspectives on Sutpen.

—   Jehlen, Myra. *Class and Character in Faulkner's South* (A34₂;
1976), pp. 51–73.

J52₂   Ringold, Francine. "The Metaphysics of Yoknapatawpha
County: 'Airy Space and Scope for Your Delirium.'" *Hartford
Studies in Literature*, 8 (1976), 223–40.
  The influence of Bergson and space-time continuums.

—   Guerard, Albert J. "*Absalom, Absalom!*: The Novel as
Impressionist Art." In A32₂ (1976), pp. 204–34.

J53₂   Rollyson, Carl E., Jr. "The Re-Creation of the Past in
Absalom, Absalom!" *Mississippi Quarterly*, 29 (Summer 1976),
361–74.
  Quentin, in ch. 8, learns the truth about Bon from Clytie not Henry.

—   Levins, Lynn Gartrell. *Faulkner's Heroic Design* (A35₂; 1976),
pp. 7–54.
  Includes J162.

J54₂   Rosenman, John B. "Anderson's *Poor White* and Faulkner's
Absalom, Absalom!" *Mississippi Quarterly*, 29 (Summer 1976),
437–38.
  Compares Wash Jones and Joe Wainsworth.

J55₂   Forrer, Richard. "*Absalom, Absalom!*: Story-Telling as a
Mode of Transcendence." *Southern Literary Journal*, 9, No. 1
(Fall 1976), 22–46.
  A humanistic reading of Faulkner's treatment of the relationship between
  past and present, this studies language, chronology, narrative structure, and
  heritage.

J56₂   Adamowski, T. H. "Children of the Idea: Heroes and Family
Romances in *Absalom, Absalom!*" *Mosaic*, 10, No. 1 (Fall
1976), 115–31.
  Sutpen's "quest for failure."

J57₂   Walters, P. S. "Hallowed Ground: Group Areas in the
Structure and Theme of *Absalom, Absalom!*" *Theoria*, 47
(October 1976), 35–55.
  Spatial patterns and details go beyond verisimilitude and atmosphere to
  perform a symbolic function for theme and characterization.

J58₂   Pinsker, Sanford. "Thomas Sutpen and Milly Jones: A Note on Paternal Design in *Absalom, Absalom!*" *Notes on Modern American Literature*, 1, No. 1 (Winter 1976), 6.

J59₂   Rollyson, Carl E., Jr. "Faulkner and Historical Fiction: *Redgauntlet* and *Absalom, Absalom!*" *Dalhousie Review*, 56 (Winter 1976), 671–81.

        Each novel has a character obsessed with his past, and each focuses on the role of consciousness in creating history.

J60₂   Polek, Fran. "From Renegade to Solid Citizen: The Extraordinary Individual and the Community." *South Dakota Review*, 15, No. 1 (Spring 1977), 61–72.

        Sutpen, Gatsby, and the Godfather.

J61₂   Rollyson, Carl E., Jr. "*Absalom, Absalom!*: The Novel as Historiography." *Literature and History*, 5 (1977), 42–54.

J62₂   Rubin, Louis D., Jr. "Scarlett O'Hara and the Two Quentin Compsons." In A43₂ (1977), pp. 168–94.

        Compares the novel with *Gone With the Wind*.

J63₂   Burns, Stuart L. "Sutpen's 'Incidental' Wives and the Question of Respectability." *Mississippi Quarterly*, 30 (Summer 1977), 445–47.

        His logic in choosing a wife is tied to his design, not to respectability.

J64₂   Piacentino, Edward J. "Another Possible Source for *Absalom, Absalom!*" *Notes on Mississippi Writers*, 10 (Winter 1977), 87–93.

        T. S. Stribling's novels.

—   Schoenberg, Estella. *Old Tales and Talking* (A45₂; 1977).

J65₂   Muhlenfeld, Elisabeth. "'We Have Waited Long Enough': Judith Sutpen and Charles Bon." *Southern Review*, 14 (January 1978), 66–80.

        The known facts about Judith and Bon differ from the version constructed by Quentin and Shreve.

J66₂   Newby, Richard L. "Matthew Arnold, the North, and *Absalom, Absalom!*" *American Notes and Queries*, 16 (March 1978), 105.

J67₂   Doxey, W. S. "Father Time and the Grim Reaper in *Absalom, Absalom!*" *Notes on Contemporary Literature*, 8, No. 3 (May 1978), 6–7.

J68₂   Kerr, Elizabeth M. "*Absalom, Absalom!*: Faust in Mississippi, or The Fall of the House of Sutpen." In A52₂ (1978), pp. 61–82. Included in A59₂ (1979), pp. 29–52.

J69₂   Watkins, Evan. "The Fiction of Interpretation: Faulkner's *Absalom, Absalom!*" In *The Critical Act: Criticism and Community.* New Haven: Yale Univ. Press, 1978, pp. 188–212.

    The novel is used to demonstrate a theory of reading as dialectical encounter with a text.

J70₂   Dickerson, Lynn. "A Possible Source for the Title *Absalom, Absalom!*" *Mississippi Quarterly*, 31 (Summer 1978), 423–24.

    A novel by Grace Lumpkin.

J71₂   Kinney, Arthur F. "Form and Function in *Absalom, Absalom!*" *Southern Review*, 14 (Autumn 1978), 677–91. Incorporated in *Faulkner's Narrative Poetics* (A54₂; 1978), pp. 194–215.

    Romance is central to the novel, and the influences go back to Faulkner's great-grandfather as well as to Dostoevsky. *Absalom* is "a novel of self-incarcerations." It deals with the "need for narrative (mythic, historical, personal, fictive)" and "is a book about self-projections."

J72₂   Rimmon-Kenan, Shlomith. "From Reproduction to Production: The Status of Narration in Faulkner's *Absalom, Absalom!*" *Degres*, 16 (1978), f–f19.

    A narratological analysis that relates the "status of narration" to three aspects of repetition: "the recurrence of events, the reproduction of events in narration, and the re-telling of a story heard from someone else." This novel "is a repetition of a repetition, itself re-enacting an absence and brought into being by this absence." Also compares narration to "transference" in psychoanalysis.

J73₂   Kestner, Joseph A. *The Spatiality of the Novel.* Detroit: Wayne State Univ. Press, 1978, pp. 162–69.

J74₂   Canellas, Maria Isabel Jesus Costa. "Time in Faulkner's *Absalom, Absalom!* as Related to Film Technique." *Estudos Anglo-Americanos*, 2 (1978), 33–44.

—   Brooks, Cleanth. *William Faulkner* (A48₂; 1978), pp. 283–300, 301–28, 423–26.

    Includes J24₂ and J46₂.

J75₂   Tobin, Patricia. "'The Shadowy Attenuation of Time': William Faulkner's *Absalom, Absalom!*" In *Time and the Novel.* Princeton: Princeton Univ. Press, 1978, pp. 107–32.

Deals with narrators' obsession with knowing origins, with the power over the imagination of the missing father, with the problems of metaphorical and metonymical interpretations of Sutpen's story by the narrators.

J76~2~ Vanderwerken, David L. "Who Killed Jay Gatsby?" *Notes on Modern American Literature*, 3 (Spring 1979), 12.

Compares *Absalom* with *The Great Gatsby*.

J77~2~ Matlack, James H. "The Voices of Time: Narrative Structure in *Absalom, Absalom!*" *Southern Review*, 15 (April 1979), 333–54.

Its relation to the oral tradition.

— Stonum, Gary Lee. *Faulkner's Career* (A60~2~; 1979), pp. 123–52.

Considers the question of design—Sutpen's, Quentin's, Faulkner's. Also studies differences between *Absalom* and the more "referential" novels that precede it: style, significance of history, "relation of the representational act to the resulting representation."

J78~2~ Brown, May Cameron, and Esta Seaton. "William Faulkner's Unlikely Detective: Quentin Compson in *Absalom, Absalom!*" *Essays in Arts and Sciences*, 8 (May 1979), 27–33.

— Wittenberg, Judith B. *Faulkner* (A61~2~; 1979), pp. 140–55.

J79~2~ Rosenzweig, Paul. "The Narrative Frames in *Absalom, Absalom!*: Faulkner's Involuted Commentary on Art." *Arizona Quarterly*, 35 (Summer 1979), 135–52.

Storytelling is related to the act of love.

J80~2~ Canine, Karen M. "The Case Hierarchy and Faulkner's Relatives in *Absalom, Absalom!*" *SECOL Bulletin* (Southeastern Conference on Linguistics), 3 (Summer 1979), 63–80.

A linguistic analysis.

— Kartiganer, Donald M. *The Fragile Thread* (A58~2~; 1979), pp. 69–108.

Includes J11~2~.

J81~2~ Parr, Susan R. "The Fourteenth Image of the Blackbird: Another Look at Truth in *Absalom, Absalom!*" *Arizona Quarterly*, 35 (Summer 1979), 153–64.

Faulkner uses a fifth narrative voice to undercut the other four. Quentin and Shreve do not present the author's view of the truth of the Sutpen story.

J82₂ Young, Thomas Daniel. "Narration as Creative Art: The Role of Quentin Compson in *Absalom, Absalom!*" In A57₂ (1979), pp. 82–102.

> Relating the Quentin of *Absalom* to the Quentin of *The Sound and the Fury*, Young argues, "Quentin creates a story in which he can participate vicariously as both brother-seducer and brother-avenger."

J83₂ Sykes, S. W. "The Novel as Conjuration: *Absalom, Absalom!* and *La route des Flandres.*" *Revue de Litterature Comparee*, 53 (July–September 1979), 348–57.

J84₂ Turner, Joseph W. "The Kinds of Historical Fiction: An Essay In Definition and Methodology." *Genre*, 12 (Fall 1979), 333–55.

> *Absalom* is an example of the inverted historical novel.

J85₂ Davis, Thadious M. "The Yoking of 'Abstract Contradictions': Clytie's Meanings in *Absalom, Absalom!*" *Studies in American Fiction*, 7 (Autumn 1979), 209–19.

> On Clytie's importance to the novel.

J86₂ Williams, J. Gary. "Quentin Finally Sees Miss Rosa." *Criticism*, 21 (Fall 1979), 331–46.

> On the importance of Rosa to Quentin's developing interest in the Sutpen story, therefore to the structure of the novel.

J87₂ Watkins, Evan. "The Politics of Literary Criticism." *Boundary 2*, 8 (Fall 1979), 31–38.

> *Absalom* is used as an example.

J88₂ Uroff, Margaret D. "The Fictions of *Absalom, Absalom!*" *Studies in the Novel*, 11 (Winter 1979), 431–45.

> On the fictions of the several narrators, especially Shreve, and on Faulkner's ambivalence towards fiction.

J89₂ Samway, Patrick, S. J. "Storytelling and the Library Scene in Faulkner's *Absalom, Absalom!*" *William Faulkner: Materials, Studies, and Criticism*, 2, No. 2 (December 1979), 1–20.

J90₂ Sugiura, Ginsaku. "Nature, History, and Entropy: A Reading of Faulkner's *Absalom, Absalom!* in Comparison with *Moby-Dick* and *V.*" *William Faulkner: Materials, Studies, and Criticism*, 2, No. 2 (December 1979), 21–33.

J91₂ Nelson, David W. "Two Novels of Speculation: William Faulkner's *Absalom, Absalom!* and Uwe Johnson's *Mutmassungen über Jakob.*" *Papers in Romance* [Seattle], 2, supp. 1 (1980), 51–57.

J92₂   Bosha, Francis J. "A Source for the Names Charles and Wash
        in *Absalom, Absalom!*" *Notes on Modern American
        Literature*, 4 (Spring 1980), 13.
            Slaves of Col. Falkner.

J93₂   Ilacqua, Alma A. "Faulkner's *Absalom, Absalom!*: An
        Aesthetic Projection of the Religious Sense of Beauty." *Ball
        State University Forum*, 21, No. 2 (Spring 1980), 34–41.

—   Powers, Lyall H. *Faulkner's Yoknapatawpha Comedy* (A68₂;
        1980), pp. 106–24.
            Argues that *Absalom*, in which Quentin is the main character, is
            "Faulkner's most searing penetration into the evil at the heart of the
            antebellum South's social organization."

J94₂   Bennett, J. A. W. "Faulkner and A. E. Housman." *Notes and
        Queries*, 27 (June 1980), 234.

J95₂   Hagopian, John V. "Black Insight in *Absalom, Absalom!*" In
        A65₂ (1980), pp. 29–36.
            Clytie not Henry is the source of Quentin's final insight.

J96₂   Hunt, John W. "Keeping the Hoop Skirts Out: Historiography
        in *Absalom, Absalom!*" In A65₂ (1980), pp. 38–47.
            On the narrative voices—Quentin, Shreve, and the authorial voice—and the
            process of reconstructing events.

J97₂   Doody, Terrence. "Quentin and Shreve/Sutpen and Bon." In
        Confession and Community in the Novel. Baton Rouge:
        Louisiana State Univ. Press, 1980, pp. 163–83.
            Emphasizes Shreve's importance.

J98₂   Herndon, Jerry A. "Faulkner: Meteor, Earthquake and
        Sword." In A63₂ (1980), pp. 175–93.
            On the Sutpen story as an analogue of Southern history (the rule of the
            sword).

J99₂   Ross, Stephen M. "Faulkner's *Absalom, Absalom!* and the
        David Story: A Speculative Contemplation." In *The David
        Myth in Western Literature*. Ed. R. J. Frontain and J. Wojcik.
        West Lafayette, Ind.: Purdue Univ. Press, 1980, pp. 136–53.

J100₂   Rose, Maxine. "From Genesis to Revelation: The Grand
        Design of William Faulkner's *Absalom, Absalom!*" *Studies in
        American Fiction*, 8 (Autumn 1980), 219–28.
            The biblical framework of the novel.

J101₂ Matthews, John T. "The Marriage of Speaking and Hearing in *Absalom, Absalom!*" *ELH*, 47 (Fall 1980), 575–94.

On the relationship between hearing and speaking among narrators, especially Rosa, and their audiences.

J102₂ Davis, Robert Con. "The Symbolic Father in Yoknapatawpha County." *Journal of Narrative Technique*, 10 (Winter 1980), 39–55.

On Sutpen and the process of the paternal symbol becoming a fiction.

J103₂ Rio-Jelliffe, R. "*Absalom, Absalom!* As Self-Reflexive Novel." *Journal of Narrative Technique*, 11 (Spring 1981), 75–90.

Discusses the theme of man's fiction-making capacity, the distortions and the creative force of the human mind.

J104₂ Davis, Thadious M. "'Be Sutpen's Hundred': Imaginative Projection of Landscape in *Absalom, Absalom!*" *Southern Literary Journal*, 13 (Spring 1981), 3–14.

The interior dimensions of the narrative interrelationships: the process of "imagining" coordinates relationships between self, past, society, and present. Especially useful to consider is the interaction between Rosa and Quentin in creating external and internal landscapes for the action.

— Jenkins, Lee Clinton. *Faulkner and Black-White Relations* (A72₂; 1981), pp. 177–219.

Analyzes the implications of Bon's blackness in the novel, as well as the limitations of Sutpen as tragic hero.

J105₂ Pitavy, François L. "The Gothicism of *Absalom, Absalom!*: Rosa Coldfield Revisited." In A71₂ (1981), pp. 199–226.

The Gothicism is crucial to the design and the meaning of the novel. Distinguishing three levels—story, narration, narrative—helps clarify its purpose. The Gothic vision "is a vision of the creative power." Gothicism is also a means for questioning the validity of created fictions.

J106₂ Robbins, Deborah. "The Desperate Eloquence of *Absalom, Absalom!*" *Mississippi Quarterly*, 34 (Summer 1981), 315–24.

Discusses the attempt of each narrator to avoid interruption or cessation of his or her narrative.

J107₂ Connolly, Thomas E. "Point of View in Faulkner's *Absalom, Absalom!*" *Modern Fiction Studies*, 27 (Summer 1981), 255–72.

Studies each narrative voice and perspective to show how the reader puts together his own "truth" out of the information, distortions, and conjectures he assimilates.

— Pilkington, John. "The Stubbornness of Historical Truth: *Absalom, Absalom!*" In *The Heart of Yoknapatawpha* (A73₂; 1981), pp. 157–88.

> Considers the genesis of the novel, the multiple ways in which it has been interpreted, and the relationships between theme and narrative method.

J108₂ Chavkin, Allan. "The Imagination as the Alternative to Sutpen's Design." *Arizona Quarterly*, 37 (Summer 1981), 116–26.

> Studies the human imagination as a central theme of the novel.

J109₂ Rose, Maxine. "Echoes of the King James Bible in the Prose Style of *Absalom, Absalom!*" *Arizona Quarterly*, 37 (Summer 1981), 137–48.

> Discusses the use of "biblical diction, cadences, syntax, and emphasis," and their effect on the tone and form of the novel.

J110₂ Introduction. *Minnesota Review*, No. 17 (Fall 1981), pp. 53–54.

> An introduction to a series of articles exploring Marxian approaches to *Absalom, Absalom!* Following the papers is a discussion transcribed and edited by Erica Harth, pp. 118–33.

J111₂ Rudich, Norman. "Faulkner and the Sin of Private Property." *Minnesota Review*, No. 17 (Fall 1981), pp. 55–57.

J112₂ Roudiéz, Leon S. "*Absalom, Absalom!* The Significance of Contradiction." *Minnesota Review*, No. 17 (Fall 1981), pp. 58–78.

> On the dialectic between the Quentin and Sutpen stories, and the attempt at understanding the post–Civil War South that grows out of that dialectic.

J113₂ Leroy, Gaylord C. "Mythopoeic Materials in *Absalom, Absalom!*: What Approach for the Marxist Critic?" *Minnesota Review*, No. 17 (Fall 1981), pp. 79–95.

> Explores complications for the Marxist critic confronting this novel, which is incompatible with a "Marxist world view."

J114₂ McClure, John. "The Syntax of Decadence in *Absalom, Absalom!*" *Minnesota Review*, No. 17 (Fall 1981), pp. 96–103.

> Combines linguistic and Marxian methods in a study of the novel's ambivalence about revealing secrets of the past.

J115₂ Markowitz, Norman. "William Faulkner's 'Tragic Legend': Southern History and *Absalom, Absalom!*" *Minnesota Review*, No. 17 (Fall 1981), pp. 104–17.

> A critical Marxian study that emphasizes Faulkner's "muddled" view of history and failure to deal with real social conflicts and relationships.

J116[2]   Ross, Stephen M. "The Evocation of Voice in *Absalom, Absalom!*" *Essays in Literature*, 8 (Fall 1981), 135–49.

> In evoking an imagined past the novel "exposes usually buried assumptions" about fictional discourse's representation of and distortion of reality.

Further commentary: A7[2] (Page), A11[2] (Hunter), A19[2] (Broughton), A28[2] (Wagner), E27[2] (Weinstein), E75[2] (Fletcher), E78[2] (Suda), E88[2] (Grover), E92[2] (Madden), G18[2] (Ford), H47[2] (McAlexander), U6[2] (Edwards), AA26[2] (Brumm), AA30[2] (Skaggs), AA44[2] (Aaron), AA55[2] (Milum), AA69[2] (Cook), AA86[2] (Rosenman), AA101[2] (Watkins), AA106[2] (Conley), AA138[2] (Goldman), AA141[2] (Berzon), AA158[2] (Palumbo), AA171[2] (Ousby), AA180[2] (King), AA203[2] (Porter), CC8[2] (Kantak), GG17[2] (Langford), HH10[2] (Polk), HH15[2] (White), II20[2] (Duncan).

K.   *The Unvanquished*

K1[2]   Ingram, Forrest L. "William Faulkner: *The Unvanquished*." In *Representative Short Story Cycles of the Twentieth Century*. The Hague: Mouton, 1971, pp. 106–42.

K2[2]   Anderson, Hilton. "Two Possible Sources for Faulkner's Drusilla Hawk." *Notes on Mississippi Writers*, 3 (Winter 1971), 108–10.

> Col. Falkner's fiction.

—   Reed, Joseph, W., Jr. *Faulkner's Narrative* (A14[2]; 1973), pp. 176–85.

K3[2]   Tucker, Edward L. "Faulkner's Drusilla and Ibsen's Hedda." *Modern Drama*, 16 (September 1973), 157–61.

K4[2]   Bledsoe, A. S. "Colonel John Sartoris' Library." *Notes on Mississippi Writers*, 7 (Spring 1974), 26–29.

K5[2]   Organ, Dennis. "The Morality of Rosa Millard: Inversion in Faulkner's *The Unvanquished*." *Publications of the Arkansas Philological Association*, 1, No. 2 (Spring 1975), 37–41.

K6[2]   Roberts, John J., and R. Leon Scott, Jr. "Faulkner's *The Unvanquished*." *Explicator*, 34 (March 1976), 49.

> Revised and reprinted in 35 (Winter 1976), 3–4. The frozen water moccasin in "Vendee."

K7[2]   Memmott, A. James. "Sartoris *Ludens*: The Play Element in *The Unvanquished*." *Mississippi Quarterly*, 29 (Summer 1976), 375–87.

Faulkner studies the play or game element in Southern culture during the
war, and its disintegration in Grumby.

—   Creighton, Joanne V. *William Faulkner's Craft of Revision*
       (A41₂; 1977), pp. 73–84.

K8₂   Wilson, G. Jennifer. "Faulkner's 'Riposte in Tertio.'"
       American Notes and Queries, 16 (February 1978), 88.

K9₂   Bradford, M. E. "Faulkner's *The Unvanquished*: The High
       Costs of Survival." *Southern Review*, 14 (July 1978), 428–37.

       Studies a sequence of protagonists through whom is unfolded a sense of
       Southern corporate identity in time.

K10₂   Milum, Richard A. "Faulkner, Scott and Another Source for
       Drusilla." *Mississippi Quarterly*, 31 (Summer 1978), 425–28.

       Rob Roy.

—   Wittenberg, Judith B. *Faulkner* (A61₂; 1979), pp. 156–66.

       The book "is Faulkner's final expression of his recurrent attempt to come
       to terms with his personal family history."

K11₂   Young, Thomas Daniel. "Pioneering on Principle, or How a
       Traditional Society May Be Dissolved." In A57₂ (1979), pp.
       34–48. Slightly revised for *The Past in the Present: A Thematic
       Study of Modern Southern Fiction*. Baton Rouge: Louisiana
       State Univ. Press, 1981, pp. 25–45.

       The novel suggests that the Civil War destroyed conventional codes of
       behavior and traditional values.

K12₂   Pryse, Marjorie. "Miniaturizing Yoknapatawpha: *The
       Unvanquished* as Faulkner's Theory of Realism." *Mississippi
       Quarterly*, 33 (Summer 1980), 343–54.

       Though the novel is basically realistic, Faulkner often miniaturizes or
       enlarges scenes or characters for thematic emphasis.

K13₂   Haynes, Jayne Isbell. "Faulkner's Verbena." *Mississippi
       Quarterly*, 33 (Summer 1980), 355–62.

       Which verbena did he intend?

—   Powers, Lyall H. *Faulkner's Yoknapatawpha Comedy* (A68₂;
       1980), pp. 125–41.

       Suggests that Bayard is a hero, "the Faulknerian standard against which"
       characters in other novels can be measured.

K14₂   Pilkington, John. "'Strange Times' in Yoknapatawpha." In
       A64₂ (1980), pp. 71–89.

       On "Skirmish at Sartoris" and Faulkner's narrative technique of
       counterpoint.

K15₂   Akin, Warren, IV. "'Blood and Raising and Background': The
        Plot of *The Unvanquished.*" *Modern Language Studies*, 11,
        No. 1 (1980), 3–11.

> Analyzes the success and failure of the novel in terms of the function of
> early sections to prepare for Bayard's crucial decision at the end, "one of
> the major incidents in the Yoknapatawpha chronicle."

K16₂   Lent, John D. "Teaching the Cycle of Short Stories." *English
        Journal*, 70 (January 1981), 55–57.

> Teaching *The Unvanquished* to high school students.

—   Jenkins, Lee Clinton. *Faulkner and Black-White Relations*
        (A72₂; 1981), pp. 107–33.

> Discusses Louvinia, Ringo, and Loosh, and considers limitations in
> Faulkner's view of blacks' self-perceptions.

—   Pilkington, John. "The Civil War and Reconstruction: *The
        Unvanquished.*" In *The Heart of Yoknapatawpha* (A73₂; 1981),
        pp. 189–215.

> Reviews the textual history, the change from stories to novel, the central role of
> Bayard, and the implications of "An Odor of Verbena."

Further commentary: A7₂ (Page), A12₂ (Leary), A19₂ (Broughton),
A22₂ (Weisgerber), A28₂ (Wagner), A34₂ (Jehlen), A35₂ (Levins), A47₂
(Williams), A54₂ (Kinney), D24₂ (Rogers), AA44₂ (Aaron), AA133₂
(Milum), AA138₂ (Goldman), AA183₂ (Wyatt), AA201₂ (Messenger).

L.   *The Wild Palms*

L1₂   Stevick, Philip. *The Chapter in Fiction: Theories of Narrative
        Division.* Syracuse: Syracuse Univ. Press, 1970, pp. 113–14.

L2₂   Monteiro, George. "'Between Grief and Nothing': Hemingway
        and Faulkner." *Hemingway Notes*, 1 (Spring 1971), 13–15.

> Also see 2 (Fall 1972), 16–17; and Robert H. Woodward, 2 (Spring 1972),
> 7–8.

L3₂   Rama, Roa, P. G. "Faulkner's *Old Man*: A Critique." *Indian
        Journal of American Studies*, 1, No. 4 (November 1971),
        43–50.

L4₂   McHaney, Thomas L. "Anderson, Hemingway, and Faulkner's
        The Wild Palms." *PMLA*, 87 (May 1972), 465–74.

> Considers several allusions to Sherwood Anderson and Ernest Hemingway,
> and the differences between Faulkner's and Hemingway's treatment of
> Anderson.

— Bedell, George C. *Kierkegaard and Faulkner* (A4$_2$; 1972), pp. 161–73.

L5$_2$ Brooks, Cleanth. "The Tradition of Romantic Love and *The Wild Palms*." *Mississippi Quarterly*, 25 (Summer 1972), 265–87.
   Paper presented by Brooks in South Carolina in 1968, and the ensuing discussion.

— Page, Sally R. *Faulkner's Women* (A7$_2$; 1972), pp. 122–35.

L6$_2$ Richards, Lewis. "Sex Under *The Wild Palms* and a Moral Question." *Arizona Quarterly*, 28 (Winter 1972), 326–32.
   Carnality and lechery replace love.

L7$_2$ Monteiro, George. "The Limits of Professionalism: A Sociological Approach to Faulkner, Fitzgerald and Hemingway." *Criticism*, 15 (Spring 1973), 145–55.
   Considers their use of the medical profession as a theme.

— McHaney, Thomas L. *William Faulkner's* The Wild Palms (A26$_2$; 1975).

L8$_2$ Springer, Mary Doyle. *Forms of the Modern Novella.* Chicago: Univ. of Chicago Press, 1975, pp. 32–46.
   Comments on "Spotted Horses" and "Old Man."

— Levins, Lynn G. *Faulkner's Heroic Design* (A35$_2$; 1976), pp. 133–44.

L9$_2$ Colson, Theodore. "Analogues of Faulkner's *The Wild Palms* and Hawthorne's 'The Birthmark.'" *Dalhousie Review*, 56 (Autumn 1976), 510–18.
   Considers several similarities—the moral theme, the psychological emphasis, hubris, the scar, and knife imagery.

L10$_2$ Collins, Carvel. "Faulkner: The Man and the Artist." In A52$_2$ (1978), pp. 217–31.
   Discusses several topics, including autobiographical elements in the fiction, with special reference to *The Wild Palms*.

— Brooks, Cleanth. *William Faulkner* (A48$_2$; 1978), pp. 205–29, 406–13.
   Calling his chapter "A Tale of Two Innocents," Brooks interprets the novel as counterpointed stories about innocence. Also deals with the traditions of romantic love (see L5$_2$).

L11₂   Cumpiano, Marion W. "The Motif of Return: Currents and Counter Currents in 'Old Man' by William Faulkner." *Southern Humanities Review*, 13 (Summer 1978), 185–93.

        Studies "Old Man" as a story about modern man's escape from freedom, an ironic quest story.

—   Wittenberg, Judith B. *Faulkner* (A61₂; 1979), pp. 167–79.

        The book reveals Faulkner's ambivalence toward involvement with women, his sense of the pain that accompanies emotional commitment.

L12₂   Foote, Horton. "On First Dramatizing Faulkner." In A57₂ (1979), pp. 49–65.

        On producing "Old Man" for television.

L13₂   Day, Douglas. "Borges, Faulkner, and *The Wild Palms.*" *Virginia Quarterly Review*, 56 (Winter 1980), 109–18.

L14₂   Lee, Dorothy H. "Denial of Time and the Failure of Moral Choice: Camus's *The Stranger*, Faulkner's *Old Man*, Wright's *The Man Who Lived Underground.*" *College Language Association Journal*, 23 (March 1980), 364–71.

L15₂   Hill, James S. "Faulkner's Allusion to Virginia Woolf's *A Room of One's Own* in *The Wild Palms.*" *Notes on Modern American Literature*, 4 (Spring 1980), 10.

L16₂   Cushman, William P. "Knowledge and Involvement in *The Wild Palms.* In A63₂ (1980), pp. 25–38.

        Analyzes each character in terms of personal involvement and means of knowing.

L17₂   MacDonald, Phyllis A. "Experiencing William Faulkner: Rhythms in *The Wild Palms.*" *Bluegrass Literary Review*, 2, No. 1 (1980), 5–17.

L18₂   Wilcox, Earl J. "Christian Coloring in Faulkner's *The Old Man.*" *Christianity and Literature*, 29, No. 2 (1980), 63–74.

Further commentary: Al2₂ (Leary), A19₂ (Broughton), A22₂ (Weisgerber), A37₂ (Wilde), A54₂ (Kinney), J94₂ (Bennett), AA61₂ (Ditsky), AA63₂ (Peckham), CC24₂ (Broughton), I110₂ (Shimura).

M.   *The Hamlet*

M1₂   Pierle, Robert C. "Snopesism in Faulkner's *The Hamlet.*" *English Studies*, 52 (June 1971), 246–52.

        Snopesism is "a habit of mind; it is materialism in its lowest form."

M2₂   Howard, Alan B. "Huck Finn in the House of Usher: The Comic and Grotesque World of *The Hamlet.*" *Southern Review* (Australia), 5 (June 1972), 125-46.
Grotesque horror and frontier humor unify the novel.

M3₂   Walton, Gerald W. "A Word List of Southern Farm Terms from Faulkner's *The Hamlet.*" *Mississippi Folklore Register*, 6 (Summer 1972), 60-75.

M4₂   Jarrett, David W. "Eustacia Vye and Eula Varner, Olympians: The Worlds of Thomas Hardy and William Faulkner." *Novel*, 6 (Winter 1973), 163-74.

M5₂   Rubin, Louis D. "The Great American Joke." *South Atlantic Quarterly*, 72 (Winter 1973), 82-94.
Frontier humor.

M6₂   Moses, Edwin. "Faulkner's *The Hamlet*: The Passionate Humanity of V. K. Ratliff." *Notre Dame English Journal*, 8 (Spring 1973), 98-109.
Ratliff's struggle with Flem is central.

M7₂   Milum, Richard A. "'The Horns of Dawn': Faulkner and a Metaphor." *American Notes and Queries*, 11 (May 1973), 134.
Metaphor of a cow.

M8₂   Creighton, Joanne V. "Suratt to Ratliff: A Genetic Approach to *The Hamlet.*" *Michigan Academician*, 6 (Summer 1973), 101-12.
Shows developing complexity in character.

M9₂   Pfeiffer, Andrew. "'No Wiser Spot on Earth': Community and the Country Store in Faulkner's *The Hamlet.*" *Notes on Mississippi Writers*, 6 (Fall 1973), 45-52.
On the community as theme and setting.

M10₂   Kindrick, Robert L. "Lizzie Dahlberg and Eula Varner: Two Modern Perspectives on the Earth Mother." *Midamerica*, 2 (1975), 93-111.

M11₂   Rubens, Philip M. "St. Elmo and the Barn Burners." *Notes on Mississippi Writers*, 7 (Winter 1975), 86-90.

M12₂   Ilacqua, Alma A. "An Artistic Vision of Election in 'Spotted Horses.'" *Cithara*, 15, No. 2 (May 1976), 33-45.

M13₂   Stineback, David C. "'The Price Had Been Necessity': William Faulkner's *The Hamlet* (1940)." In *Shifting World: Social Change and Nostalgia in the American Novel*. Lewisburg, Pa.: Bucknell Univ. Press, 1976, pp. 142–55.

> There is tension between social change (Flem's usurpation) and nostalgia (Ratliff's voice).

M14₂   Chapdelaine, Annick. "Perversion as Comedy in *The Hamlet*." *Delta* [Montpellier], 3 (November 1976), 95–104.

> On Faulkner's comic methods.

M15₂   Bruss, Elizabeth W. "The Game of Literature and Some Literary Games." *New Literary History*, 8 (Autumn 1977), 153–62.

> Includes *The Hamlet* as an example of a literary game.

M16₂   Fink, Robert A. "Comedy Preceding Horror: *The Hamlet*'s Not So Funny Horses." *CEA Critic*, 40, No. 4 (May 1978), 27–30.

> Humor is used to magnify horror.

M17₂   Burch, Beth. "A Miltonic Echo in Faulkner's *The Hamlet*." *Notes on Contemporary Literature*, 8, No. 4 (September 1978), 3–4.

M18₂   Tien, Morris Wei-hsin. "Faulkner's World as Reflected in *The Hamlet*." *American Studies* [Taiwan], 8 (December 1978), 99–124.

M19₂   McDermott, John V. "Mrs Armstid: Faulkner's Moral 'Snag.'" *Studies in Short Fiction*, 16 (Summer 1979), 179–82.

> On "Spotted Horses."

—   Kartiganer, Donald M. *The Fragile Thread* (A58₂; 1979), pp. 109–29.

> A novel of energy, surprise, and vitality, it is his only major novel "in which he describes a genuine meeting of the community and the individual."

M20₂   Male, Roy R. *Enter, Mysterious Stranger: American Cloistral Fiction*. Norman: Univ. of Oklahoma Press, 1979, pp. 52–55.

> On "Spotted Horses" and the pattern of a stranger entering a community.

—   Powers, Lyall H. *Faulkner's Yoknapatawpha Comedy* (A68₂; 1980), pp. 145–61.

> Emphasizes themes of love, barter, nature and the land, and evil.

M21₂   Portch, Stephen R. "All Pumped Up: A Real Horse Trick in
        Faulkner's *The Hamlet.*" *Studies in American Fiction*, 9
        (Spring 1981), 93–95.

—   Pilkington, John. "Materialism in the Country: *The Hamlet.*"
        In *The Heart of Yoknapatawpha* (A73₂; 1981), pp. 217–41.
> Reviews the development of Snopes material, the theme of human greed,
> and the implications of Snopesism.

M22₂   Lucente, Gregory L. *The Narrative of Realism and Myth:
        Verga, Lawrence, Faulkner, Pavese.* Baltimore: Johns Hopkins
        Univ. Press, 1981, pp. 123–34.
> A section called "Southern Literature/Southern History: Flem in Hell, or
> The Trickster Tricked" considers the relationship between realism and
> myth. Comments elsewhere in the book cover the network of romance,
> realism, myth, humor, and irony in Faulkner's work.

M23₂   Heck, Francis S. "Faulkner's 'Spotted Horses': A Variation of
        a Rabelaisian Theme." *Arizona Quarterly*, 37 (Summer 1981),
        167–72.
> Compares the "Sheep Dingdong" episode by Rabelais.

M24₂   Higgs, Robert J. *Laurel & Thorn: The Athlete in American
        Literature.* Lexington: Univ. Press of Kentucky, 1981.
> Brief discussion of Labove.

Further commentary: A32₂ (Guerard), A44₂ (Kawin), L8₂ (Springer),
AA30₂ (Skaggs), AA69₂ (Cook), AA78₂ (Simpson), AA112₂
(McGinnis), AA127₂ (Gray), AA133₂ (Milum), AA201₂ (Messenger),
KK35₂ (Kiell).

N.   *Go Down, Moses*

N1₂   Tyner, Troi. "The Function of the Bear Ritual in Faulkner's
       Go Down, Moses." *Journal of the Ohio Folklore Society*, 3
       (1968), 19–40.

N2₂   Stephens, Rosemary. "Mythical Elements of 'Pantaloon in
       Black'." *University of Mississippi Studies in English*, 11 (1970),
       45–51.

N3₂   Cate, Hollis L. "Faulkner's V-Shaped Land in 'Delta
       Autumn.'" *Research Studies* [Washington State Univ.] 38
       (June 1970), 156.
> On the funnel-shaped symbol.

N4₂   Nelson, Malcolm A. "'Yr Stars Fell' in *The Bear.*" *American Notes and Queries*, 9 (March 1971), 102–03.
       Also see 12 (September 1973), 4–5.

N5₂   Hamilton, Gary D. "The Past in the Present: A Reading of *Go Down, Moses.*" *Southern Humanities Review*, 5 (Spring 1971), 171–81.
       The juxtaposition of past and present unifies the book.

N6₂   Sachs, Viola. *Le Sacré et le Profane: "The Bear" de William Faulkner.* Paris: Université de Paris, 1971.
       A pedagogical project—responses of French undergraduates, in English, plus analysis.

N7₂   Maud, Ralph. "Faulkner, Mailer, and Yogi Bear." *Canadian Review of American Studies*, 2 (Fall 1971), 69–75.
       Compares the initiation story with that in *Why Are We in Vietnam?*

N8₂   McDonald, Walter R. "Faulkner's 'The Bear': Part IV." *CEA Critic*, 34 (January 1972), 31–32.
       On Ike's statement that "Sam Fathers set me free."

N9₂   Pinsker, Sanford. "The Unlearning of Ike McCaslin: An Ironic Reading of William Faulkner's 'The Bear.'" *Topic*, Spring 1972, pp. 35–51.
       Ike's education is impractical.

N10₂   Sequeira, Isaac. "*The Bear*: The Initiation of Ike McCaslin." *Osmania Journal of English Studies*, 9, No. 1 (1972), 1–10.

N11₂   Brogunier, Joseph. "A Source for the Commissary Entries in *Go Down, Moses.*" *Texas Studies in Literature and Language*, 14 (Summer 1972), 545–54.
       The diary of a Mississippi planter.

—   Early, James. *The Making of* Go Down, Moses (A5₂; 1972).

N12₂   Dabney, Lewis M. "'Was': Faulkner's Classic Comedy of the Frontier." *Southern Review*, 8 (Autumn 1972), 736–48.

N13₂   Taylor, Walter. "Faulkner's Pantaloon: The Negro Anomaly at the Heart of *Go Down, Moses.*" *American Literature*, 44 (November 1972), 430–44.
       "Pantaloon in Black" reveals Faulkner's ambivalence toward racial problems, especially in his characterization of Rider.

N14₂   Beauchamp, Gorman. "The Rite of Initiation in Faulkner's *The Bear.*" *Arizona Quarterly*, 28 (Winter 1972), 319–25.

N15$_2$ Adamowski, T. H. "Isaac McCaslin and the Wilderness of the Imagination." *Centennial Review*, 17 (Winter 1973), 92–112.
Even in the wilderness scenes Ike is out of step with his community, even before his discoveries in the commissary.

N16$_2$ Stone, William B. "Ike McCaslin and the Grecian Urn." *Studies in Short Fiction*, 10 (Winter 1973), 93–94.

N17$_2$ Sachs, Viola. "*The Bear*." In *The Myth of America* (See J21$_2$; 1973), pp. 125–42.
The story recreates a vision of a primeval American past and man's loss of a second chance. The values of the New Canaan are self-destructive.

N18$_2$ Bell, Haney H., Jr. "The Relative Maturity of Lucius Priest and Ike McCaslin." *Aegis*, 2 (1973), 15–21.
"The Bear" is a more serious initiation story than *The Reivers*.

— Reed, Joseph W., Jr. *Faulkner's Narrative* (A14$_2$; 1973), pp. 185–200.

N19$_2$ Ruotolo, Lucio P. "Isaac McCaslin." *Six Existential Heroes: The Politics of Faith.* Cambridge: Harvard Univ. Press, 1973, pp. 57–78.
On Ike's existential education.

N20$_2$ Bell, Haney H., Jr. "Sam Fathers and Ike McCaslin and the World in Which Ike Matures." *Costerus*, 7 (1973), 1–12.

N21$_2$ Noble, Donald R. "Faulkner's 'Pantaloon in Black': An Aristotelian Reading." *Ball State University Forum*, 14, No. 3 (Summer 1973), 16–19.

N22$_2$ Devlin, Albert J. "'How Much It Takes to Compound a Man': A Neglected Scene in *Go Down, Moses*." *Midwest Quarterly*, 14 (Summer 1973), 408–21.
Sophonsiba's discovery that her brother has a mulatto housekeeper at Warwick becomes important to Ike's moral education.

N23$_2$ Nelson, Raymond S. "Apotheosis of the Bear." *Research Studies* [Washington State Univ.], 41 (September 1973), 201–04.

N24$_2$ Creighton, Joanne V. "Revision and Craftsmanship in the Hunting Trilogy of *Go Down, Moses*." *Texas Studies in Literature and Language*, 15 (Fall 1973), 577–92.
Compares magazine and book versions.

N25₂   Devlin, Albert J. "Faulknerian Chronology: Puzzles and
       Games." *Notes on Mississippi Writers*, 5 (Winter 1973),
       98–102.
       An inconsistency in part 4 of "The Bear."

N26₂   Zender, Karl F. "A Hand of Poker: Game and Ritual in
       Faulkner's 'Was.'" *Studies in Short Fiction*, 11 (Winter 1974),
       53–60.

N27₂   Taylor, Walter. "Horror and Nostalgia: The Double
       Perspective of Faulkner's 'Was.'" *Southern Humanities
       Review*, 8 (Winter 1974), 74–84.
       The story is a tableau based on a paradox, sentimental romance and
       Gothic terror in the same situation.

N28₂   Brunauer, Dalma H. "Worshiping the Bear-God." *Christianity
       and Literature*, 23, No. 3 (Spring 1974), 7–35.
       Shamanism and bear-worship.

N29₂   Creighton, Joanne V. "Revision and Craftsmanship in
       Faulkner's 'The Fire and the Hearth.'" *Studies in Short
       Fiction*, 11 (Spring 1974), 161–72.
       Revisions of magazine versions enrich Lucas' character and integrate the
       story into the novel.

N30₂   Hess, Judith W. "Traditional Themes in Faulkner's 'The
       Bear.'" *Tennessee Folklore Society Bulletin*, 40 (June 1974),
       57–64.
       Faulkner uses folklore to develop the theme of tradition and
       modernization.

N31₂   Mukerji, Nirmal. "Ike McCaslin and the Measure of Heroism."
       Punjab University Research Bulletin, 5, No. 1 (1974), 15–21.

—   Dabney, Lewis M. *The Indians of Yoknapatawpha* (A20₂;
       1974), pp. 118–57.

N32₂   Ackerman, R. D. "The Immolation of Isaac McCaslin." *Texas
       Studies in Literature and Language*, 16 (Fall 1974), 557–65.
       Ike sees from the perspective of nature's unity, Roth from the perspective
       of chaotic civilization.

N33₂   Knight, Karl F. "'Spintrius' in Faulkner's 'The Bear.'" *Studies
       in Short Fiction*, 12 (Winter 1975), 31–32.
       On Percival Brownlee.

N34₂   Blanchard, Leonard A. "The Failure of the Natural Man: Faulkner's 'Pantaloon in Black.'" *Notes on Mississippi Writers*, 8 (Spring 1975), 28–32.

N35₂   Thornton, Weldon. "Structure and Theme in Faulkner's *Go Down, Moses*." *Costerus*, 3 (1975), 73–112.
        Studies the unity of the book through the themes of freedom and responsibility, and through the technique of "latent juxtaposition."

N36₂   Kolodny, Annette. *The Lay of the Land: Metaphor as Experience and History in American Life and Letters*. Chapel Hill: Univ. of North Carolina Press, 1975, pp. 140–45.
        A sympathetic view of Ike, who refuses to prey upon the land.

N37₂   Umphlett, Wiley Lee. "Ike McCaslin and the 'Best Game of All.'" In *The Sporting Myth and the American Experience*. Lewisburg, Pa.: Bucknell Univ. Press, 1975, pp. 58–69.
        Ike transcends the evils of his society and becomes "one of the most positive characters in all modern fiction."

N38₂   Stoneback, H. R. "Faulkner's Blues: 'Pantaloon in Black.'" *Modern Fiction Studies*, 21 (Summer 1975), 241–45.
        The song "Easy Rider" may be a source.

N39₂   Ingrasci, Hugh J. "Strategic Withdrawal or Retreat: Deliverance from Racial Oppression in Kelley's *A Different Drummer* and Faulkner's *Go Down, Moses*." *Studies in Black Literature*, 6, No. 3 (Fall 1975), 1–6.

N40₂   Benert, Annette. "The Four Fathers of Isaac McCaslin." *Southern Humanities Review*, 9 (Fall 1975), 423–33.
        The influence of history and of Cass, Sam, Carothers, and Buck on Ike's actions.

N41₂   Hiers, John T. "Faulkner's Lord-to-God Bird in 'The Bear.'" *American Literature*, 47 (January 1976), 636–37.

N42₂   Kern, Alexander C. "The Growth and Achievement of Faulkner's 'The Bear.'" *Platte Valley Review*, 4 (April 1976), 26–45.

N43₂   Cowley, Malcolm. "Ike McCaslin and the Wilderness." In A33₂ (1976), pp. 89–97.
        Also covers Faulkner's mixed attitude toward Ike.

N44₂   Hochberg, Mark R. "The Unity of *Go Down, Moses*." *Tennessee Studies in Literature*, 21 (1976), 58–65.
        The book has a coherent tragic pattern.

—   Beck, Warren. *Faulkner* (A29$_2$; 1976), pp. 334–582.
        A long discussion of the major themes and methods, story by story.

N45$_2$ Sams, Larry Marshall. "Isaac McCaslin and Keats's 'Ode on a
        Grecian Urn.'" *Southern Review*, 12 (Summer 1976), 632–39.
        "The poem furnishes a key to Faulkner's intention."

—   Levins, Lynn Gartrell. *Faulkner's Heroic Design* (A35$_2$; 1976),
        pp. 75–94.

N46$_2$ Idei, Yasuko. "Faulkner's *Go Down, Moses*: An Interrelation
        between Content and Structure." *Kyushu American Literature*,
        17 (September 1976), 29–41.

—   Jehlen, Myra. *Class and Character in Faulkner's South* (A34$_2$;
        1976), pp. 1–17, 97–126.
        Considers Faulkner's attempt to find a more satisfactory way to present
        black experience and interracial relations in fiction.

N47$_2$ Scafella, Frank. "Models of the Soul: Authorship as Moral
        Action in Four American Novels." *Journal of the American
        Academy of Religion*, 44 (September 1976), 459–75.

N48$_2$ Pounds, Wayne. "Symbolic Landscapes in 'The Bear': 'Rural
        Myth and Technological Fact.'" *Gypsy Scholar*, 4 (Winter
        1977), 40–52.
        Ike is an escapist, misunderstanding the nature of his Eden.

N49$_2$ Schamberger, J. Edward. "Renaming Percival Brownlee in
        Faulkner's 'Bear.'" *College Literature*, 4 (Winter 1977), 92–94.

N50$_2$ Alsen, Eberhard. "An Existentialist Reading of Faulkner's
        'Pantaloon in Black.'" *Studies in Short Fiction*, 14 (Spring
        1977), 169–78.
        Rider, in death triumphantly asserting freedom and individuality, defies a
        cruel God and a cruel society.

N51$_2$ Stone, Edward. "More on *Moby-Dick* and 'The Bear.'" *Notes
        on Modern American Literature,* 1, No. 2 (Spring 1977), 13.

—   Creighton, Joanne V. *William Faulkner's Craft of Revision*
        (A41$_2$; 1977), pp. 85–148.
        Includes N24$_2$ and N29$_2$.

N52$_2$ Cleman, John L. "'Pantaloon in Black': Its Place in *Go Down,
        Moses*." *Tennessee Studies in Literature*, 22 (1977), 170–81.
        Its thematic connections with other stories.

N53[2]   Lofquist, A. J. "More in the Name of Brownlee in Faulkner's *The Bear*." *College Literature*, 5 (Winter 1978), 62–64.

N54[2]   Rollyson, Carl E. "Faulkner as Historian: The Commissary Books in *Go Down, Moses*." *Markham Review*, 7 (Winter 1978), 31–36.
> A close study of the entries and Ike's interpretations.

—   Capps, Jack L., ed. Go Down, Moses: *A Concordance to the Novel* (A49[2]; 1978).

N55[2]   Davis, Walter A. "The Act of Interpretation: Faulkner's 'The Bear' and the Problems of Practical Criticism." In *The Act of Interpretation: A Critique of Literary Reason*. Chicago: Univ. of Chicago Press, 1978, pp. 1–61.
> Uses "The Bear" as an example in developing a theory of radical pluralism.

—   Kinney, Arthur F. *Faulkner's Narrative Poetics* (A54[2]; 1978), pp. 215–41.
> Emphasizes the unfolding consciousness of Ike, but in relation to other problems in the novel. Describes how the novel "radiates from the emblematic core scene in the commissary."

N56[2]   Akin, Warren, IV. "'The Normal Human Feelings': An Interpretation of Faulkner's 'Pantaloon in Black.'" *Studies in Short Fiction*, 15 (Fall 1978), 397–404.
> Relates the story to the rest of the book, and says that it renders grief sympathetically.

N57[2]   James, Stuart. "The Ironic Voices of Faulkner's *Go Down, Moses*." *South Dakota Review*, 16, No. 3 (Autumn 1978), 80–101.
> Faulkner's "Puritan vision of the world and man" is presented by means of several ironic narrative voices.

N58[2]   Walker, David. "Out of the Old Time: 'Was' and *Go Down, Moses*." *Journal of Narrative Technique*, 9 (Winter 1979), 1–11.
> Relates the story to the rest of the book.

—   Kartiganer, Donald M. *The Fragile Thread* (A58[2]; 1979), pp. 130–39.
> Emphasizes Ike's attempt to transfer the meaning of the wilderness rituals to his own community.

N59[2]   Morris, Wesley. *Friday's Footprint: Structuralism and the Articulated Text*. Columbus: Ohio State Univ. Press, 1979, pp. 1–83.

Uses the book as an example in developing a methodology of applied structuralism.

— Wittenberg, Judith B. *Faulkner* (A61$_2$; 1979), pp. 190-204.

The book is transitional, showing Faulkner's shift from the personal to the social and from consciousness to conscience.

N60$_2$ Cowley, Malcolm. "Magic in Faulkner." In A57$_2$ (1979), pp. 3-19.

Discusses magical, mythic, and mythopoeic elements in Faulkner, emphasizing this novel.

— Kerr, Elizabeth M. "*Go Down, Moses*: Paradise Lost, or, The Secret of the Ledgers." In *William Faulkner's Gothic Domain* (A59$_2$; 1979), pp. 137-61.

N61$_2$ Aiken, Charles S. "A Geographical Approach to William Faulkner's 'The Bear.'" *Geographical Review*, 71 (October 1981), 446-59. Originally published in the Proceedings of the Southern Studies Session of the 34th Annual Meeting of the Southeastern Division, Association of American Geographers, Memphis, 1979.

Analyzes the fictional setting and the theme of change in relation to actual geographical changes in Lafayette County.

N62$_2$ Canfield, J. Douglas. "Faulkner's Grecian Urn and Ike McCaslin's Empty Legacies." *Arizona Quarterly*, 36 (Winter 1980), 359-84.

On the myths Ike inherits and the myths he makes to mystify the situation, and on Faulkner's complicity in the process.

N63$_2$ Howell, John M. "Hemingway, Faulkner, and 'The Bear.'" *American Literature*, 52 (March 1980), 115-26.

Faulkner's debt to *For Whom the Bell Tolls*.

N64$_2$ Stein, Paul S. "Ike McCaslin: Traumatized in a Hawthornian Wilderness." *Southern Literary Journal*, 12, No. 2 (Spring 1980), 65-82.

Ike creates his own myth of the wilderness.

N65$_2$ Church, Margaret. "Faulkner and Frazer: The Bear." *International Fiction Review*, 7 (Summer 1980), 126.

N66$_2$ Zender, Karl. "Reading in 'The Bear.'" In A65$_2$ (1980), pp. 91-99.

On the ledger entries, and the importance of the act of reading.

— Powers, Lyall H. *Faulkner's Yoknapatawpha Comedy* (A68$_2$; 1980), pp. 162-91.

Relates the self-destructiveness of evil and the theme of the second chance to the pathos of Ike's failure and the thematic opposition between Ike and Lucas Beauchamp.

N67₂   Martin, Terence. "The Negative Character in American Fiction." In *Towards a New American Literary History*. Ed. L. J. Budd et al. Durham: Duke Univ. Press, 1980, pp. 230–43.
Covers Ike McCaslin.

—   King, Richard H. *A Southern Renaissance* (AA180₂; 1980), pp. 130–45.

N68₂   Seay, James. "The Southern Outdoors: Bass Boats and Bear Hunts." In *The American South: Portrait of a Culture*. Ed. L. D. Rubin. Baton Rouge: Louisiana State Univ. Press, 1980, pp. 118–28.
The novel explores changes in the Southern landscape.

N69₂   Saunders, Barbara A. "'Sold My Benjamin': The Benjamin Reference in *Go Down, Moses*." *Notes on Contemporary Literature*, 10, No. 4 (September 1980), 2–3.

N70₂   Brezianu, Andrei. "'The Unknown Gate': 'Ochi de Urs' by Mikhail Sadoveanu and 'The Bear' by William Faulkner." *Synthesis* [Bucharest], 7 (1980), 123–30.

N71₂   Holsberry, Carmen W. "Faulkner, Fitzgerald, and Pynchon: Modernism and Postmodernism." *English Journal*, 70 (February 1981), 25–30.
Uses "The Bear" as an example.

N72₂   Cooley, John. "The Garden in the Machine: Three Postmodern Pastorals." *Michigan Academician*, 13 (Spring 1981), 405–20.
Faulkner's book is compared with fiction by Vonnegut, Brautigan, and Coover.

N73₂   Southard, Bruce. "Syntax and Time in Faulkner's *Go Down, Moses*." *Language & Style*, 14 (Spring 1981), 107–15.
Studies embedded sentences and embedded narratives.

N74₂   Zender, Karl. "Faulkner at Forty: The Artist at Home." *Southern Review*, 17 (April 1981), 288–302.
Closely studies the link between Faulkner and both Lucas and Ike. In "The Bear" there is "a parable of the career of the artist as Faulkner understood it." The story suggests a major shift in his sense of the artist's "relationship with society."

—   Jenkins, Lee Clinton. *Faulkner and Black-White Relations* (A72₂; 1981), pp. 221–60.

Considers the book as the culmination of central Faulknerian themes such as "man's appropriation and violation of the land . . . and his violation of the human rights of others." Explores the importance of racial patterns, and suggests that the book was Faulkner's most serious attempt to understand blacks' perceptions of themselves.

$N75_2$ Ford, Daniel G. "Mad Pursuit in *Go Down, Moses.*" *College Literature*, 8, No. 2 (1981), 115–26.

Discusses the theme of pursuit in relation to time, motion, and stasis.

—   Pilkington, John. "Pensioners of History: *Go Down, Moses.*" *The Heart of Yoknapatawpha* ($A73_2$; 1981), pp. 243–88.

Reviews the textual history of the book, then explicates each story separately with some attention to relationships between them.

$N76_2$ Stewart, Jack F. "Structure, Language, and Vision in Faulkner's 'The Old People.'" *Ball State University Forum*, 22 (Summer 1981), 51–57.

Considers the story as a "microcosmic epic" built on Ike's vision of a oneness with the forces of nature.

$N77_2$ Bassett, John Earl. "*Go Down, Moses*: Experience and the Forms of Understanding." *Kentucky Review*, 3, No. 1 (1981), 3–22.

The book "explores the relationship between" human fictions and the experiences "on which they are based," the distance between understanding and what is being understood.

Further commentary: $A7_2$ (Page), $A9_2$ (Boecker), $A11_2$ (Hunter), $A12_2$ (Leary), $A19_2$ (Broughton), $A22_2$ (Weisgerber), $A28_2$ (Wagner), $A60_2$ (Stonum), $E91_2$ (Fujihara), $J111_2$ (Rudich), $AA26_2$ (Brumm), $AA78_2$ (Simpson), $AA82_2$ (Culley), $AA101_2$ (Watkins), $AA103_2$ (Rose), $AA133_2$ (Milum), $AA141_2$ (Berzon), $AA147_2$ (Alexander), $AA164_2$ (Werner), $AA186_2$ (Oberhelman), $AA188_2$ (McKethan), $AA208_2$ (Nilon), $GG21_2$ (Capps), $HH49_2$ (Covici), $II56_2$ (Langman), $KK9_2$ (Hays).

O.   *Intruder in the Dust*

$O1_2$ Skerry, Philip J. "*The Adventures of Huckleberry Finn* and *Intruder in the Dust*: Two Conflicting Myths of the American Experience." *Ball State University Forum*, 13, No. 1 (Winter 1972), 4–13.

O2₂   Monaghan, David M. "Faulkner's Relationship to Gavin Stevens in *Intruder in the Dust*." *Dalhousie Review*, 52 (Autumn 1972), 449–57.

Faulkner satirizes Steven's position, and counters it with Chick's.

O3₂   Hutchinson, D. "The Style of Faulkner's *Intruder in the Dust*." *Theoria*, 39 (October 1972), 33–47.

Stylistic devices are important in the portrayal of Chick's adolescent perspective. Faulkner combines the setting of a regional novel, the action of a detective story, and the point of view of the Bildungsroman.

O4₂   Degenfelder, E. Pauline. "The Film Adaptation of Faulkner's *Intruder in the Dust*." *Literature/Film Quarterly*, 1 (Spring 1973), 138–48. Revised for *The Modern American Novel and the Movies*. Ed. G. Peary and R. Shatzkin. New York: Ungar, 1978, pp. 178–86.

O5₂   Kearney, J. A. "Paradox in Faulkner's *Intruder in the Dust*." *Theoria*, 49 (May 1973), 55–67.

The unity of form and theme is seen through the emphasis on the paradox that freedom is often false freedom or escape, and the point that there is a difference between compulsiveness and commitment.

—   Reed, Joseph W., Jr. *Faulkner's Narrative* (A14₂; 1973), pp. 201–11.

O6₂   Sequeira, Isaac. "*Intruder in the Dust*." *Bulletin of the Ramakrishna Mission Institute of Culture*, March 1974, pp. 64–68.

O7₂   Kane, Patricia. "Only too Rhetorical Rhetoric: A Reading of *Intruder in the Dust*." *Notes on Contemporary Literature*, 4, No. 3 (May 1974), 2–3.

O8₂   Samway, Patrick, S.J. "New Material for Faulkner's *Intruder in the Dust*." In A21₂ (1974), pp. 107–12.

A revision Faulkner sent to Random House in 1949.

O9₂   Rigsby, Carol R. "Chick Mallison's Expectations and *Intruder in the Dust*." *Mississippi Quarterly*, 29 (Summer 1976), 389–99.

The novel shows a youth struggling with conscience, community values, and current stereotypes.

O10₂   Samway, Patrick. "Faulkner's Hidden Story in *Intruder in the Dust*." *Delta* [Montpellier], 3 (November 1976), 63–81.

A section Faulkner once considered as a separate story.

O11$_2$ Heller, Terry L. "*Intruder in the Dust*: The Representation of
            Racial Problems in Faulkner's Novel and in the MGM Film
            Adaptation." *Coe Review*, No. 8 (1977), pp. 79–90.
            Covers simplifications of the novel in the film.

—   Fadiman, Regina K. *Faulkner's* Intruder in the Dust (A51$_2$;
            1978).

O12$_2$ Rabinowitz, Peter J. "The Click of the Spring: The Detective
            Story as Parallel Structure in Dostoyevsky and Faulkner."
            Modern Philology, 76 (May 1979), 355–69.
            It is a "discovery novel."

—   Kerr, Elizabeth M. "*Intruder in the Dust*: The Perilous Quest,
            or, The Secret of the Grave." In *William Faulkner's Gothic
            Domain* (A59$_2$; 1979), pp. 162–83.

O13$_2$ Samway, Patrick, S.J. "*Intruder in the Dust*: A Re-
            Evaluation." In A63$_2$ (1980), pp. 83–113.

—   Powers, Lyall H. *Faulkner's Yoknapatawpha Comedy* (A68$_2$;
            1980), pp. 192–203.
            Emphasizes thematic connections with *Go Down, Moses* and the optimistic
            implications of Faulkner's use of Chick Mallison.

—   Samway, Patrick H., S.J. *Faulkner's* Intruder in the Dust: *A
            Critical Study of the Typescripts* (A69$_2$; 1980).

—   Jenkins, Lee Clinton. *Faulkner and Black-White Relations*
            (A72$_2$; 1981), pp. 261–79.
            Studies racial themes, Charles's learning, and Lucas' role "as a moral agent
            bringing into focus the pattern of rural conventions of the society at large."

Further commentary: Al$_2$ (Peavy), A7$_2$ (Page), A9$_2$ (Boecker), A12$_2$
(Leary), A22$_2$ (Weisgerber), A28$_2$ (Wagner), A34$_2$ (Jehlen), A44$_2$
(Kawin), A58$_2$ (Kartiganer), A61$_2$ (Wittenberg), AA30$_2$ (Skaggs),
AA54$_2$ (Carey), AA141$_2$ (Berzon), AA147$_2$ (Alexander).

P.   *Knight's Gambit*

P1$_2$ Canby, Vincent. "The Screen: 'Tomorrow.'" *New York Times*,
            April 10, 1972, p. 44.
            "Tomorrow" was made into a film in 1972. Two reviews comparing the
            movie with the story are one in the *New York Times* (April 23, 1972, Sec.
            2, p. 16) and one by Andrew Sarris in the *Village Voice* (June 8, 1972,
            p. 61). The Lee County Library in Tupelo, Mississippi, has a file of
            clippings about local filming of the movie. See the article by Barbera (P8$_2$).

P2₂   Howell, Elmo. "Faulkner's Enveloping Sense of History: A Note on 'Tomorrow.'" *Notes on Contemporary Literature*, 3 (March 1973), 5–6.

P3₂   Volpe, Edmond L. "Faulkner's 'Knight Gambit': Sentimentality and the Creative Imagination." *Modern Fiction Studies*, 24 (Summer 1978), 232–39.
      The story shows much about the role of sentimentality in Faulkner's fiction.

P4₂   Rollyson, Carl E., Jr. "Faulkner into Film: 'Tomorrow' and 'Tomorrow.'" *Mississippi Quarterly*, 32 (Summer 1979), 437–52.
      Compares the film with the novel.

P5₂   Foote, Horton. "*Tomorrow*: The Genesis of a Screenplay." In A57₂ (1979), pp. 149–62.

P6₂   Volpe, Edmond L. "'Monk': The Detective Story and the Human Heart." In A65₂ (1980), pp. 86–90.
      Shows links between the detective story and Faulkner's narrative art.

P7₂   Skei, Hans. "Faulkner's *Knight's Gambit*: Detection and Ingenuity." *Notes on Mississippi Writers*, 13, No. 2 (1981), 79–93.
      Studies all six detective stories.

P8₂   Barbera, Jack. "Tomorrow and Tomorrow and *Tomorrow*." *Southern Quarterly*, 19 (Spring–Summer 1981), 183–97.
      A favorable analysis of the movie that compares it with the short story and Horton Foote's dramatic version.

Further commentary: AA81₂ (Grossman), CC4₂ (Gidley).

Q.   *Requiem for a Nun*

Q1₂   Polk, Noel. "Faulkner's 'The Jail' and the Meaning of Cecelia Farmer." *Mississippi Quarterly*, 25 (Summer 1972), 305–25.
      The Cecelia Farmer passage is concerned not only with human endurance and perseverance but also with the purposes of art.

Q2₂   Holmes, Edward M. "Requiem for a Scarlet Nun." *Costerus*, 5 (1972), 35–49.
      Compares *The Scarlet Letter*.

Q3₂   Broughton, Panthea R. "*Requiem for a Nun*: No Part in Rationality." *Southern Review*, 8 (Autumn 1972), 749–62.

> The novel's structure is a metaphorical expression of its central awareness—a mystical sense of human illimitability, a vision of transcendence.

—   Weisgerber, Jean. *Faulkner and Dostoevsky* (A22$_2$; 1974), pp. 287–301.

Q4$_2$ Polk, Noel. "The Textual History of Faulkner's *Requiem for a Nun*." *Proof*, 4 (1975), 109–28.

—   Beck, Warren. *Faulkner* (A29$_2$; 1976), pp. 583–635.
> An extensive explication, focusing on the book as both succinct drama and impressionistic prose, and on its inconclusive handling of good and evil.

Q5$_2$ Ruppersburg, Hugh Michael. "The Narrative Structure of Faulkner's *Requiem for a Nun*." *Mississippi Quarterly*, 31 (Summer 1978), 387–406.
> The book must be read not as a play but as a novel with a unique dramatic narrative mode, in which the narrator is one of Faulkner's most versatile and powerful lyric voices.

Q6$_2$ Wilson, Paule A. "Faulkner and Camus: *Requiem for a Nun*." *Odyssey*, 3, No. 2 (April 1979), 3–9.

—   Capps, Jack L., ed. Requiem for a Nun: *A Concordance to the Novel* (A56$_2$; 1979).

Q7$_2$ Polk, Noel. "The Nature of Sacrifice: *Requiem for a Nun* and *A Fable*." In A65$_2$ (1980), pp. 100–111.
> A thematic discussion of the real and the ideal, self-sacrifice, obedience to a higher law, and "the attempt to define individual freedom in the context of an increasingly oppressive world."

—   Powers, Lyall H. *Faulkner's Yoknapatawpha Comedy* (A68$_2$; 1980), pp. 204–17.
> Emphasizes the theme of the Second Chance in relation to man's inability to escape "Evil of the Past."

Q8$_2$ Polk, Noel. "Nun Out of the Habit: Nancy Mannigoe, Gavin Stevens, and *Requiem for a Nun*.'" *Recherches anglaises et américaines*, 13 (1980), 64–75.
> Focusing on Temple as the moral center of the novel, Polk attacks criticism that approves of Gavin's perspective on the situation and sentimentalizes Nancy.

Q9$_2$ Samway, Patrick, S.J. "The Rebounding Images of Faulkner's *Sanctuary* and *Requiem for a Nun*." *Recherches anglaises et américaines*, 13 (1980), 90–108.

Considers the following patterns of imagery in the novel: music, pools, women/children.

—   Polk, Noel. *Faulkner's* Requiem for a Nun*: A Critical Study* (A74$_2$; 1981).

Further commentary: A7$_2$ (Page), A9$_2$ (Boecker), A12$_2$ (Leary), A14$_2$ (Reed), A19$_2$ (Broughton), A47$_2$ (Williams), A54$_2$ (Kinney), A58$_2$ (Kartiganer), A61$_2$ (Wittenberg), D39$_2$ (Millgate), G15$_2$ (Degenfelder), G19$_2$ (Kinney), AA24$_2$ (Millgate), AA63$_2$ (Peckham), AA82$_2$ (Culley).

R. *A Fable*

R1$_2$ Ziolkowski, Theodore. *Fictional Transfigurations of Jesus.* Princeton: Princeton Univ. Press, 1972, pp. 270-98.

R2$_2$ Hutten, Robert W. "A Major Revision in Faulkner's *A Fable.*" *American Literature*, 45 (May 1973), 297-99.
> On the lawyer's speech given to the marshal.

R3$_2$ Meriwether, James B. "A Note on *A Fable.*" *Mississippi Quarterly*, 26 (Summer 1973), 416-17.
> A statement by Faulkner about the novel. Included in A21$_2$.

R4$_2$ Raisor, Philip. "Up from Adversity: William Faulkner's *A Fable.*" *South Dakota Review*, 11, No. 2 (Summer 1973), 3-15.
> The novel is about the intellectual sanctions and moral sources making affirmation possible.

R5$_2$ Ratner, Marc. "Dualism in Faulkner's *A Fable*: Humanization versus Dehumanization." *Prague Studies in English*, 15 (1973), 117-34.

—   Weisgerber, Jean. *Faulkner and Dostoevsky* (A22$_2$; 1974), pp. 301-21.

R6$_2$ Wegelin, Christof. " 'Endure' and 'Prevail': Faulkner's Modification of Conrad." *Notes and Queries*, 21 (October 1974), 375-76.

R7$_2$ Berrone, Louis. "A Dickensian Echo in Faulkner." *The Dickensian*, 71 (May 1975), 100-101.

R8$_2$ Bond, Adrienne. " 'Eneas Africanus' and Faulkner's Fabulous Racehorse." *Southern Literary Journal*, 9, No. 2 (Spring 1977), 3-15.
> Harry Stillwell Edwards' tale was a source for Faulkner.

R9₂   Ilacqua, Alma A. "Faulkner's *A Fable.*" *Notes on Mississippi Writers*, 10 (Spring 1977), 37–46.
        Calvinist ideas of evil, redemption, and regeneration.

R10₂   Chittick, Kathryn A. "The Fables in William Faulkner's *A Fable.*" *Mississippi Quarterly*, 30 (Summer 1977), 403–15.
        Investigates the novel's fictional origins, the network of references mythic and biblical, and patterns of repetition and parallelism.

—   Brooks, Cleanth. *William Faulkner* (A48₂; 1978), pp. 230–50, 414–23.
        Attributes the book's weakness to an uncertain fusion of fabulous and realistic elements.

R11₂   Simpson, Lewis P. "Yoknapatawpha and Faulkner's Fable of Civilization." In A53₂ (1978), pp. 122–45.
        Explores the novel in relation to an American myth and to the Faulknerian theme of the internalization of history in the self.

R12₂   Magee, Rosemary M. "*A Fable* and the Gospels: A Study in Contrasts." *Research Studies* [Washington State Univ.], 47 (June 1979), 98–107.
        On the contrast between the story of the corporal and the story of Jesus.

R13₂   Chittick, Kathryn. "'Telling It Again and Again': *Notes on a Horsethief.*" *Mississippi Quarterly*, 32 (Summer 1979), 423–35.
        On the transformation of the profane into the sacred.

R14₂   MacMillan, Duane J. "His 'Magnum O': Stoic Humanism in Faulkner's *A Fable.*" In *The Stoic Strain in American Literature.* Ed. D. J. MacMillan. Toronto: Univ. of Toronto Press, 1979, pp. 135–54.

R15₂   Bahr, Howard L. "Exciting Find on a Rowan Oak Wall Uncovers *A Fable* Outline False Start." *Faulkner Newsletter*, April–June 1981, pp. 1, 3.
        A recent discovery of additional writing on the wall.

—   Polk, Noel, and Kenneth Privratsky, eds. A Fable: *A Concordance to the Novel* (A75₂; 1981).

R16₂   Fowler, Doreen. "The Old Verities in Faulkner's Fable." *Renascence*, 34 (Autumn 1981), 41–51.
        Relates themes in *A Fable* to those in Faulkner's other novels.

Further commentary: A9$_2$ (Boecker), A12$_2$ (Leary), A14$_2$ (Reed), A28$_2$ (Wagner), A32$_2$ (Guerard), A54$_2$ (Kinney), A58$_2$ (Kartiganer), A60$_2$ (Stonum), A61$_2$ (Wittenberg), Q7$_2$ (Polk), AA5$_2$ (Brumm), AA63$_2$ (Peckham).

S. *The Town*

S1$_2$ Gregory, Eileen. "Faulkner's Typescripts of *The Town*." *Mississippi Quarterly*, 26 (Summer 1973), 361–86.

    Analyzes differences between typescript and text, and reprints materials such as letters on versos of the typescript. Included in A21$_2$.

S2$_2$ Wilson, Raymond J., III. "Imitative Flem Snopes and Faulkner's Causal Sequence in *The Town*." *Twentieth Century Literature*, 26 (Winter 1980), 432–44.

    The novel's central action is Flem's "steady adoption of Jefferson's behavior, rather than his corruption of it."

S3$_2$ Moses, Edwin. "Comedy in *The Town*." In A63$_2$ (1980), pp. 59–73.

    Considers comic elements in relation to the "collision between illusion and reality."

—   Powers, Lyall H. *Faulkner's Yoknapatawpha Comedy* (A68$_2$; 1980), pp. 218–32.

T. *The Mansion*

T1$_2$ Creighton, Joanne V. "The Dilemma of the Human Heart in *The Mansion*." *Renascence*, 25 (Autumn 1972), 35–45.

    On the paradox of a murder being the ultimate life-affirming act.

T2$_2$ Gregory, Eileen. "The Temerity to Revolt: Mink Snopes and the Dispossessed in *The Mansion*." *Mississippi Quarterly*, 29 (Summer 1976), 401–21.

    The dominant tone is comic. The death of Flem affirms the perseverance of good in society because Flem has come to symbolize the demonic life-denying force of stasis and because the act is placed in a mythical context.

—   Powers, Lyall H. *Faulkner's Yoknapatawpha Comedy* (A68$_2$; 1980), pp. 233–49.

U.   *The Snopes Trilogy*

U1₂   Barnett, Suzanne B. "Faulkner's Relation to the Humor of the
       Old Southwest." *Journal of the Ohio Folklore Society*, 2
       (Winter 1967), 149–65.
           Compares Faulkner with George Washington Harris.

U2₂   Maddocks, Gladys. "William Faulkner and the Evolution of V.
       K. Ratliff." *Proceedings of the Conference of College Teachers
       of English of Texas*, 33 (September 1968), 24–28.

U3₂   Kane, Patricia. "Adaptable and Free: Faulkner's Ratliff."
       Notes on Contemporary Literature, 1, No. 3 (May 1971), 9–11.

U4₂   Carey, Glenn O. "William Faulkner: The Rise of the
       Snopeses." *Studies in the Twentieth Century*, 8 (Fall 1971),
       27–64.
           General discussion of the Snopeses.

U5₂   Sharma, P. P. "The Snopes Theme in Faulkner's Larger
       Context." *Indian Journal of American Studies*, 1, No. 4
       (November 1971), 33–41.

U6₂   Edwards, Duane. "Flem Snopes and Thomas Sutpen: Two
       Versions of Respectability." *Dalhousie Review*, 51 (Winter
       1971), 559–70.
           A comic and a tragic version of similar rise and fall stories in the South.

—   Page, Sally R. *Faulkner's Women* (A7₂; 1972), pp. 153–73.
           Argues that the three novels set a male principle (for example, Flem)
           against a female principle (Eula, Linda), with which Faulkner sympathizes.

U7₂   Norris, Nancy. "*The Hamlet, The Town* and *The Mansion*: A
       Psychological Reading of the Snopes Trilogy." *Mosaic*, 7, No.
       1 (Fall 1973), 213–35.
           Studies incestuous wishes and the device of narrative displacement (Ratliff,
           Labove, Gavin for Jody); anxieties about disintegration; and revenge
           against the father.

—   Leary, Lewis. *William Faulkner of Yoknapatawpha County*
       (A12₂; 1973), pp. 150–70.

U8₂   Smith, Gerald J. "A Note on the Origin of Flem Snopes."
       Notes on Mississippi Writers, 6 (Fall 1973), 56–57.

—   Reed, Joseph W., Jr. *Faulkner's Narrative* (A14₂; 1973), pp.
       218–57.

Studies Faulkner's narrative methods—the function of the different first-person speakers, the purpose of the embedded tales, the counterpoint between different tones or modes, the variations from conventional narrative structure.

U9$_2$ Crawford, John W. "Bred and Bawn in a Briar Patch—Deception in the Making." *South Central Bulletin*, 34 (Winter 1974), 149–50.

> On Flem Snopes.

U10$_2$ Trimmer, Joseph F. "V. K. Ratliff: A Portrait of the Artist in Motion." *Modern Fiction Studies*, 20 (Winter 1975), 451–67.

> Ratliff's major role is not as agent-hero but as observer-narrator, the artist testing ideas against the flux of experience. Unlike Gavin he can adjust theories to fit reality.

— Wagner, Linda W. *Hemingway and Faulkner* (A28$_2$; 1975), pp. 218–28.

U11$_2$ Rice, Michael. "Myth and Legend: The Snopes Trilogy: *The Hamlet, The Town* and *The Mansion*." *Unisa English Studies* [South Africa], 14, No. 1 (April 1976), 18–22.

— Jehlen, Myra. *Class and Character in Faulkner's South* (A34$_2$; 1976), pp. 133–74.

> Argues that in the trilogy Faulkner finally assumes a conservative stance toward class relationships.

U12$_2$ Freidman, Alan Warren. "Faulkner's Snopes Trilogy: Omniscience as Impressionism." *Delta* [Montpellier], 3 (November 1976), 125–51. Included in *Multivalence: The Moral Quality of Form in the Modern Novel*. Baton Rouge: Louisiana State Univ. Press, 1978, pp. 141–77.

> Analyzes the function of each of the participant-narrators, Ratliff, Gavin, and Chick, and the importance of the impressionistic authorial perspective with which the trilogy concludes.

— Levins, Lynn Gartrell. *Faulkner's Heroic Design* (A35$_2$; 1976), pp. 55–75, 144–60, 168–74.

> Considers the "heroic" dimensions of Eula and Flem, the episode of Ike Snopes and the cow, and the character of Mink Snopes.

U13$_2$ McFarland, Holly. "The Mask Not Tragic . . . Just Damned: The Women in Faulkner's Trilogy." *Ball State University Forum*, 18, No. 2 (Spring 1977), 27–50.

> The female characters are positive forces, restoring a natural order to a world in which nature has been violated.

—   Creighton, Joanne V. *William Faulkner's Craft of Revision*
       (A41$_2$; 1977), pp. 18–72.

U14$_2$ Richardson, W. M. "Snopesian Man." In *Crisis and
       Consciousness*. Ed. R. M. Faris. Amsterdam: Gruner, 1977,
       pp. 63–71.

—   Williams, David. *Faulkner's Women* (A47$_2$; 1977), pp.
       197–226.

U15$_2$ Brooks, Cleanth. "Gavin Stevens and the Chivalric Tradition."
       In A52$_2$ (1978), pp. 19–32.
           Relates the quixotic Gavin to traditions of chivalric love as described in the
           books of Denis de Rougemont.

U16$_2$ Edwards, C. H. "A Conjecture on the Name *Snopes*." *Notes
       on Contemporary Literature*, 8, No. 5 (November 1978), 9–10.

—   Kerr, Elizabeth M. "*Snopes*: From Rags to Riches; The Knight
       of the Rueful Countenance; The Revenger's Tragedy." In
       William Faulkner's Gothic Domain (A59$_2$; 1979), pp. 184–219.

—   Stonum, Gary Lee. *Faulkner's Career* (A60$_2$; 1979), pp.
       153–94.
           Considers the importance of social forms and literary forms to the trilogy,
           arguing for example that "*The Mansion* rewrites the entire trilogy as . . . a
           pastoral elegy."

U17$_2$ Balla, P. E. "Knoxville Town and Snopes City." *Appalachian
       Heritage*, 7 (Fall 1979), 18–22.
           Compares the impact of T.V.A. on Knoxville with the effect of Snopesism
           and situations in Poe's "The Masque of the Red Death."

—   Wittenberg, Judith B. *Faulkner* (A61$_2$; 1979), pp. 179–89,
       226–35.

U18$_2$ Polk, Noel. "Faulkner and Respectability." In A64$_2$ (1980), pp.
       110–33.
           Respectability is a theme he handles with complexity and subtlety.

U19$_2$ Rankin, Elizabeth D. "Chasing Spotted Horses: The Quest for
       Human Dignity in Faulkner's Snopes Trilogy." In A63$_2$ (1980),
       pp. 139–56.
           The episode of the horses is a metaphor for the human condition in the
           trilogy.

U20$_2$ Stroble, Woodrow. "Flem Snopes: A Crazed Mirror." In A63$_2$
       (1980), pp. 195–212.

> Emphasizes change in tone in the later novels, Ratliff's reduced role, and the changing ethical perspective on Flem.

U21[2] Bell, Brenda H. "Mike Snope's Wife and the Critics: A Study in Bias." *Publications of the Missouri Philological Association,* 5 (1980), 1–5.

U22[2] Haselswerdt, Marjorie B. "I'd Rather Be Ratliff: A Maslovian Study of Faulkner's *Snopes.*" *Literary Review,* 24 (Winter 1981), 308–27.

> Discusses Ratliff in terms of Abraham Maslov's model of "the self-actualizing person," and as a positive norm in the trilogy.

Further commentary: A9[2] (Boecker), A11[2] (Hunter), A19[2] (Broughton), A22[2] (Weisgerber), A54[2] (Kinney), AA13[2] (Hauck), AA104[2] (Cook), KK9[2] (Hays).

V. *The Reivers*

V1[2] Brown, Calvin S. "Faulkner's Three-in-One Bridge in *The Reivers.*" *Notes on Contemporary Literature,* 1, No. 2 (March 1971), 8–10.

V2[2] Devlin, Albert J. "*The Reivers*: Readings in Social Psychology." *Mississippi Quarterly,* 25 (Summer 1972), 327–37.
> The story is an initiation experience handled with complexity and sophistication.

V3[2] Shepherd, Allen. "Code and Comedy in Faulkner's *The Reivers.*" *Literatur in Wissenschaft und Unterricht,* 6 (March 1973), 43–51.
> Compares *The Reivers* with Sherwood Anderson's "I Want to Know Why."

V4[2] Travis, Mildred K. "Echoes of *Pierre* in *The Reivers.*" *Notes on Contemporary Literature,* 3, No. 2 (September 1973), 11–13.

V5[2] Hasley, Louis. "Reivers' Progress." *CEA Critic,* 36, No. 2 (January 1974), 24–25.
> A 59-line poem referring to the novel.

V6[2] Bradford, M. E. "What Grandfather Said: The Social Testimony of Faulkner's *The Reivers.*" *Occasional Review* (San Diego), February 1974, pp. 5–15.

V7[2] Moses, Edwin. "Faulkner's *The Reivers*: The Art of Acceptance." *Mississippi Quarterly,* 27 (Summer 1974), 307–18.

Through the methods of point of view, allusion, rhetoric, and
characterization, the novel "embodies Faulkner's theme of acceptance
artfully and realistically."

V8₂   Howe, Irving. *William Faulkner: A Critical Study*. 3rd ed.
Chicago: Univ. of Chicago Press, 1975, pp. 295–300.

The third edition makes only minor revisions, adds a chapter on *The
Reivers*, a concluding note, and a brief comment on *Flags in the Dust*.

V9₂   Smith, Gerald J. "Medicine Made Palatable: An Aspect of
Humor in *The Reivers*." *Notes on Mississippi Writers*, 8 (Fall
1975), 58–62.

Compares Otis with Flem Snopes and Jason Compson as "*foci* of
Faulkner's most humorous efforts," satiric attacks on materialism.

V10₂   Tanner, Gale. "Sentimentalism and *The Reivers*: A Reply to
Ben Merchant Vorpahl." *Notes on Mississippi Writers*, 9
(Spring 1976), 50–58.

V11₂   Dettelbach, Cynthia G. *In the Driver's Seat: The Automobile
in American Literature and Popular Culture*. Westport, Ct.:
Greenwood Press, 1976, pp. 17–30.

—   Williams, David. *Faulkner's Women* (A47₂; 1977), pp. 227–41.

Considers "the re-emergence of the feminine archetype in a Memphis
whorehouse."

V12₂   McCarron, William E. "Shakespeare, Faulkner, and Ned
William McCaslin." *Notes on Contemporary Literature*, 7, No.
5 (November 1977), 8–9.

—   Wittenberg, Judith B. *Faulkner* (A61₂; 1979), pp. 236–48.

Emphasizes the triumph of Lucius as hero and of the code of the
gentleman.

V13₂   Nelson, Erik C. "Faulkner's Noble Prince." *Arizona Quarterly*,
35 (Summer 1979), 129–34.

Compares Lucius Priest and Shakespeare's Prince Hal.

V14₂   Carothers, James B. "The Road to *The Reivers*." In A71₂
(1981), pp. 95–124.

It is "a fully realized articulation of themes and techniques Faulkner
employed throughout his developing career." He began planning it in 1940.

Further commentary: A7₂ (Page), A12₂ (Leary), A14₂ (Reed), A22₂
(Weisgerber), A28₂ (Wagner), A35₂ (Levins), A44₂ (Kawin), A54₂
(Kinney), H5₂ (Griffith), N18₂ (Bell), AA112₂ (McGinnis), KK22₂
(Robinson).

III. Studies of Short Stories, Poetry, and Miscellaneous Writings

W. Reviews of Collections

Uncollected Stories. Edited by Joseph Blotner. New York: Random House, 1979.

W1₂   Bailey, Paul. "Working from Within." *Times Literary Supplement*, January 2, 1981, p. 8.

W2₂   Barkham, John. Syndicated review.

W3₂   Boozer, William. "Hefty Faulkner Collection Has Some Jewels." *Nashville Banner*, November 10, 1979, p. 5. Another review by Boozer appeared in the *Memphis Commercial Appeal*, November 11, 1979, p. G6.

W4₂   Bradford, M. E. "The Rest of Faulkner." *National Review*, March 21, 1980, pp. 361–62.

W5₂   Brooks, Cleanth. "His Somewhat Lesser Sound and Fury." *Saturday Review*, November 10, 1979, pp. 51–53.

W6₂   Brown, Calvin S. Review. *Georgia Review*, 34 (Spring 1980), 221–23.

W7₂   Busby, Mark. "Faulkner: Even the Lesser Work Shines." *Houston Chronicle*, December 23, 1979, Zest, p. 18.

W8₂   Bushnell, Scott. Syndicated Associated Press review dated January 13, 1980.

W9₂   Carothers, James B. "A Newest Faulkner Collection Invokes a Sympathetic, Intelligent Reading." *Kansas City Star*, November 11, 1979, p. D12.

W10₂   Carter, Ron. "A Gold Mine for Faulkner Scholars." *Richmond Times-Dispatch*, January 27, 1980, p. G5.

W11₂   Charles, Isabel. Review. *The Critic*, May 1, 1980, pp. 3–4.

W12₂   Covici, Pascal, Jr. Review. *Dallas Lone Star Book Review*.

W13₂   Cowley, Malcolm. "Faulkner's Frugal Imagination." *Washington Post*, November 4, 1979, Books, pp. 1, 12.

W14₂   Dickerson, James. "'New' Faulkner Works Show His Development as Writer." *Jackson* [Miss.] *Clarion-Ledger*, January 6, 1980, p. G8.

W15₂   Donald, David H. Review. *New Republic*, December 15, 1979, p. 36.

W16₂   Fadiman, Regina K. "Miscellany from the Lumber Room." *Southern Literary Journal*, 12, No. 2 (Spring 1980), 137–44.

W17₂   Ferguson, James. "A Treasury of Stories by Faulkner." *Louisville Courier Journal*, February 24, 1980, p. D3.

W18₂   Frakes, James R. "Great Faulkner Tales, Bad Poems." *Cleveland Plain Dealer*, February 3, 1980, p. C22. Also reviews *Mississippi Poems*.

W19₂   Garrison, David. Review. *Minnesota Daily*, Janury 14, 1980, p. 12.

W20₂   Gillespie, Stan. "A Gold Mine of Faulkneriana." *Chattanooga Times*, December 16, 1979, p. B4.

W21₂   Goodin, Gayle. "Faulkner's Artistic Cosmos." *Jackson* [Tenn.] *Sun*, April 13, 1980, p. B4.

W22₂   Gray, Paul. "Tales in the Marketplace." *Time*, November 5, 1979, pp. 105–06.

W23₂   Gribbin, Daniel V. "At Last, the Fugitive Faulkner Tales." *Roanoke Times & World-News*, December 16, 1979, p. F4.

W24₂   Gullason, Thomas A. Review. *Studies in Short Fiction*, 18 (Spring 1981), 189–91.

W25₂   Hardwick, Elizabeth. "Unknown Faulkner." *New York Times Book Review*, November 4, 1979, pp. 1, 48–49.

W26₂   Harris, Roger. "Faulkner Traces an Artful Path in Uncollected Tales." *Newark Star-Ledger*, November 4, 1979, Sec. 4, p. 28.

—   Heller, Terry. Review (see HH321₂).

W27₂   Jones, Malcolm. Review. *Greensboro Daily News*, January 6, 1980, p. G5.

W28₂   Jordan, Peter. "Faulkner's Uncollected Stories Mainly for Full-Fledged Fans." *Nashville Tennessean*, December 9, 1979, p. F10.

W29₂   Kamenetz, Rodger. "Even Most 'Minor' Faulkner Is of Major Interest." *Baltimore Sun*, December 2, 1979, p. D5.

W30₂   Kirsch, Robert. "Feeling the Early Faulkner Fabric." *Los Angeles Times*, January 1, 1980, Sec. 5, p. 4.

W31₂   Krisher, Trudy. "Faulkner: The Stories." *Dayton Journal-Herald*, November 17, 1979, pp. 22–23.

W32₂   Lee, Hermione. "Exhausting the Possibilities." *New Statesman*, October 31, 1980, p. 17.

W33₂   Leighton, Betty. "Faulkner: More Pieces Gathered." *Winston-Salem Journal*, January 13, 1980, p. C4.

W34₂   Meriwether, James B. "William Faulkner: Curious Volume Not Aimed at General Reader." *The State* [Columbia, S.C.], January 20, 1980, Magazine, p. 12.

W35₂   McNally, Peter. "Faulkner Obscurities Find Their Way into Special Edition." *Hartford Courant*, November 25, 1979, p. G8.

W36₂   Milazzo, Lee. "Finally, a Collection of Faulkner's Stories." *Dallas Morning News*, November 4, 1979, p. G4.

W37₂   Morris, Willie. "Faulkner Genius on Display in Vintage Stories." *Chicago Tribune*, November 11, 1979, Sec. 7, p. 1.

W38₂   O'Connell, Shaun. "Odds and Ends from Faulkner." *Boston Sunday Globe*, January 6, 1980, p. C7.

W39₂   Powell, Larry. Review. *Savannah News-Press*, January 13, 1980, Magazine, p. F5.

W40₂   Robertson, William K. "Faulkner and His Sense of Place." *Miami Herald*, November 25, 1979, pp. E1, E7.

W41₂   Ruppersburg, Hugh M. "New Volume of Faulkner Stories Doesn't Spark Much Sound or Fury." *Atlanta Journal-Constitution*, December 9, 1979, p. E4.

W42₂   Samway, Patrick. Review. *America*, January 12, 1980, pp. 26–28.

W43₂   Smith, Henry Nash. "Leftovers of Faulkner's Masterful Career." *Chicago Sun-Times*, October 28, 1979, Show, p. 12.

W44₂   Thompson, Francis J. "Still the Sole Owner of Yoknapatawpha." *Tampa Tribune-Times*, November 18, 1979, p. C5.

W45₂   Wells, Robert W. "Between the Lines." *Milwaukee Journal*, December 30, 1979, Pt. 5, p. 5.

W46$_2$ Willingham, David. Review. *Cleveland* [Tenn.] *Daily Banner*, March 9, 1980, p. 9.

W47$_2$ Yardley, Jonathan. "The Early Marks of Faulkner's Genius." *Baltimore News-American*, November 25, 1979, p. H9. Also appeared in the *Washington Star*.

X.   Critical Commentary[1]

"Artist at Home"

X1$_2$ Bradford, M. E. "An Aesthetic Parable: Faulkner's 'Artist at Home.'" *Georgia Review*, 27 (Summer 1973), 175–81.

  It is a hyperbolic parable depending on careful control of tone and perspective.

X2$_2$ Peterson, Richard F. "An Early Judgment of Anderson and Joyce in Faulkner's 'Artist at Home.'" *Kyushu American Literature*, 18 (October 1977), 19–23.

X3$_2$ Owens, Tony J. "Faulkner, Anderson, and 'Artist at Home.'" *Mississippi Quarterly*, 32 (Summer 1979), 393–412.

  The story is a culmination of Faulkner's earlier "artistic portraits and an anticipation of larger and related themes of perception, responsibility, and action." Influenced by Sherwood Anderson and in part using him as a model, it deals with "the tragic consequences of fragmentation."

"Barn Burning"

X4$_2$ Bowen, James K., and James A. Hamby. "Colonel Sartoris Snopes and Gabriel Marcel: Allegiance and Commitment." *Notes on Mississippi Writers*, 3 (Winter 1971), 101–07.

  An existentialist approach to the story.

X5$_2$ Johnston, Kenneth G. "Time of Decline: Pickett's Charge and the Broken Clock in Faulkner's 'Barn Burning.'" *Studies in Short Fiction*, 11 (Fall 1974), 434–36.

X6$_2$ Nicolet, William P. "Faulkner's 'Barn Burning.'" *Explicator*, 34 (November 1975), 25.

  Sardines and deviled ham are symbols.

X7$_2$ Volpe, Edmond L. "'Barn Burning': A Definition of Evil." In A63$_2$ (1980), pp. 75–82.

  On Sarty's emotional conflict.

---

[1]Commentary on short stories that are parts of novels, such as "Odor of Verbena" and "Pantaloon in Black," is listed under the novel.

X8₂   Hadley, Charles. "Seeing and Telling: Narrational Functions in the Short Story." In *Discourse and Style, II.* Ed. J. P. Petit. Lyon, France: L'Hermès, 1980, pp. 63–68.

Also covers "That Will Be Fine."

X9₂   Hogan, Michael. "Grammatical Tenuity in Fiction." *Language and Style*, 14 (Winter 1981), 13–19.

Uses the story as an example in discussing the progressive form of verbs in fiction.

X10₂   Bradford, M. E. "Family and Community in Faulkner's 'Barn Burning.'" *Southern Review*, 17 (April 1981), 332–39.

Discusses Sarty's struggle to reconcile conflicting claims of self, family, and community.

"Beyond"

X11₂   Simpson, Hassell A. "Wilbur Daniel Steele's Influence on Faulkner's Revision of 'Beyond.'" *Mississippi Quarterly*, 34 (Summer 1981), 335–39.

"The Brooch"

X12₂   Hult, Sharon S. "William Faulkner's 'The Brooch': The Journey to the Riolama." *Mississippi Quarterly*, 27 (Summer 1974), 291–305.

On Faulkner's use of W. H. Hudson's *Green Mansions.*

X13₂   Garrison, Joseph M., Jr. "Faulkner's 'The Brooch': A Story for Teaching." *College English*, 36 (September 1974), 51–57.

"Carcassonne"

X14₂   Milum, Richard A. "Faulkner's 'Carcassonne': The Dream and the Reality." *Studies in Short Fiction*, 15 (Spring 1978), 133–38.

Faulkner dramatizes the romantic dream-making of youth.

X15₂   Hamblin, Robert W. "'Carcassonne': Faulkner's Allegory of Art and the Artist." *Southern Review*, 15 (April 1979), 355–65.

The protagonist is "a poet struggling with the need to articulate his inner vision."

X16₂   Bradford, M. E. "The Knight and the Artist: Tasso and Faulkner's 'Carcassonne.'" *South Central Bulletin*, 41 (Winter 1981), 88–90.

"Dr. Martino"

X17₂   Lang, Beatrice. "'Dr. Martino': The Conflict of Life and Death." *Delta* [Montpellier], 3 (November 1976), 23–32, 34.

Emphasizes the issue of "closure and finality" in the story.

"Dry September"

X18₂ Johnson, Ira. "Faulkner's 'Dry September' and Caldwell's 'Saturday Afternoon': An Exercise in Practical Criticism." In *Tradition et innovation. littérature et paralittérature: Actes du Congrès de Nancy* (1972). Sec. des Anglicistes de l'Enseignement Superieur. Paris: Didier, n.d., pp. 269–78.

X19₂ Faulkner, Howard J. "The Stricken World of 'Dry September.'" *Studies in Short Fiction*, 10 (Winter 1973), 47–50.
On the symbolism of the moon, and the role of Hawkshaw.

X20₂ McDermott, John V. "Faulkner's Cry for a Healing Measure: 'Dry September.'" *Arizona Quarterly*, 32 (Spring 1976), 31–34.
The central theme is the need for spiritual reconciliation.

X21₂ Winslow, Joan D. "Language and Destruction in Faulkner's 'Dry September.'" *College Language Association Journal*, 20 (March 1977), 380–86.
The story revolves around language misused and the failure of verbal tactics.

X22₂ Daniels, Edgar F., and Ralph H. Wolfe. "Beneath the Dust of 'Dry September.'" In *Itinerary 3: Criticism*. Ed. F. Baldanza. Bowling Green, Ohio: Bowling Green Univ. Press, 1977, pp. 159–60.

X23₂ Széky, Annámaria R. "The Lynching Story." *Studies in English and American* [Budapest], 4 (1978), 181–99.

X24₂ Pryse, Marjorie. "Faulkner's 'Dry September' and 'Red Leaves': Caste and Outcast." *The Mark and the Knowledge* (See H58₂; 1979), pp. 92–107.
A new look at the community and outsiders is provided by the story.

X25₂ Stewart, Jack F. "The Infernal Climate of Faulkner's 'Dry September.'" *Research Studies* [Washington State Univ.], 47 (December 1979), 238–43.
Considers the thematic significance of weather and climate.

"Elly"

X26₂ Skei, Hans. "The Trapped Female Breaking Loose: William Faulkner's 'Elly' (1934)." *American Studies in Scandinavia*, 11 (1979), 15–24.

"Golden Land"

X27[2] Spatz, Jonas. *Hollywood in Fiction: Some Versions of the American Myth*. New York: Humanities Press, 1970, pp. 116–19.

"Miss Zilphia Gant"

X28[2] Pitavy, François L. "A Forgotten Faulkner Story. 'Miss Zilphia Gant.'" *Studies in Short Fiction*, 9 (Spring 1972), 131–42.

Studies revisions, especially in the narrative voice, and considers connections with *Light in August*.

X29[2] Morell, Giliane. "Prisoners of the Inner World: Mother and Daughter in *Miss Zilphia Gant*." *Mississippi Quarterly*, 28 (Summer 1975), 299–305.

The story is a five-act tragedy with links to *Sanctuary* and "A Rose for Emily."

— Brooks, Cleanth. *William Faulkner* (A48[2]; 1978), pp. 152–65.

Compares Miss Zilphia's obsessions with those of Emily Grierson.

"Mistral"

X30[2] Shepherd, Allen. "Hemingway's 'An Alpine Idyll' and Faulkner's 'Mistral.'" *University of Portland Review*, Fall 1973, pp. 63–68.

X31[2] Paddock, Lisa. "'Trifles with a tragic profundity': The Importance of 'Mistral.'" *Mississippi Quarterly*, 32 (Summer 1979), 413–22.

The story is an early handling of the theme of the complexity of truth and making sense of things.

X32[2] Morrison, Gail M. "Faulkner's Priests and Fitzgerald's 'Absolution.'" *Mississippi Quarterly*, 32 (Summer 1979), 461–65.

Also covers "The Priest."

"A Mountain Victory"

X33[2] Meriwether, James B., ed. "An Unpublished Episode from 'A Mountain Victory.'" *Mississippi Quarterly*, 32 (Summer 1979), 481–83.

"My Grandmother Millard . . ."

X34[2] Ditsky, John. "Faulkner's Harrykin Creek: A Note." *University of Windsor Review*, Fall–Winter 1976, pp. 88–89.

On the real Hurricane Creek.

"A Rose for Emily"

X35₂ Nebeker, Helen E. "Chronology Revised." *Studies in Short Fiction*, 8 (Summer 1971), 471–73.

X36₂ Sullivan, Ruth. "The Narrator in 'A Rose for Emily.'" *Journal of Narrative Technique*, 1 (September 1971), 159–78.
Understanding the narrator is crucial.

X37₂ Holland, Norman N. "Fantasy and Defense in Faulkner's 'A Rose for Emily.'" *Hartford Studies in Literature*, 4 (1972), 1–31.
Detailed psychoanalytic interpretation.

X38₂ Barnes, Daniel R. "Faulkner's Miss Emily and Hawthorne's Old Maid." *Studies in Short Fiction*, 9 (Fall 1972), 373–77.
"The White Old Maid" was an influence.

X39₂ Wilson, G. R., Jr. "The Chronology of Faulkner's 'A Rose for Emily' Again." *Notes on Mississippi Writers*, 5 (Fall 1972), 44, 56–62.

X40₂ Heller, Terry. "The Telltale Hair: A Critical Study of William Faulkner's 'A Rose for Emily.'" *Arizona Quarterly*, 28 (Winter 1972), 301–18.
The town victimizes Emily. The story deals with barriers to sympathy and understanding, as well as the means to overcome them.

X41₂ Levitt, Paul. "An Analogue for Faulkner's 'A Rose for Emily.'" *Papers on Language and Literature*, 9 (1973), 91–94.
Compares John Crowe Ransom's "Emily Hardcastle, Spinster."

X42₂ Barber, Marion. "The Two Emily's: A Ransom Suggestion to Faulkner?" *Notes on Mississippi Writers*, 5 (Winter 1973), 103–05.
"Emily Hardcastle, Spinster" may be a source.

X43₂ Edwards, C. Hines, Jr. "Three Literary Parallels to Faulkner's 'A Rose for Emily.'" *Notes on Mississippi Writers*, 7 (Spring 1974), 21–25.
Compares works by Dickens, Browning, and Poe.

X44₂ Kobler, J. F. "Faulkner's 'A Rose for Emily.'" *Explicator*, 32 (April 1974), 65.
On the significance of calling the main character "Miss Emily," "Poor Emily," or "Emily."

X45$_2$ Tefs, Wayne A. "Norman N. Holland and 'A Rose for Emily':
Some Questions Concerning Psychoanalytic Criticism." *The*
Sphinx, 1, No. 2 (Summer 1974), 50–57.
>   A response to Holland's article (X37$_2$), with a comment also by Ralph
>   Smith.

X46$_2$ Davis, William V. "Another Flower for Faulkner's Bouquet:
Theme and Structure in 'A Rose for Emily.'" *Notes on*
Mississippi Writers, 7 (Fall 1974), 34–38.
>   On the emphasis on time in the story.

X47$_2$ Holland, Norman N. *5 Readers Reading*. New Haven: Yale
Univ. Press, 1975.
>   Includes a slightly revised version of Holland's earlier article (X37$_2$), and
>   also uses the story as the main example in his "fantasy-defense model of
>   the literary experience," now seen as existing "in the union of reader and
>   text." This is based on an experiment with the responses of five students to
>   "A Rose for Emily."

X48$_2$ Muller, Gilbert H. "Faulkner's 'A Rose for Emily.'"
Explicator, 33 (May 1975), 79.
>   On the imagery of art.

X49$_2$ López Landeira, Ricardo. "'Aura,' 'The Aspern Papers,' 'A
Rose for Emily': A Literary Relationship." *Journal of Spanish*
Studies: Twentieth Century, 3 (Fall 1975), 125–43.

X50$_2$ Hendricks, William O. "'A Rose for Emily': A Syntagmatic
Analysis." *PTL: A Journal for Descriptive Poetics and Theory*
of Literature, 2 (April 1977), 257–95.
>   A structuralist analysis of the story.

X51$_2$ Fetterley, Judith. *The Resisting Reader: A Feminist Approach*
to American Fiction. Bloomington: Indiana Univ. Press, 1978,
pp. 34–45.
>   Discusses the influence of Emily's upbringing and her father on her
>   character, and argues that "the grotesque aspects . . . are a result of its
>   violation of the expectations generated by the conventions of sexual
>   politics."

X52$_2$ Garrison, Joseph M., Jr. "Bought Flowers in 'A Rose for
Emily.'" *Studies in Short Fiction*, 16 (Fall 1979), 341–44.
>   The story criticizes a certain kind of narrative method.

X53$_2$ Perry, Menakhem. "Literary Dynamics: How the Order of a
Text Creates Its Meanings." *Poetics Today*, 1 (Autumn 1979),
35–64, 311–61.

One section is subtitled "The Devices of Meaning Construction in 'A Rose for Emily.'" This is a semiotic study of "the semantic dynamics of a text." It analyzes basic elements of the story and some critical responses in order to study how a reader constructs meaning ("hypotheses") out of the text. It also considers the narrator, the extent to which Emily is a "type," and the "difference between what a character is and how it is perceived."

X54$_2$ Hunter, William B., Jr. "A Chronology for Emily." *Notes on Modern American Literature*, 4 (Summer 1980), 18.

X55$_2$ Scherting, Jack. "Emily Grierson's Oedipus Complex: Motif, Motive, and Meaning in Faulkner's 'A Rose for Emily.'" *Studies in Short Fiction*, 17 (Fall 1980), 397–406.
She transfers the desire for her father to Homer Barron.

X56$_2$ Lupack, Barbara Tepa. "The Two Tableaux in Faulkner's 'A Rose for Emily.'" *Notes on Contemporary Literature*, 11, No. 3 (May 1981), 6–7.
The contrast between an early and a late tableau clarifies central conflicts in the story.

X57$_2$ Weaks, Mary Louise. "The Meaning of Miss Emily's Rose." *Notes on Contemporary Literature*, 11, No. 5 (November 1981), 11–12.
The rose is "Emily's means of escape from reality." Homer and the bedchamber are substitutes for the rose.

"That Evening Sun"

X58$_2$ Manglaviti, Leo M. J. "Faulkner's 'That Evening Sun' and Mencken's 'Best Editorial Judgment.'" *American Literature*, 43 (January 1972), 649–54.
Revisions in 1931 for *American Mercury*.

X59$_2$ Davis, Scottie. "Faulkner's Nancy: Racial Implications in 'That Evening Sun.'" *Notes on Mississippi Writers*, 5 (Spring 1972), 30–32.
Nancy is vindictive and masochistic. The Compsons are not responsible for her problem.

X60$_2$ Bethea, Sally. "Further Thoughts on Racial Implications in Faulkner's 'That Evening Sun.'" *Notes on Mississippi Writers*, 6 (Winter 1974), 87–92.
Response to Scottie Davis (X59$_2$).

X61$_2$ Coburn, Mark D. "Nancy's Blues: Faulkner's 'That Evening Sun.'" *Perspective*, 17 (Winter 1974), 207–16.
The story depends on a mixture of tragic and comic elements.

X62₂ Johnston, Kenneth G. "The Year of Jubilee: Faulkner's 'That Evening Sun.'" *American Literature*, 46 (March 1974), 93–100.

The story assesses the condition of Southern blacks a generation after the Civil War.

X63₂ Brown, May Cameron. "Voice in 'That Evening Sun': A Study of Quentin Compson." *Mississippi Quarterly*, 29 (Summer 1976), 347–60.

Quentin is a sensitive and reliable narrator through whom the reader senses the evil and fear of the adult world and a child's initiation into it.

X64₂ Garrison, Joseph M., Jr. "The Past and the Present in 'That Evening Sun.'" *Studies in Short Fiction*, 13 (Summer 1976), 371–73.

The first paragraph establishes Quentin's sentimental attachment to the past and his moral blindness.

X65₂ Rosenman, John B. "The Heaven and Hell Archetype in Faulkner's 'That Evening Sun' and Bradbury's 'Dandelion Wine.'" *South Atlantic Bulletin*, 43 (May 1978), 12–16.

X66₂ Momberger, Philip. "Faulkner's 'The Village' and 'That Evening Sun': The Tale in Context." *Southern Literary Journal*, 11, No. 1 (Fall 1978), 20–31.

Studies the story's placement in *Collected Stories*.

X67₂ Hamblin, Robert W. "Before the Fall: The Theme of Innocence in Faulkner's 'That Evening Sun.'" *Notes on Mississippi Writers*, 11 (Winter 1979), 86–94.

X68₂ Pitcher, E. W. "Motive and Metaphor in Faulkner's 'That Evening Sun.'" *Studies in Short Fiction*, 18 (Spring 1981), 131–35.

The story deals with the unclear understanding of black experience by whites, but it works through the theme of understanding by reaching backwards in time to perceive a network of intersecting lives and events.

"There Was a Queen"

X69₂ Castille, Philip. "'There Was a Queen' and Faulkner's Narcissa Sartoris." *Mississippi Quarterly*, 28 (Summer 1975), 307–15.

Narcissa's "pragmatic and successful coping with life" is admirable in the story. She "embodies life and power."

"Thrift"

X70₂ Skei, Hans H. "A Forgotten Faulkner Story: 'Thrift.'" *Mississippi Quarterly*, 32 (Summer 1979), 453–60.

Relates the story to Faulkner's other World War I fiction.

33

33

"Turnabout"

X71[2] Hogue, Peter. "Hawks and Faulkner: *Today We Live.*" *Literature/Film Quarterly*, 9, No. 1 (1981), 51–58.

Discusses the film version of "Turnabout."

"Uncle Willy"

X72[2] Volpe, Edmond L. "Faulkner's 'Uncle Willy': A Childhood Fable." *Mosaic*, 12, No. 1 (Fall 1978), 177–81.

The Indian Stories

X73[2] O'Nan, Martha. "William Faulkner's 'Du Homme.'" *Laurel Review*, 10, No. 2 (1970), 26–28.

Discusses "A Justice."

X74[2] Funk, Robert W. "Satire and Existentialism in Faulkner's 'Red Leaves.'" *Mississippi Quarterly*, 25 (Summer 1972), 339–48.

The first half of the story is a satire on the cultural effects of slavery; the second half is an existential statement on confronting death from a black person's perspective.

X75[2] Langford, Beverly Y. "History and Legend in William Faulkner's 'Red Leaves.'" *Notes on Mississippi Writers*, 6 (Spring 1973), 19–24.

Considers a possible historical model.

X76[2] Beidler, Peter G. "A Darwinian Source for Faulkner's Indians in 'Red Leaves.'" *Studies in Short Fiction*, 10 (Fall 1973), 421–23.

X77[2] Gage, Duane. "William Faulkner's Indians." *American Indian Quarterly*, 1 (Spring 1974), 27–33.

— Dabney, Lewis M. *The Indians of Yoknapatawpha* (A20[2]; 1974), pp. 3–117.

X78[2] Muller, Gilbert H. "The Descent of the Gods: Faulkner's 'Red Leaves' and the Garden of the South." *Studies in Short Fiction*, 11 (Summer 1974), 243–49.

The story formulates the South's failure to establish a new Eden; it also argues for the restoration of an ecumenical function in life.

X79[2] Bradford, M. E. "That Other Patriarchy: Observations on Faulkner's 'A Justice.'" *Modern Age*, 18 (Summer 1974), 266–71.

Emphasizes irony in the title, the duplicity of Doom, and the pattern of measurement and justice.

X80₂ Milum, Richard A. "Ikkemotubbe and the Spanish Conspiracy." *American Literature*, 46 (November 1974), 389–91.

> Discusses the historical allusion to Wilkinson and the "Spanish Conspiracy."

X81₂ Milum, Richard A. "The Title of Faulkner's 'Red Leaves.'" *American Notes and Queries*, 13 (December 1974), 58–59.

X82₂ Pryse, Marjorie L. "Race: Faulkner's 'Red Leaves.'" *Studies in Short Fiction*, 12 (Spring 1975), 133–38.

> It is a story about the isolation of the scapegoat. Also see X24₂.

X83₂ Volpe, Edmond L. "Faulkner's 'Red Leaves': The Deciduation of Nature." *Studies in American Fiction*, 3 (Autumn 1975), 121–31.

> "Faulkner elevates a story about cultural impingement to a terrifying existential confrontation with the reality of death."

X84₂ Clark, William B. "A Tale of Two Chiefs: William Faulkner's Ikkemotubbe and Washington Irving's Blackbird." *Western American Literature*, 12 (Fall 1977), 223–25.

> Considers a parallel between "A Justice" and a passage in *Astoria*.

X85₂ Krefft, James H. "A Possible Source for Faulkner's Indians: Oliver La Farge's *Laughing Boy*." *Tulane Studies in English*, 23 (1978), 187–92.

X86₂ Bradford, M. E. "Faulkner's 'A Courtship': An Accommodation of Cultures." *South Atlantic Quarterly*, 80 (July 1981), 355–59.

> Discusses the relationship and competition between David and Ikkemotubbe, and the conflict between Saxon-Celt and Chickasaw-Choctaw cultures.

General Commentary on Short Stories

X87₂ Meriwether, James B. "Two Unknown Faulkner Short Stories." *Recherches Anglaises et Américaines*, 4 (1971), 23–30.

> "Two Dollar Wife" and "Sepulture South."

X88₂ Knieger, Bernard. "Faulkner's 'Mountain Victory,' 'Doctor Martino,' and 'There Was a Queen.'" *Explicator*, 30 (February 1972), 45.

> Questions explications in *Crowell's Handbook of Faulkner*.

X89₂ Voss, Arthur. "Virtuoso Storyteller." In *The American Short Story: A Critical Survey*. Norman: Univ. of Oklahoma Press, 1973, pp. 242–61.

—   Leary, Lewis. *William Faulkner of Yoknapatawpha County* (A12$_2$; 1973), pp. 133–49.

X90$_2$ Brooks, Cleanth. "A Note on Faulkner's Early Attempts at the Short Story." *Studies in Short Fiction*, 10 (Fall 1973), 381–88.
         Influence of Sherwood Anderson and Irvin S. Cobb.

—   Reed, Joseph W., Jr. *Faulkner's Narrative* (A14$_2$; 1973), pp. 12–57.

X91$_2$ Burns, Landon C. "The 1976 Supplement to a Cross-Referenced Index of Short Fiction Anthologies and Author-Title Listings." *Studies in Short Fiction*, 13 (Spring 1976), 222–23.
         Updated in each Spring issue.

X92$_2$ Showett, H. K. "A Note on Faulkner's Title, *These Thirteen*." *Notes on Mississippi Writers*, 9 (Fall 1976), 120–22.

X93$_2$ Cassill, R. V. Instructor's Handbook to *The Norton Anthology of Short Fiction*. New York: Norton, 1977, pp. 69–77.
         Discusses "A Rose for Emily," "Golden Land," and "Barn Burning."

—   Skei, Hans H. *Bold and Tragical and Austere* (A46$_2$; 1977).

X94$_2$ Walker, Warren S. *Twentieth-Century Short Story Explication*. Hamden, Conn.: Shoe String Press, 1977, pp. 190–208.
         Checklist of explications.

X95$_2$ Putzel, Max. "Faulkner's Short Story Sending Schedule." *Papers of the Bibliographical Society of America*, 71 (1977), 98–105.

X96$_2$ Skei, Hans H. "William Faulkner's Short Story Sending Schedule and His First Short Story Collection, *These 13*: Some Ideas." *Notes on Mississippi Writers*, 11 (Winter 1979), 64–72.

X97$_2$ Kinney, Arthur F. "Faulkner's Narrative Poetics and *Collected Stories*." In A65$_2$ (1980), pp. 58–79.
         On the composition and arrangement of the stories.

X98$_2$ Watson, James G. "Short Story Fantasies and the Limits of Modernism." In A65$_2$ (1980), pp. 80–85.
         On "Carcassonne" and other fantasy stories.

X99₂   Watson, James G. "Faulkner's Short Stories and the Making
         of Yoknapatawpha County," In A64₂ (1980), pp. 202–25.
         Patterns of time, place, and theme in collections of stories.

X100₂   Johnson, Glen M. "*Big Woods*: Faulkner's Elegy for
         Wilderness." *Southern Humanities Review*, 14 (Summer 1980),
         249–58.

X101₂   Allen, Walter. *The Short Story in English*. New York: Oxford
         Univ. Press, 1981, pp. 181–88.

X102₂   Magill, F. N., ed. *Critical Survey of Short Fiction*. Englewood
         Cliffs, N.J.: Salem Press, 1981.
         Faulkner is discussed in several articles.

         Commentary on Poetry and Miscellaneous Writings[1]
X103₂   Gidley, Mick. "Faulkner and Children." *Signal*, September
         1970, pp. 91–102.
         On *The Wishing Tree*.

X104₂   Polk, Noel. "William Faulkner's *Marionettes*." *Mississippi
         Quarterly*, 26 (Summer 1973), 247–80.
         Included in A21₂. Covers themes and techniques, but also shows the work
         is a self-conscious display of Faulkner's reading in the French Symbolists
         as well as English and American writers.

X105₂   McHaney, Thomas L. "The Elmer Papers: Faulkner's Comic
         Portrait of the Artist." *Mississippi Quarterly*, 26 (Summer
         1973), 281–311. Included in A21₂.
         Covers comic and satiric aspects, discusses Bergson's influence, and
         compares text with other versions as well as Faulkner's later fiction.

X106₂   Lang, Beatrice. "An Unpublished Faulkner Story: 'The Big
         Shot.'" *Mississippi Quarterly*, 26 (Summer 1973), 312–24.
         Faulkner's gangster story is "a study of destiny and fate" and of "the teller
         and the tale."

X107₂   Cantrell, Frank. "An Unpublished Faulkner Short Story:
         'Snow.'" *Mississippi Quarterly*, 26 (Summer 1973), 325–30.
         Discusses psychological and metaphorical patterns.

X108₂   Butterworth, Keen. "A Census of Manuscripts and Typescripts
         of William Faulkner's Poetry." *Mississippi Quarterly*, 26
         (Summer 1973), 333–59. Revised in A21₂.

[1]Some stories printed for the first time in *Uncollected Stories of William Faulkner* (1979)
are covered in this section. The very few reviews of such volumes as *Mayday, Marionettes*, and
Mississippi Poems are also included here.

X109₂   Millgate, Michael. "Faulkner on the Literature of the First World War." *Mississippi Quarterly*, 26 (Summer 1973), 387–93. Revised in A21₂.

> Reprints and discusses an unpublished essay, "Literature and War," that refers to Sassoon, Barbusse, Brooke, and Mottram.

X110₂   Polk, Noel. "'Hong Li' and *Royal Street*: The New Orleans Sketches in Manuscript." *Mississippi Quarterly*, 26 (Summer 1973), 394–95. Included in A21₂.

> A booklet collected by Faulkner in 1926 included ten of the eleven *Double Dealer* pieces plus one other.

X111₂   Meriwether, James B., ed. "And Now What's To Do." *Mississippi Quarterly*, 26 (Summer 1973), 399–402. Included in A21₂.

> An unfinished manuscript from around 1926.

X112₂   Meriwether, James B., ed. "Nympholepsy." *Mississippi Quarterly*, 26 (Summer 1973), 403–09. Included in A21₂.

> A prose manuscript from 1925.

X113₂   Gresset, Michel. "Faulkner's 'The Hill.'" *Southern Literary Journal*, 6, No. 2 (Spring 1974), 3–18.

> Considers the importance of this early sketch in terms of distancing, symbolism, use of setting, and arrested motion.

X114₂   Foley, Ivan M., Jr. "First Sketches of a Master." *Richmond Mercury*, April 3, 1974, Book Review, pp. 15, 20, 18.

> On *New Orleans Sketches*.

X115₂   Meriwether, James B., ed. "Faulkner's Ode to the Louver." *Mississippi Quarterly*, 27 (Summer 1974), 333–35.

> Faulkner's satire on himself and Mencken. Also reprinted in this issue is "Faulkner's Speech at the Teatro Municipal, Caracas, in 1961," p. 337.

X116₂   Boozer, William. *William Faulkner's First Book:* The Marble Faun *Fifty Years Later*. Memphis: Pigeon Roost Press, 1975.

> A 40-page commemorative pamphlet, this describes known existing copies of the book and discusses sales and purchases of copies.

X117₂   Meriwether, James B., ed. "Mac Grider's Son." *Mississippi Quarterly*, 28 (Summer 1975), 347–51.

> A 1934 article by Faulkner.

X118₂   Collins, Carvel. "A Fourth Book Review by Faulkner." *Mississippi Quarterly*, 28 (Summer 1975), 339–46.

> A 1925 review of *Ducdame*, a novel by John Cowper Powys.

X119₂   Wasson, Ben. "A Memory of Marionettes." Prefatory essay to
        Marionettes: A Play in One Act. Oxford, Miss.: Yoknapa-
        tawpha Press, 1975.

X120₂   Meriwether, James B. "Faulkner's Essays on Anderson." In
        A38₂ (1976), pp. 159–81.
            Compares the 1925 and 1953 essays on Sherwood Anderson.

X121₂   Meriwether, James B., ed. "The Priest." *Mississippi Quarterly*,
        29 (Summer 1976), 445–50.

X122₂   Momberger, Philip. "A Reading of Faulkner's 'The Hill.'"
        Southern Literary Journal, 9, No. 2 (Spring 1977), 16–29. "The
        Hill" is concerned with the theme of separation and
        involvement, and the sense of identity.

X123₂   Polk, Noel. Introduction to *The Marionettes*. Charlottesville:
        Univ. Press of Virginia, 1977.

X124₂   Collins, Carvel. Afterword to *Mayday*. South Bend, Ind.:
        Univ. of Notre Dame Press, 1977.
            Discusses sources, themes, and relationships to Faulkner's later work.

X125₂   Kreiswirth, Martin. "Faulkner as Translator: His Versions of
        Verlaine." *Mississippi Quarterly*, 30 (Summer 1977), 429–32.

X126₂   Wood, Marilyn. "William Faulkner's 'Mayday.'" *Book Forum*,
        3, No. 3 (1977), 390–91.

—   Brooks, Cleanth. *William Faulkner* (A48₂; 1978), pp. 32–66.
            On Faulkner's early prose.

X127₂   Brodsky, Louis Daniel, ed. "Eunice." *Mississippi Quarterly*, 31
        (Summer 1978), 449–52.
            A poem written around 1920.

X128₂   Ditsky, John. "William Faulkner's *The Wishing Tree*:
        Maturity's First Draft." *The Lion and the Unicorn*, Spring
        1978, pp. 56–64.

X129₂   Meriwether, James B., ed. "Frankie and Johnny." *Mississippi
        Quarterly*, 31 (Summer 1978), 453–64.

X130₂   Morrison, Gail M. "'Time, Tide, and Twilight': *Mayday* and
        Faulkner's Quest Toward *The Sound and the Fury*."
        Mississippi Quarterly, 31 (Summer 1978), 337–57.
            Studies similarities between *Mayday* and Quentin Compson's story.

X131₂ Yonce, Margaret. "'Shot Down Last Spring': The Wounded Aviators of Faulkner's Wasteland." *Mississippi Quarterly*, 31 (Summer 1978), 359–68.

> Discusses "The Lilacs" as a dramatic monologue of a divided psyche, similar to Eliot's "Prufrock."

X132₂ Bonner, Thomas, Jr. "'Once Aboard the Lugger'—an Uncollected Faulkner Story." *Notes on Modern American Literature*, 3 (Winter 1978), 8.

X133₂ Hamblin, Robert W. "*The Marble Faun*: Chapter One of Faulkner's Continuing Dialectic on Life and Art." *Publications of the Missouri Philological Association*, 3 (1978), 80–90.

X134₂ Blotner, Joseph. Introduction to *Mississippi Poems*. Oxford, Miss.: Yoknapatawpha Press, 1979.

> There is also an Afterword by L. D. Brodsky. See X150₂.

—   Stonum, Gary Lee. *Faulkner's Career* (A60₂; 1979), pp. 41–60.

> On Faulkner's early poetry.

X135₂ Sensibar, Judith L., ed. "Pierrot and the Marble Faun: Another Fragment." *Mississippi Quarterly*, 32 (Summer 1979), 473–76.

X136₂ Meriwether, James B., ed. "Don Giovanni." *Mississippi Quarterly*, 32 (Summer 1979), 484–95.

X137₂ Blotner, Joseph. Introduction to "A Portrait of Elmer." *Georgia Review*, 33 (Fall 1979), 533–34.

> Blotner also writes a short introduction and extensive notes for *Uncollected Stories of William Faulkner* (New York: Random House, 1979).

X138₂ Wittenberg, Judith. Introduction to "Evangeline." *Atlantic Monthly*, November 1979, p. 67.

X139₂ Clothier, Peter. "Faulkner as a Young Poet." *Los Angeles Times*, December 23, 1979, Books, p. 6.

> On *Mississippi Poems*.

X140₂ Boozer, William. "Faulkner's Unrequited Love." *Detroit News*, March 23, 1980, p. G2.

> On *Mayday*.

X141₂ Larson, Charles R. "An Early Fable from Faulkner." *Chicago Tribune*, April 6, 1980, Sec. 7, p. 3.

> On *Mayday*.

X142$_2$ Beaver, Harold. "Mississippian Knights." *Times Literary Supplement*, July 18, 1980, p. 821.
　　　　On *Mayday*.

X143$_2$ Schwartz, Richard A. Review. In A65$_2$ (1980), pp. 167–68.
　　　　On *Marionettes*.

X144$_2$ Polk, Noel. "William Faulkner's 'Hong Li' on Royal Street." *Library Chronicle of the University of Texas*, No. 13 (1980), pp. 27–30.
　　　　Reprints "Hong Li" and discusses its background and significance.

X145$_2$ Morton, Bruce. "The Irony and Significance of Two Early Faulkner and Hemingway Poems Appearing in the *Double Dealer*." *Zeitschrift für Anglistik und Amerikanistik*, No. 3 (1980), pp. 254–58.
　　　　On "Portrait."

X146$_2$ Meriwether, James B., ed. "The Uncut Text of Faulkner's Review of *Test Pilot*." *Mississippi Quarterly*, 33 (Summer 1980), 385–89.

X147$_2$ Hamblin, R. W., and L. D. Brodsky. "'L'Après-Midi D'Un Faune': The Evolution of a Poem." *Studies in Bibliography*, 33 (1980), 254–63.

X148$_2$ Kreiswirth, Martin. "Faulkner's *The Marble Faun:* Dependence and Independence." *English Studies in Canada*, 6 (Fall 1980), 333–44.
　　　　On the use of seasonal patterns and pastoral conventions.

X149$_2$ Morrow, Patrick D. Review. *Southern Humanities Review*, 15 (Spring 1981), 174.
　　　　On *Mississippi Poems*.

X150$_2$ Collins, Carvel. Introduction to *Helen: A Courtship*. Oxford, Miss.: Yoknapatawpha Press, 1981.
　　　　Helen, with Collins' long biographical introduction, and *Yoknapatawpha Poems*, with Blotner's introduction (X134$_2$), were printed together in a trade edition by Tulane Univ. Press in 1981.

X151$_2$ Brodsky, Louis Daniel. "Additional Manuscripts of Faulkner: 'A Dead Dancer.'" *Studies in Bibliography*, 34 (1981), 267–70.
　　　　On manuscripts of Faulkner's poem in Brodsky's collection.

X152₂ Garrett, George. Afterword to *The Road to Glory*. By Joel
Sayre and William Faulkner. Ed. M. J. Bruccoli. Carbondale:
Southern Illinois Univ. Press, 1981.

The movie script.

X153₂ Folks, Jeffrey J. "William Faulkner's 'The Rosary' and
Florence L. Barclay." *Studies in Short Fiction*, 18 (Fall 1981),
445–47.

Faulkner's sketch is a parody of a novel by Barclay.

X154₂ Boozer, William. "*Helen: A Courtship* Joins *Mayday* in
Facsimile and Trade Editions." *Faulkner Newsletter*,
July–September 1981, pp. 1, 4.

Further commentary: A7₂ (Page), A22₂ (Weisgerber), U18₂ (Polk:
"Uncle Willy"), X29₂ (Morell: "A Rose for Emily"), AA40₂ (Putzel:
early prose), AA103₂ (Rose: "Red Leaves"), AA104₂ (Cook: "The Tall
Men"), AA110₂ (Brooks: poetry, early prose), CC20₂ (Lind:
Marionettes), HH298₂ (Kinney: *Mayday*), HH303₂ (Brown: *Mayday*),
II56₂ (Langman: "Golden Land"), KK6₂ (Zolla: Indian stories).

IV. Topical Studies

AA. General Studies

AA1₂   Mickelson, Joel C. "Faulkner's Military Figures of Speech." *Wisconsin Studies in Literature*, 4 (1967), 46–55.

AA2₂   Mottram, Eric. "Mississippi Faulkner's Glorious Mosaic of Impotence and Madness." *Journal of American Studies*, 2 (April 1968), 121–29.

AA3₂   Peskin, S. G. "William Faulkner: A 'Failed' Poet." *Unisa English Studies*, May 1969, pp. 39–45.

AA4₂   Feild, Claire. "Defense Mechanisms Employed by the Faulkner White Racist and Their Effect on the Faulkner Negro." *Research in the Teaching of English*, 4 (Spring 1970), 20–36.

AA5₂   Brumm, Ursula. *American Thought and Religious Typology.* New Brunswick, N.J.: Rutgers Univ. Press, 1970, pp. 206–20.
   Considers religious typology in *The Sound and the Fury, Light in August,* and *A Fable.*

AA6₂   Alexandrescu, Sorin. "William Faulkner and the Greek Tragedy." *Romanian Review*, 24 (1970), 102–10.
   Compares forms and themes in Faulkner's novels with those in Greek tragedy, for example, destiny, order and hierarchy, hybris, community norms.

AA7₂   Smith, Lewis, A. "William Faulkner and the Racist Virus." *Annual Reports of Studies* [Doshisha Women's College, Kyoto, Japan], 21 (1970), 388–98.

AA8₂   Hoadley, Frank M. "The Theme of Atonement in the Novels of William Faulkner." *Northwest Review*, 10 (Summer 1970), 30–43.
   In treating the theme of atonement, Faulkner moves during his career from an extremely pessimistic position "to a theme of man's moral regeneration in the later novels."

AA9₂   Hancock, Maxine. "Fire: Symbolic Motif in Faulkner." *English Quarterly*, 3 (Fall 1970), 19–23.

AA10₂   Alexandrescu, Sorin. "A Project in the Semantic Analysis of the Characters in William Faulkner's Work." *Semiotica*, 4 (1971), 37–51.
   A "typological analysis of Faulkner's universe."

AA11₂   Glicksberg, Charles I. "Faulkner's World of Love and Sex."
         In *The Sexual Revolution in Modern American Literature*.
         The Hague: Martinus Nijhoff, 1971, pp. 96–120.

> A conservative and humanistic writer, Faulkner makes use of violence,
> horror, frustration, and troubled lovers as he deals with man's demonic
> and animal elements. This entry is a renumbering of KK119.

AA12₂   Goldman, Arnold. "Faulkner and the Revision of
         Yoknapatawpha History." In *The American Novel and the
         Nineteen Twenties*. Ed. M. Bradbury and D. Palmer.
         London: E. Arnold, 1971, pp. 165–95.

> Studies Faulkner's process of revising and rearranging in successive
> novels the stories and background of his fictional county.

AA13₂   Hauck, Richard B. "The Prime Maniacal Risibility: William
         Faulkner." In *A Cheerful Nihilism: Confidence and "The
         Absurd" in American Humorous Fiction*. Bloomington:
         Indiana Univ. Press, 1971, pp. 167–200.

> Faulkner's comic vision of the absurd, with special reference to the
> Snopes Trilogy and *As I Lay Dying*.

AA14₂   Schorer, Mark. "William Faulkner." In *Atlantic Brief Lives*.
         Ed. L. Kronenberger and E. M. Beck. Boston: Little, Brown,
         1971, pp. 267–79.

AA15₂   Brooks, Cleanth. "Faulkner's Treatment of the Racial
         Problem: Typical Examples." In *A Shaping Joy: Studies in
         the Writer's Craft*. New York: Harcourt Brace Jovanovich,
         1971, pp. 230–46.

> This is a talk delivered in 1967, mostly on *Light in August* but covering
> other works. The book also reprints J136 and X120.

AA16₂   Lawson, Lewis A. "William Faulkner." In *The Politics of
         Twentieth Century Novelists*. Ed. G. A. Panichas. New
         York: Hawthorn Books, 1971, pp. 278–95.

> Considers Faulkner's originally conservative outlook, his developing
> social criticism, and his extraction of values out of chaos.

AA17₂   Blackley, Charles. "William Faulkner's County: A
         Chronological Guide to Yoknapatawpha." *TAIUS* [Texas A
         & I Univ.], 4, No. 1 (September 1971), 73–86.

AA18₂   Gidley, Mick. "Another Psychologist, A Physiologist and
         William Faulkner." *Ariel*, 2, No. 4 (1971), 78–86.

> On the influence of Havelock Ellis and Louis Berman.

AA19₂   Nolte, W. H. "Mencken, Faulkner, and Southern
         Moralism." *South Carolina Review*, 4 (December 1971),
         45–61.
> On similarities in their views of the causes and ramifications of Southern
> moralism.

AA20₂   Bradford, M. E. "Faulkner's Last Words and 'The American
         Dilemma.'" *Modern Age*, 16 (Winter 1972), 77–82.
> Discusses a Faulkner speech in 1962 which focused on the "abuse of
> language" by modern man.

AA21₂   Dabney, Lewis M. "Faulkner, the Red and the Black."
         Columbia Forum, 1 (Spring 1972), 52–54.

AA22₂   Brooks, Cleanth. "Faulkner and History." *Mississippi
         Quarterly*, 25 (Spring 1972), Supplement, pp. 3–14.
> Discusses the novels' and the characters' concern for the meaning of
> history, and also Faulkner in relation to millennial and gnostic impulses
> in American literature.

AA23₂   Meriwether, James B. "Faulkner's 'Mississippi.'" *Mississippi
         Quarterly*, 25 (Spring 1972), Supplement, pp. 15–24.
> Uses Faulkner's essay to demonstrate the relationship between fact and
> fiction in Faulkner's imagination.

AA24₂   Millgate, Michael. "'The Firmament of Man's History':
         Faulkner's Treatment of the Past." *Mississippi Quarterly*, 25
         (Spring 1972), Supplement, pp. 25–35.
> Faulkner is less interested in history as a reconstruction of the past than
> he is in history "as the embodiment of what people believe happened in
> the past."

AA25₂   Boswell, George W. "Superstition and Belief in Faulkner."
         Costerus, 6 (1972), 1–22.
> On Faulkner's use of local folk materials.

AA26₂   Brumm, Ursula. "Forms and Functions of History in the
         Novels of William Faulkner." *Archiv für das Studium der
         Neueren Sprachen und Literaturen*, 209 (1972), 43–56.

AA27₂   Ditsky, John M. "Uprooted Trees: Dynasty and the Land in
         Faulkner's Novels." *Tennessee Studies in Literature*, 17
         (1972), 151–58.
> The basis of dynasty shifts from property to a heritage of traditional
> values.

AA28₂ Magny, Claude-Edmonde. "Faulkner, or Theological Inversion." In *The Age of the American Novel: The Film Aesthetic of Fiction Between the Two Wars.* New York: F. Ungar, 1972, pp. 178–224.

> This was published in French in 1948, and a section was translated in 1966 (see CC7).

AA29₂ Palievsky, Pyotr. "Faulkner's Road to Realism." In *Soviet Criticism of American Literature in the Sixties* (GG7₂; 1972), pp. 150–68.

> Published in Russian in 1965.

AA30₂ Skaggs, Merrill M. *The Folk of Southern Fiction.* Athens: Univ. of Georgia Press, 1972, pp. 221–34.

> On types of "plain folk."

AA31₂ Yoshida, Michiko. "The Voices and Legends in Yoknapatawpha County." *Studies in English Literature* [Japan], 1972, pp. 174–76.

AA32₂ Zellegrow, Ken. "Faulkner's Flying Tales—a View of the Past." *Descant*, 16 (Summer 1972), 42–48.

> On doomed, alienated pilots in Faulkner's fiction.

AA33₂ Antoniadis, Roxandra. "Faulkner and Balzac: The Poetic Web." *Comparative Literature Studies*, 9 (September 1972), 303–26.

> Considers similarities: reappearing characters, thematic use of setting, narrative techniques, and mythic dimensions.

AA34₂ Howell, Elmo. "Faulkner and Scott and the Legacy of the Lost Cause." *Georgia Review*, 26 (Fall 1972), 314–25.

> Scott had a clearer attitude toward the Jacobite cause than Faulkner had toward the South. Scott's fiction has a grander concept, even if Faulkner's is more lyrical and probing.

AA35₂ Carey, Glenn O. "William Faulkner: Man's Fatal Vice." *Arizona Quarterly*, 28 (Winter 1972), 293–300.

> On Faulkner as an antiwar writer.

AA36₂ Taylor, Walter. "Faulkner's Curse." *Arizona Quarterly*, 28 (Winter 1972), 333–38.

> The "curse" in Faulkner's world finally comes down to white treatment of Negroes, even if related to themes of self-aggrandisement and property abuse.

AA37₂ Howell, Elmo. "William Faulkner's Graveyard." *Notes on Mississippi Writers*, 4 (Winter 1972), 115–18.
Epitaphs in the fiction and in an Oxford cemetery.

AA38₂ Dillon, Richard T. "Some Sources for Faulkner's Version of the First Air War." *American Literature*, 44 (January 1973), 629–37.
The popular fiction of James W. Bellah and Elliott W. Springs.

AA39₂ Robinson, Clayton. "Faulkner and Welty and the Mississippi Baptists." *Interpretations: Studies in Language and Literature*, 5, No. 1 (1973), 51–54.

AA40₂ Putzel, Max. "Evolution of Two Characters in Faulkner's Early and Unpublished Fiction." *Southern Literary Journal*, 5, No. 2 (Spring 1973), 47–63.
Development of characters from the early sketches to the first novels.

AA41₂ O'Brien, Matthew C. "William Faulkner and the Civil War in Oxford, Miss." *Journal of Mississippi History*, 35 (May 1973), 167–74.
Faulkner's use of Oxford's actual part in the war.

AA42₂ Dahl, James. "William Faulkner on Individualism." *West Georgia College Review*, 6 (May 1973), 3–9.

AA43₂ Pladott, Dinnah. "Absurd and Romantic Elements in the Writing of William Faulkner." Diss. Tel-Aviv, 1973.

AA44₂ Aaron, Daniel. "William Faulkner." In *The Unwritten War: American Writers and the Civil War*. New York: Knopf, 1973, pp. 310–26.
On Faulkner's (ironic but compassionate) handling of the war as historical event, mirror of character, and buried experience.

AA45₂ Brooks, Cleanth, R. W. B. Lewis, and Robert Penn Warren. *American Literature: The Makers and the Making*. Vol. II. New York: St. Martin's Press, 1973, pp. 2559–65.

AA46₂ Cowley, Malcolm. "Faulkner: The Yoknapatawpha Story." In *A Second Flowering*. New York: Viking, 1973, pp. 130–55.
The *Portable Faulkner* (1946) introduction with minor revisions plus an afterword.

AA47₂ Jacobs, Robert D. "Faulkner's Humor." In *The Comic Imagination in American Literature*. Ed. L. D. Rubin, Jr. New Brunswick: Rutgers Univ. Press, 1973, pp. 305–18.

AA48₂   Kazin, Alfred. "The Secret of the South: Faulkner to Percy." In *Bright Book of Life: American Novelists and Storytellers from Hemingway to Mailer*. Boston: Little, Brown, 1973, pp. 23–42.

AA49₂   Lehan, Richard. *A Dangerous Crossing: French Literary Existentialism and the Modern American Novel*. Carbondale: Southern Illinois Univ. Press, 1973, pp. 68–79.

AA50₂   Adams, Percy G. "Faulkner, French Literature, and 'Eternal Verities.'" In A17₂ (1973), pp. 7–24.
> The French influence, particularly Balzac, on Faulkner, and Faulkner's influence on French literature.

AA51₂   Aytür, Necla. "Faulkner in Turkish." In A17₂ (1973), pp. 25–39.
> Problems of translating Faulkner into Turkish.

AA52₂   Carlock, Mary Sue. "Kaleidoscopic Views of Motion." In A17₂ (1973), pp. 95–113.
> Like Henry Adams, Faulkner was intrigued by the flux of life, and frequently developed women characters—Caddy, Addie, Eula—as embodiments of force, vitality, and human energy.

AA53₂   Stewart, David H. "Faulkner, Sholokhov, and Regional Dissent in Modern Literature." In A17₂ (1973), pp. 135–50.
> Modern regionalism is a reaction to the emergent superstate.

AA54₂   Carey, Glenn O. "William Faulkner on the Automobile as Social-Sexual Symbol." *CEA Critic*, 36, No. 2 (January 1974), 15–17.
> The automobile is a symbol of sex and man's spiritual deterioration in several novels.

AA55₂   Milum, Richard A. "Faulkner and the Cavalier Tradition: The French Bequest." *American Literature*, 45 (January 1974), 580–89.
> French cavalier backgrounds as seen in Faulkner's Indians, the old Frenchman, and Sutpen's story.

AA56₂   Cowley, Malcolm. "William Faulkner." *Encyclopedia Britannica*, 15th edition, 1974, Macropaedia, Vol. 7, pp. 195–97.

AA57₂   Antoniadis, Roxandra V. "The Dream as Design in Balzac and Faulkner." *Zagadnienia Rodzajow Litearackich*, 17, No. 2 (1974), 45–58.

"Inspiration and rationality, dream and design, are coexistent in the creative process experienced by both authors"; but whereas Balzac analyzes more critically the "mystery" of creativity, Faulkner is more concerned with the moral role of the artist.

AA58[2] Prasad, V. R. N. "William Faulkner and the Southern Syndrome." In *Indian Studies in American Fiction*. Ed. M. K. Naik et al. Delhi: Macmillan, India, 1974, pp. 185-202.

On the theme of endurance and survival in a changing culture.

AA59[2] Richter, Barbara. "*Per Ardua ad Astra*: Perversity in the Morality Puzzle of William Faulkner." *Revista de la Universidad de Costa Rica*, 39 (1974), 139-47.

AA60[2] Walhout, Clarence P. "The Earth Is the Lord's: Religion in Faulkner." *Christian Scholar's Review*, 4, No. 1 (1974), 26-35.

AA61[2] Ditsky, John M. "'Dark, Darker Than Fire': Thematic Parallels in Lawrence and Faulkner." *Southern Humanities Review*, 8 (Fall 1974), 497-505.

AA62[2] Korenman, Joan S. "Faulkner's Grecian Urn." *Southern Literary Journal*, 7, No. 1 (Fall 1974), 3-23.

References to the poem by Keats throughout Faulkner's fiction.

AA63[2] Peckham, Morse. "The Place of Sex in the Work of William Faulkner." *Studies in the Twentieth Century*, No. 14 (Fall 1974), pp. 1-20.

Tension between Idealism and Biology in *A Fable, Requiem for a Nun*, and *The Wild Palms*.

AA64[2] Reed, Richard. "The Role of Chronology in Faulkner's Yoknapatawpha Fiction." *Southern Literary Journal*, 7, No. 1 (Fall 1974), 24-48.

Lays out chronology, and discusses inconsistencies.

AA65[2] Chabot, C. Barry. "Faulkner's Rescued Patrimony." *Review of Existential Psychology and Psychiatry*, 13, No. 3 (1974), 274-86.

A psychoanalytic study dealing with Faulkner's discovery of his personal voice, and the role of time, place, and the past in his fiction.

AA66[2] Kent, George E. "The Black Woman in Faulkner's Works, with the Exclusion of Dilsey." *Phylon*, 35 (December 1974), 430-41.

Faulkner's emphasis is usually on the response of a white consciousness not on the black woman.

AA67₂ Spivey, Herman E. "Faulkner and the Adamic Myth:
       Faulkner's Moral Vision." *Modern Fiction Studies*, 19
       (Winter 1974), 497–505.

    Faulkner rejected the concept of Adamic innocence, but insisted on
    man's freedom of choice and individual responsibility.

AA68₂ Brooks, Cleanth. "Faulkner's Criticism of Modern America."
       Virginia Quarterly Review, 51 (Spring 1975), 294–308.

    Faulkner's Southern background gave him a good vantage point for
    criticizing the modern world and the loss of community.

AA69₂ Cook, Richard M. "Popeye, Flem, and Sutpen: The
       Faulknerian Villain as Grotesque." *Studies in American
       Fiction*, 3 (Spring 1975), 3–14.

AA70₂ Harold, Brent. "The Value and Limitation of Faulkner's
       Fictional Method." *American Literature*, 47 (May 1975),
       212–29.

    Discusses his methods in relation to themes, and illustrates his
    limitations in handling social and economic themes.

AA71₂ Brumm, Ursula. "The Historical Novel and Historicist
       Criticism: Notes on the Critical Reception of Scott and
       Faulkner." In *Geschichte und Gesellschaft in der
       amerikanische Literatur*. Ed. K. Schubert and U. Müller-
       Richter. Heidelberg: Quelle & Meyer, 1975, pp. 102–13.

AA72₂ Day, Martin S. "William Faulkner." In *A Handbook of
       American Literature*. New York: Crane, Russak, 1975, pp.
       508–23.

AA73₂ Geher, István. "Olé, Grandfather: The Presence of a Missing
       Link in William Faulkner's Life and Work." *Studies in
       English and American* [Budapest], 2 (1975), 215–75.

AA74₂ Brumm, Ursula. "William Faulkner and the Rebirth of
       Dixie." In *American Literature Since 1900*. Ed. M. Cunliffe.
       London: Barrie & Jenkins, 1975, pp. 214–41.

AA75₂ McCormick, John. "William Faulkner, the Past, and
       History." In *Fiction as Knowledge: The Modern Post-
       Romantic Novel*. New Brunswick: Rutgers Univ. Press, 1975,
       pp. 88–108.

    On Faulkner's handling of history in his fiction.

AA76[2] Momberger, Philip. "Faulkner's 'Country' as Ideal
Community." In *Individual and Community: Variations on a
Theme in American Fiction*. Ed. K. H. Baldwin and D. K.
Kirby. Durham, N.C.: Duke Univ. Press, 1975, pp. 112–36.
Faulkner emphasizes man's need for community, and provides models.

AA77[2] Brooks, Cleanth. "Faulkner and the Muse of History."
Mississippi Quarterly, 28 (Summer 1975), 265–79. Included
in A48[2] (1978), pp. 251–82.
On Faulkner's sense of history, the theme of man's failure to cope with
change, and Faulkner's skepticism about Southern and American myths
and dreams.

AA78[2] Simpson, Lewis P. "Faulkner and the Southern Symbolism
of Pastoral." *Mississippi Quarterly*, 28 (Fall 1975), 401–15.
Faulkner repudiates the pastoral tradition, and "surrenders" to a
historical view of Southern experience. "All belongs to history, including
the Grecian urn."

AA79[2] Strandberg, Victor. "Between Truth and Fact: Faulkner's
Symbols of Identity." *Modern Fiction Studies*, 21 (Autumn
1975), 445–57.
Faulkner's characters feel a need to construct a bridge between the facts
of their appearance to others and the truth of their appearance to self.

AA80[2] Simpson, Lewis P. "The Loneliness of William Faulkner."
Southern Literary Journal, 8, No. 1 (Fall 1975), 126–43.
An essay-review of Blotner's biography, this also discusses "On Privacy,"
Faulkner's sense of himself as a modern artist, and the influence on him
of Hollywood and World War II.

AA81[2] Grossman, Joel M. "The Source of Faulkner's 'Less Oft Is
Peace.'" *American Literature*, 47 (November 1975), 436–38.
On an allusion to Shelley.

AA82[2] Culley, Margaret M. "Judgment in Yoknapatawpha
Fiction." *Renascence*, 28 (Winter 1976), 59–70.
On the eschatological mode, apocalyptic vision, and the relation between
past and future.

AA83[2] Petesch, Donald A. "Faulkner on Negroes: The Conflict
between the Public Man and the Private Art." *Southern
Humanities Review*, 10 (Winter 1976), 55–64.
Studies confusions and contradictions in Faulkner's public statements on
race relations.

AA84[2] Carey, Glenn O. "Faulkner and His Carpenter's Hammer." *Arizona Quarterly*, 32 (Spring 1976), 5–15.
On Faulkner as a social critic. Included in A63[2].

AA85[2] Cole, Hunter M. "Welty on Faulkner." *Notes on Mississippi Writers*, 9 (Spring 1976), 28–49.
An annotated list of Eudora Welty's public statements on Faulkner.

AA86[2] Rosenman, John B. "A Matter of Choice: The Locked Door Theme in Faulkner." *South Atlantic Bulletin*, 41, No. 2 (May 1976), 8–12.
Studies a recurring image.

AA87[2] Kerr, Elizabeth M. "The Evolution of Yoknapatawpha." In A33[2] (1976), pp. 23–62.
A general overview of the gradual "organic" development of Faulkner's fictional county from 1926 to 1962.

AA88[2] Blotner, Joseph. "William Faulkner: Seminar." In A33[2] (1976), pp. 63–78.
Answers questions from the audience about Faulkner's life and fiction.

AA89[2] Flynn, Peggy. "The Sister Figure and 'Little Sister Death' in the Fiction of William Faulkner." In A33[2] (1976), pp. 99–117.
On Faulkner's female characters, particularly the recurring sister figure.

AA90[2] Cowley, Malcolm, et al. "Faulkner's Mississippi: Land into Legend: Panel Discussion." In A33[2] (1976), pp. 119–33.
Questions from the audience to Cowley, Evans Harrington, and Elizabeth Kerr.

AA91[2] Blotner, Joseph, et al. "William Faulkner's Mississippi: Panel Discussion." In A33[2] (1976), pp. 135–40.
Questions answered by Blotner, Elizabeth Kerr, Gerald Walton, Jack Stone, Bill Lamb.

AA92[2] Blotner, Joseph, et al. "The Riches of Yoknapatawpha: Panel Discussion." In A33[2] (1976), pp. 141–61.
Questions answered by Blotner, Malcolm Cowley, Elizabeth Kerr, Evans Harrington, Gerald Walton, James Webb.

AA93[2] Blotner, Joseph. "The Sole Owner and Proprietor." In A38[2] (1976), pp. 1–20.
Surveys Faulkner's personal relationship to his fictional county.

AA94[2] Adams, Richard P. "Faulkner: The European Roots." In A38[2] (1976), pp. 21–41.

Considers the influence of European culture, including troubadours, on Faulkner.

AA95₂   Morimoto, Shin'ichi. "Freedom from Burden: Two Phases in William Faulkner's Novels." *Sophia English Studies*, 1 (1976), 71–88.

AA96₂   Rubin, Louis D., Jr. "William Faulkner: The Discovery of a Man's Vocation." In A38₂ (1976), pp. 43–68.

Examines Faulkner's perception of his vocation, with emphasis on the relationship between sexuality and artistic talent, and the dialectic of action and sensibility in his fiction.

AA97₂   Zlobin, G. "A Struggle Against Time." In *20th Century American Literature: A Soviet View*. Trans. R. Vroon. Moscow: Progress, 1976, pp. 285–305.

AA98₂   Landor, M. "Faulkner's Creative Method in the Making." In *20th Century American Literature: A Soviet View*. Trans. R. Vroon. Moscow: Progress, 1976, pp. 306–30.

AA99₂   Simpson, Lewis P. "Faulkner and the Legend of the Artist." In A38₂ (1976), pp. 69–100.

Faulkner works out of the self-conscious romantic myth of the artist in his own way, especially in relation to the dialectic between Pan (nature) and antinatural modern forces.

AA100₂   Page, Sally R. "Faulkner's Sense of the Sacred." In A38₂ (1976), pp. 101–21.

Faulkner's fiction prophesies a new age of hopefulness about human life and its importance.

AA101₂   Watkins, Floyd C. "Habet: Faulkner and the Ownership of Property." In A38₂ (1976), pp. 123–37.

In contrast with the extremes of Ike McCaslin and Thomas Sutpen, Faulkner believed in responsible ownership of property.

AA102₂   Brooks, Cleanth. "William Faulkner and William Butler Yeats: Parallels and Affinities." In A38₂ (1976), pp. 139–58. Also in A48₂ (1978), pp. 329–44.

Studies their comparable uses of regional cultures and their interest in oral tradition and man's relation to nature and history.

AA103₂   Rose, Alan Henry. "The Limits of Humanity in the Fiction of William Faulkner." In *Demonic Vision: Racial Fantasy and Southern Fiction*. Hamden, Conn.: Archon Books, 1976, pp. 101–18.

Studies the influence on Faulkner of traditional Southern visions of the Negro as demonic.

—   Beck, Warren. *Faulkner* (A29₂; 1976). See annotation to
        A29₂.

AA104₂ Cook, Sylvia Jenkins. "Faulkner's Celebration of the Poor-
        White Paradox." In *From Tobacco Road to Route 66: The
        Southern Poor White in Fiction*. Chapel Hill: Univ. of
        North Carolina Press, 1976, pp. 39–63.
        From a generally conservative perspective, Faulkner uses traditional
        figures but humanizes the stereotypes.

AA105₂ Blotner, Joseph. "The Faulkners and the Fictional Families."
        Georgia Review, 30 (Fall 1976), 572–92.
        Considers the correspondence between fictional characters and actual
        persons.

AA106₂ Conley, Timothy K. "Beardsley and Faulkner." *Journal of
        Modern Literature*, 5 (September 1976), 339–56.
        Studies Beardsley's influence on Faulkner.

AA107₂ Sharma, P. P. "William Faulkner's South and the Other
        South." *Indian Journal of American Studies*, 7, No. 1
        (January 1977), 79–93. Included in A63₂ (1980), pp. 123–37.
        Compares the South of the Fugitives and the South of Welty with
        Faulkner's South.

AA108₂ Cowley, Malcolm. "The Etiology of Faulkner's Art."
        Sewanee Review, 13 (January 1977), 83–95.
        A critical study of John Irwin's psychoanalytic approach to Faulkner.

AA109₂ Aiken, Charles S. "Faulkner's Yoknapatawpha County:
        Geographical Fact into Fiction." *Geographical Review*, 67
        (January 1977), 1–21.
        On Faulkner's use of the terrain and demography of northeast
        Mississippi.

AA110₂ Brooks, Cleanth. "The Image of Helen Baird in Faulkner's
        Early Poetry and Fiction." *Sewanee Review*, 85 (Spring
        1977), 218–34.

AA111₂ Petesch, Donald A. "Some Notes on the Family in
        Faulkner's Fiction." *Notes on Mississippi Writers*, 10 (Spring
        1977), 11–18.

AA112₂ McGinnis, Wayne D. "Faulkner's Use of the Mule: Symbol
        of Endurance and Derision." *Notes on Mississippi Writers*,
        10 (Spring 1977), 19–26.

AA113₂ Wagner, Linda W. "Tension and Technique: The Years of Greatness." *Studies in American Fiction*, 5 (Spring 1977), 65–77.

AA114₂ Wasiolek, Edward. "Dostoevsky, Camus, and Faulkner: Transcendence and Mutilation." *Philosophy and Literature*, 1 (Spring 1977), 131–46.
> All three writers use patterns of mutilation based on outrage.

AA115₂ Polek, Fran. "Tick-tocks, Whirs, and Broken Gears: Time and Identity in Faulkner." *Renascence*, 29 (Summer 1977), 193–200.
> Compares those characters associated with "natural" (circular) time with those associated with "mechanical" (linear) time.

AA116₂ Jenkins, Lee Clinton. "Faulkner, the Mythic Mind, and the Blacks." *Literature and Psychology*, 27, No. 2 (1977), 74–91.
> On mythic and agitated lyrical elements in Faulkner's style, and the association of blacks with a curse. Incorporated into A72₂ (1981).

AA117₂ Millgate, Michael. "Faulkner and History." In A43₂ (1977), pp. 22–39.
> "Faulkner is not so much interested in history as a factual record as he is in history as a text for the study of man."

AA118₂ Foote, Shelby. "Faulkner's Depiction of the Planter Aristocracy." In A43₂ (1977), pp. 40–61.
> Faulkner did not deal with aristocrats much because there were none in Mississippi.

AA119₂ Turner, Darwin T. "Faulkner and Slavery." In A43₂ (1977), pp. 62–85.
> Faulkner's opposition to slavery was abstract, lacking in a real vision of brutality in practice.

AA120₂ Foote, Shelby, Darwin T. Turner, and Evans Harrington. "Faulkner and Race." In A43₂ (1977), pp. 86–103.
> A panel discussion in which Turner talks about Dilsey at length.

AA121₂ Tuttleton, James W. "'Combat in the Erogenous Zone': Women in the American Novel between the Two World Wars." In *What Manner of Woman: Essays on American Life and Literature*. Ed. M. Springer. New York: New York Univ. Press, 1977, pp. 271–96.

AA122₂ Pilkington, John. "Nature's Legacy to William Faulkner." In A43₂ (1977), pp. 104–27.

Puts Faulkner into a tradition of nature romance and makes comparisons with Cooper.

AA123[2]   Wagner, Linda W. "Faulkner and (Southern) Women." In A43[2] (1977), pp. 128–46.

Traces a pattern of development in Faulkner's characterization of women.

AA124[2]   Wagner, Linda W., Victoria F. Black, and Evans Harrington. "Faulkner and Women." In A43[2] (1977), pp. 147–51.

A panel discussion, with other comments by Elizabeth Kerr.

AA125[2]   Foote, Shelby. "Faulkner and War." In A43[2] (1977), pp. 152–67.

Foote answers questions on Faulkner's handling of war, the historical novel, and other topics.

AA126[2]   Millgate, Michael. "Faulkner and the South: Some Reflections." In A43[2] (1977), pp. 195–210.

Emphasizes Faulkner's conscious literary use of "the South."

AA127[2]   Gray, Richard. "The Individual Talent: William Faulkner and the Yoknapatawpha Novels." In *The Literature of Memory: Modern Writers of the American South.* Baltimore: Johns Hopkins Univ. Press, 1977, pp. 197–256.

Includes sections on Faulkner's relationship to the South, his treatment of farmers as characters, and the plantation myth.

AA128[2]   Blotner, Joseph. "Romantic Elements in Faulkner." In *Romantic and Modern: Revaluations of Literary Tradition.* Ed. G. Bornstein. Pittsburgh: Univ. of Pittsburgh Press, 1977, pp. 207–21.

Considers such romantic elements as the influence of the past, the emphasis on nature and individualism, character types connected with romanticism, and the imagination's shaping power.

AA129[2]   Paliyevsky, Pyotr. "Faulkner's America." *Soviet Literature,* No. 8 (1977), pp. 177–80.

AA130[2]   Anastasyev, Nikolai. "The Necessity of Faulkner." *Soviet Literature,* No. 8 (1977), pp. 180–83.

AA131[2]   Wagner, Linda W. "Codes and Codicils: Faulkner's Last Novels." In *Itinerary 3: Criticism.* Ed. F. Baldanza. Bowling Green, Ohio: Bowling Green Univ. Press, 1977, pp. 1–9.

AA132[2]   Taylor, Walter. "Faulkner: Nineteenth-Century Notions of
           Racial Mixture and the Twentieth-Century Imagination."
           South Carolina Review, 10, No. 1 (November 1977), 57–68.
           Compares Faulkner's characters with stereotypes in books by Thomas
           Dixon, William Gilmore Simms, and others.

AA133[2]   Milum, Richard A. "Cavaliers, Calvinists, and the Wheel of
           Fortune: The Gambling Instinct in Faulkner's Fiction."
           Notes on Mississippi Writers, 11 (Spring 1978), 3–14.
           On the frequent gambling scenes and imagery.

AA134[2]   Brooks, Cleanth. "The Sense of Community in
           Yoknapatawpha Fiction." In A52[2] (1978), pp. 3–18.

AA135[2]   Jackson, Blyden. "Faulkner's Depiction of the Negro." In
           A52[2] (1978), pp. 33–47.

AA136[2]   Kerr, Elizabeth M. "The Women of Yoknapatawpha." In
           A52[2] (1978), pp. 83–100.

AA137[2]   Collins, Carvel, et al. "Faulkner's Mississippi: Land into
           Legend." In A52[2] (1978), pp. 205–15.
           A panel discussion by Collins, Evans Harrington, Elizabeth Kerr, Blyden
           Jackson, and Carl Petersen.

AA138[2]   Goldman, Arnold. "Faulkner's Images of the Past: From
           Sartoris to *The Unvanquished*." *Yearbook of English
           Studies*, 8 (1978), 109–24.
           The transition from naturalism to humanism is seen in Faulkner's
           treatment of the past.

AA139[2]   Campbell, Leslie Jean. "Exercises in Doom: Yoknapatawpha
           County Weddings." *Publications of the Arkansas
           Philological Association*, 4, No. 2 (Spring 1978), 2–7.

AA140[2]   Dickerson, Mary Jane. "Faulkner's Golden Steed."
           Mississippi Quarterly, 31 (Summer 1978), 369–80.
           Faulkner's use of horses and horse imagery reveals much about his
           complex vision of the "entwined creative-destructive energies in human
           relationships."

AA141[2]   Berzon, Judith R. *Neither White Nor Black: The Mulatto
           Character in American Fiction*. New York: New York Univ.
           Press, 1978, pp. 86–92, 225–35.

AA142[2]   Morris, Wright. "William Faulkner." In *Earthly Delights,
           Unearthly Adornments*. New York: Harper & Row, 1978,
           pp. 131–40.

Considers the emotions behind Faulkner's imaginatively extravagant style.

AA143$_2$ Brown, Calvin S. "Faulkner's Localism." In A53$_2$ (1978), pp. 3–24.

Reviews Faulkner's use of specific local flora, fauna, dialects, and traditions.

AA144$_2$ Guerard, Albert J. "The Faulknerian Voice." In A53$_2$ (1978), pp. 25–42.

Faulkner's unique expression of temperament and self includes comedy of mind, misogyny, and sexual fantasy.

AA145$_2$ Simpson, Lewis P. "Sex and History: Origins of Faulkner's Apocrypha." In A53$_2$ (1978), pp. 43–70.

The tension between cosmological and historical modes of existence is a nexus for Faulkner's fiction. A crisis in sexuality is at the center of his treatment of the modern internalization of history in the self.

AA146$_2$ Lind, Ilse Dusoir. "Faulkner's Women." In A53$_2$ (1978), pp. 89–104.

Explores Faulkner's emphasis on physical and biological factors, and describes the influence of books by Havelock Ellis and Louis Berman.

AA147$_2$ Alexander, Margaret Walker. "Faulkner and Race." In A53$_2$ (1978), pp. 105–21.

Emphasizing Lucas Beauchamp, this discusses Faulkner as the first white Southern writer to grapple seriously with the prejudices of his time and place.

AA148$_2$ Brown, Calvin S. "Faulkner's Universality." In A53$_2$ (1978), pp. 146–66.

Explores universal themes in the fiction, but argues Faulkner did not know classical literature and myth well.

AA149$_2$ Debreczeny, Paul. "The Device of Conspicuous Silence in Tolstoi, Cexov, and Faulkner." In *American Contributions to the Eighth International Congress of Slavists, Zagreb and Ljubljana, September 3–9, 1978.* Ed. V. Terras. Columbus: Slavica, 1978, Vol. 2 Lit., pp. 125–45.

AA150$_2$ Donald, Miles. "The Fate of the Traditional Novel: William Faulkner and John Updike." In *The American Novel in the Twentieth Century.* London: David & Charles, 1978, pp. 73–90.

AA151$_2$ Mansfield, Luther Stearns. "The Nature of Faulkner's Christianity." *Descant*, 22, No. 3 (1978), 40–48.

AA152₂ Millgate, Michael. "Faulkner's Masters." *Tulane Studies in English*, 23 (1978), 143–55.
>Considers several major influences including Joyce, Melville, Conrad, and Balzac.

AA153₂ Asselineau, Roger. "The French Face of William Faulkner." *Tulane Studies in English*, 23 (1978), 157–73.
>Studies French influences on Faulkner, and his popularity in France.

AA154₂ Weinstein, Philip M. "Precarious Sanctuaries: Protection and Exposure in Faulkner's Fiction." *Studies in American Fiction*, 6 (Autumn 1978), 173–91.
>Considers the implicit assumption of a chasm between self and not-self in Faulkner's fiction, and the development in the later novels from sanctuaries as escapes to sanctuary as transcendence.

AA155₂ Fried, Barbara H. *The Spider in the Cup: Yoknapatawpha County's Fall into the Unknowable.* The LeBaron Russell Briggs Prize Honors Essay in English, 1977. Cambridge, Mass.: Harvard University, 1978.

AA156₂ Weston, Robert V. "Faulkner and Lytle: Two Modes of Southern Fiction." *Southern Review*, 15 (January 1979), 34–51.
>Compares Andrew Lytle.

AA157₂ Boswell, George W. "Epic, Drama, and Faulkner's Fiction." *Kentucky Folklore Record*, 25 (January–June 1979), 16–27.
>Considers the influence of epic and drama on Faulkner's fiction.

AA158₂ Palumbo, Donald. "The Concept of God in Faulkner's *Light in August, The Sound and the Fury, As I Lay Dying,* and *Absalom, Absalom!*" *South Central Bulletin* [SCMLA], 34 (Winter 1979), 142–46.

AA159₂ Johnson, Robert L. "William Faulkner, Calvinism, and the Presbyterians." *Journal of Presbyterian History*, 57 (Spring 1979), 66–81.

AA160₂ Gidley, M. "William Faulkner and Some Designs of Naturalism." *Studies in American Fiction*, 7 (Spring 1979), 75–82.
>The influence of biological naturalism on Faulkner's fiction.

AA161₂ Going, William T. "Faulkner's Other State: His Fictional View of Alabama." *Ball State University Forum*, 20, No. 2 (Spring 1979), 49–52.

AA162₂   Ford, Dan. "Maybe Happen Is Never Once: Some Critical
          Thought on Faulkner's Use of Time." *Publications of the
          Arkansas Philological Association*, 5, Nos. 2–3 (Spring–Fall
          1979), 9–15.

AA163₂   Tanaka, Hisao. "Hawthorne and Faulkner." *Kyushu
          American Literature*, No. 20 (June 1979), pp. 63–65.

AA164₂   Werner, Craig. "Beyond Realism and Romanticism: Joyce,
          Faulkner and the Tradition of the American Novel."
          Centennial Review, 23 (Summer 1979), 242–62.

AA165₂   Connolly, Thomas E. "Joyce and Faulkner." *James Joyce
          Quarterly*, 16 (Summer 1979), 513–15.

AA166₂   Vincent, Sybil K. "Sweet and Bitter Sweat: William
          Faulkner's Work Ethic." *Markham Review*, 8 (Summer
          1979), 66–69.

AA167₂   Aiken, Charles S. "Faulkner's Yoknapatawpha County: A
          Place in the American South." *Geographical Review*, 69
          (July 1979), 331–48.
          Uses maps, historical descriptions, pictures of actual places.

AA168₂   Brown, Calvin S. "Faulkner as Aphorist." *Revue de
          Littérature Comparée*, 53 (July–September 1979), 277–98.
          Discusses the function of aphorisms in universalizing the significance of
          actions as well as in establishing tone and rhythm.

AA169₂   Straumann, Heinrich. "Black and White in Faulkner's
          Fiction." *English Studies*, 60 (August 1979), 452–70.
          A general survey of race relations in Faulkner's fiction, this emphasizes
          the suspense and tension created by Faulkner's ambivalence on racial
          issues.

AA170₂   Simpson, Lewis. "Southern Fiction." In *Harvard Guide to
          Contemporary American Writing*. Ed. D. Hoffman.
          Cambridge: Harvard Univ. Press, 1979, pp. 156–67.

AA171₂   Ousby, Ian. *A Reader's Guide to Fifty American Novels*.
          London: Heinemann, 1979, pp. 279–303.
          Includes *The Sound and the Fury*, *As I Lay Dying*, *Sanctuary*, and
          Absalom, Absalom!

AA172₂   Kawin, Bruce. "Faulkner's Film Career: The Years with
          Hawks." In A57₂ (1979), pp. 163–81.
          Draws on Kawin's own interviewing of Howard Hawks to survey the
          relationship between Faulkner and Hawks in Hollywood.

AA173[2]   Kenner, Hugh. "Faulkner and the Avant-Garde." In A57?
           (1979), pp. 182–96.

> Considers influences on Faulkner of Imagism and other aspects of
> international modernism.

AA174[2]   Tanaka, Hisao. "Hawthorne and Faulkner." *Chu-Shikoku
           Studies in American Literature*, 15 (1979), 17–35.

> Hawthorne and Faulkner were concerned with similar themes and used
> some of the same methods. Both used ambiguity in creative ways; both
> used the romance and Gothicism in order to explore psychological
> themes.

AA175[2]   Sasiki, Midori. "Southern Appalachian English: The
           Language of Faulkner's Country People." *Chu-Shikoku
           Studies in American Literature*, 15 (1979), 37–46.

AA176[2]   Ryan, Steven T. "Faulkner and Quantum Mechanics."
           Western Humanities Review, 33 (Autumn 1979), 329–39.

> Discusses Faulkner's methods in relation to modern scientific theories.

AA177[2]   Gretlund, Jan N. "The Wild Old Green Man of the Woods:
           Katherine Anne Porter's Faulkner." *Notes on Mississippi
           Writers*, 12 (Winter 1980), 67–79.

> Porter's comments on Faulkner.

AA178[2]   Boswell, George W. "Pet Peeves of William Faulkner."
           Mississippi Folklore Register, 14 (Spring 1980), 24–29.

> On the human failings Faulkner most often criticized.

AA179[2]   Church, Margaret. "Two Views of Time: James Joyce and
           William Faulkner." *University of Dayton Review*, 14 (Spring
           1980), 65–69.

AA180[2]   King, Richard H. *A Southern Renaissance: The Cultural
           Awakening of the American South 1930-1955.* New York:
           Oxford Univ. Press, 1980, pp. 77–85, 111–45.

> Includes sections on Faulkner's use of the past, Quentin Compson, and
> *Go Down, Moses.*

AA181[2]   Milum, Richard A. "Continuity and Change: The Horse, the
           Automobile and the Airplane in Faulkner's Fiction." In A63[2]
           (1980), pp. 157–74.

> Considers symbolic and thematic implications of all three, in relation to
> the cavalier/modern dichotomy.

AA182[2]   Howell, John M. "Faulkner, Prufrock, and Agamemnon:
           Horses, Hell, and High Water." In A63[2] (1980), pp. 213–29.

> On the influence of and allusions to Eliot's poetry.

AA183₂   Wyatt, David. "Faulkner and the Burdens of the Past." In
          Prodigal Sons: A Study in Authorship and Authority.
          Baltimore: Johns Hopkins Univ. Press, 1980, pp. 72–100.

> "Faulkner's struggle for a revenge against time was also an ambition
> which changed through time."

AA184₂   Onoe, Masaji. "Some T. S. Eliot Echoes in Faulkner."
          William Faulkner: Materials, Studies, and Criticism [Japan],
          3, No. 1 (July 1980), 1–15.

AA185₂   Wittenberg, Judith B. "Faulkner and Eugene O'Neill."
          Mississippi Quarterly, 33 (Summer 1980), 327–41.

> Considers the influence of O'Neill's work.

AA186₂   Oberhelman, Harley D. *The Presence of Faulkner in the
          Writings of García Márquez.* Graduate Studies, Texas Tech
          Univ., No. 22. Lubbock: Texas Tech Press, 1980.

> Monograph on similarities and influence.

AA187₂   Simpson, Lewis P. "William Faulkner of Yoknapatawpha."
          In *The American South: Portrait of a Culture.* Ed. L. D.
          Rubin, Jr. Baton Rouge: Louisiana State Univ. Press, 1980,
          pp. 227–44.

AA188₂   MacKethan, Lucinda H. "Faulkner's Sons of the Fathers:
          How to Inherit the Past." In *The Dream of Arcady: Place
          and Time in Southern Literature.* Baton Rouge: Louisiana
          State Univ. Press, 1980, pp. 153–80.

> Traces a pattern of self-destructive attempts by characters to seize a
> dream of the past and make it relevant to a fragmented modern world.

AA189₂   Millgate, Michael. "'A Cosmos of My Own': The Evolution
          of Yoknapatawpha." In A64₂ (1980), pp. 23–43.

> The genesis and discovery of Faulkner's unified legend.

AA190₂   Watson, James G. "Faulkner: The House of Fiction." In
          A64₂ (1980), pp. 134–58.

> On houses as setting and symbol, and architectural imagery.

AA191₂   Polk, Noel. "'I Taken an Oath of Office Too': Faulkner and
          the Law." In A64₂ (1980), pp. 139–78.

> On law and lawbreakers in the fiction.

AA192₂   McHaney, Thomas L. "Faulkner's Curious Tools." In A64₂
          (1980), pp. 179–201.

> Discusses unlikely catalysts of noble actions, such as Nub Gowrie, in
> relation to the Nobel Prize speech.

AA193₂ McHaney, Thomas L. "Watching for the Dixie Limited: Faulkner's Impact Upon the Creative Writer." In A64₂ (1980), pp. ?26 47.
  Considers attitudes of contemporary and younger writers toward Faulkner.

AA194₂ Lind, Ilse Dusoir. "Faulkner and Nature." In A65₂ (1980), pp. 112–21.
  Considers nature as a complex source of setting, theme, and symbol.

AA195₂ Strandberg, Victor. "William James and Faulkner's God." In A65₂ (1980), pp. 122–35.
  Faulkner's religious vision was similar to that of James.

AA196₂ Reed, Joseph. "Faulkner, Ford, Ives, and the Sense of Canon." In A65₂ (1980), pp. 136–51.
  Compares George Ives and John Ford as canon-builders.

AA197₂ Gallagher, Susan. "To Love and Honor: Brothers and Sisters in Faulkner's Yoknapatawpha County." *Essays in Literature*, 7 (Fall 1980), 213–44.
  Considers the frequency of brother-sister pairs, and their thematic function.

AA198₂ Tran, Qui Phiet. *William Faulkner and the French New Novelists*. Arlington: Carrolton, 1980. An 85-page study of influence.

AA199₂ Meeks, Elizabeth. "Reflections of the Milieu in Names of William Faulkner's Characters." *Southern Studies*, 20 (Spring 1981), 91–96.
  Local sources for names of characters.

AA200₂ Mortimer, Gail L. "Significant Absences: Faulkner's Rhetoric of Loss." *Novel*, 14 (Spring 1981), 232–50.
  Faulkner's preoccupation with the past can be best understood by studying rhetorical devices that control the narrative. These emphasize certain "significant absences" that reveal the development of this preoccupation out of a profound sense of loss.

AA201₂ Messenger, Christian. "Faulkner: The Play Spirit." In *Sport and Spirit of Play in American Fiction: Hawthorne to Faulkner*. New York: Columbia Univ. Press, 1981, pp. 262–90.
  Faulkner's use of play, contest, and the play spirit is discussed in relation to *Sartoris* and *The Unvanquished*. Games and rituals, play and freedom, in *The Hamlet*, are related to central themes. In other chapters

Messenger discusses "Frank Merriwell in Frenchman's Bend" (Labove), pp. 218–24, and compares Ike McCaslin with Hemingway's character Santiago, pp. 291–309.

— Strandberg, Victor. *A Faulkner Overview: Six Perspectives* (A77$_2$; 1981). See annotation to A77$_2$.

AA202$_2$ Wagner, Linda W. "William Faulkner." In *American Novelists, 1910–1945. Dictionary of Literary Biography.* Ed. J. J. Martine. Detroit: Gale Research, 1981, pp. 282–302.

AA203$_2$ Porter, Carolyn. "William Faulkner: Innocence Historicized." In *Seeing and Being: The Plight of the Participant Observer in Emerson, James, Adams, and Faulkner.* Middletown, Conn.: Wesleyan Univ. Press, 1981, pp. 207–76.

Chapters on "Faulkner's America," which reestablishes a framework for considering the typicality of Thomas Sutpen "and explores Faulkner's relation to the paternalistic plantation tradition"; and on "The Reified Reader," which analyzes Faulkner's "increasingly complex strategies for undermining the reader's detached contemplative stance" in *The Sound and the Fury, Light in August,* and *As I Lay Dying.*

AA204$_2$ Folks, Jeffrey J. "William Faulkner and the Silent Film." *Southern Quarterly,* 19 (Spring–Summer 1981), 171–82.

Considers the influence of silent films on Faulkner's early fiction.

AA205$_2$ Hamblin, Robert W. "'Saying No to Death': Toward William Faulkner's Theory of Fiction." In A71$_2$ (1981), pp. 3–35.

Faulkner's theory of fiction is based on his idea that through art man can defy time, death, and mortality. Memory and imagination, not "realism," are the means by which man accomplishes this end.

AA206$_2$ Douglas, Ellen. "Faulkner's Women." In A71$_2$ (1981), pp. 149–67.

Faulkner's attitude toward women is consistent throughout his career. Generally he accepts his region's conventional images of women, and his misogyny is closely tied to his own love/hate relationship with the South.

AA207$_2$ Nilon, Charles H. "Cooper, Faulkner, and the American Venture." In A71$_2$ (1981), pp. 168–98.

A comparative study of "aristocrats" in the fiction of Cooper and Faulkner.

AA208$_2$ Nilon, Charles H. "Blacks in Motion." In A71$_2$ (1981), pp. 227–51.

Studies black characters by focusing on patterns of motion, journeys in
time and space, and the narrative methods presenting such motion—
especially in *Go Down, Moses*.

AA209[2]   Carothers, James B. "The Myriad Heart: The Evolution of
the Faulkner Hero." In A71[2] (1981), pp. 252–83.

Applies a "developmental method" to the study of Faulkner's career,
emphasizing changes and repetitions in the presentation of heroes and
heroic action between 1926 and 1962.

AA210[2]   Douglas, Ellen. "Faulkner in Time." In A71[2] (1981), pp.
284–301.

Tells the effect of the first reading of Faulkner on a young Southern
writer in the 1930s and 1940s.

AA211[2]   Bleikasten, André. "Fathers in Faulkner." In *The Fictional
Father: Lacanian Readings of the Text*. Ed. Robert Con
Davis. Amherst: Univ. of Massachusetts Press, 1981, pp.
115–46.

The book also includes a section from John Irwin's study of Faulkner
(A25[2]), and an article on fathers in Joyce by J. M. Rabaté that draws
comparisons with Faulkner.

AA212[2]   Kort, Wesley A. "Social Time in Faulkner's Fiction."
Arizona Quarterly, 37 (Summer 1981), 101–15.

Studies several novels in terms of "social times," a term Kort uses to
explore the tension between continuity and the preservation of identity,
on the one hand, and changes over time, on the other.

AA213[2]   Kreiswirth, Martin. "The Will to Create: Faulkner's
Apprenticeship to Willard Huntington Wright." *Arizona
Quarterly*, 37 (Summer 1981), 149–65.

Studies the influence on Faulkner of Wright's *The Creative Will*.

AA214[2]   Watson, James G. "Literary Self-Criticism." *Southern
Quarterly*, 20 (Fall 1981), 46–63.

Works such as "Afternoon of a Cow" and *Mayday* show Faulkner's
capacity for self-parody.

AA215[2]   Ilacqua, Alma A. "From Purveyor of Perversion to
Defender of the Faithful: A Summary of Critical Studies on
Faulkner's Theological Vision." *Language Quarterly*, 20
(Fall–Winter 1981), 35–38.

BB. Biographical Articles

BB1₂   Webb, James W. "Rowan Oak, Faulkner's Golden Bough."
University of Mississippi Studies in English, 6 (1965), 39–47.

BB2₂   Commins, Dorothy B. "William Faulkner in Princeton."
Journal of Historical Studies, 2 (1969), 179–85.

BB3₂   Emerson, O. B. "Faulkner and His Friend: An Interview
with Emily W. Stone." *Comment* [Univ. of Alabama],
Spring 1971, pp. 31–37.

BB4₂   Williams, Joan. *The Wintering*. New York: Harcourt Brace
Jovanovich, 1971.
>
> A novel based in part on the author's friendship with Faulkner in the 1950s.

BB5₂   Olson, Ted. "Faulkner and the Colossus of Maroussi."
South Atlantic Quarterly, 71 (Spring 1972), 205–12.
>
> Reminiscence of a dinner in Greece attended by both Faulkner and George Katsimbalis.

BB6₂   Hand, Barbara. "Faulkner's Widow Recounts Memories of
College Weekends in Charlottesville." *Cavalier Daily*, April
21, 1972, pp. 1, 4.

BB7₂   McHaney, Thomas L. "The Falkners and the Origin of
Yoknapatawpha County: Some Corrections." *Mississippi
Quarterly*, 25 (Summer 1972), 249–64.
>
> Background of the Falkner family, and correction of earlier scholarship.

BB8₂   Pitts, Stella. "Faulkner Views on South, Integration Cost
Him Approval, Says Brother." *New Orleans Times-Picayune*,
July 9, 1972, Sec. 3, p. 8.
>
> Interview with Jack Falkner.

BB9₂   Pfeiffer, Andrew H. "Eye of the Storm: The Observers'
Image of the Man Who Was Faulkner." *Southern Review*, 8
(Autumn 1972), 763–73.
>
> Discusses attempts by many observers to make sense of Faulkner's personality.

BB10₂   Faulkner, Jim. "Auntee Owned Two." *Southern Review*, 8
(Autumn 1972), 836–44.
>
> Memoir by Faulkner's nephew.

BB11₂   Pitts, Stella. "Faulkner's Oxford Ten Years Later." *New
Orleans Times-Picayune*, September 17, 1972, Dixie, pp.
10–14.

BB12₂ Vare, Robert. "Oxford, Miss., Which Faulkner Transcended,
Is As He Left It." *New York Times*, January 14, 1973, Sec.
10, pp. 3, 11.

BB13₂ Martin, H. "Caravan to Faulkner County . . . And Beyond."
Southern Living, May 1973, pp. 116–25.

BB14₂ Falkner, Murry C. "The Coming of the Motor Car."
Southern Review, 10 (January 1974), 170–80.
Reminiscence by Faulkner's brother.

BB15₂ Fox, Thomas. "Faulkner's 'Sanctuary.'" *Memphis
Commercial Appeal*, March 3, 1974, Sec. 6, p. 6.
On Rowan Oak.

BB16₂ Pitts, Stella. "624 Pirates Alley: Faulkner Lived Here." *New
Orleans Times-Picayune*, March 17, 1974, Sec. 3, p. 10.
On Faulkner in New Orleans. A related article appeared November 26,
1972, Dixie, pp. 42–46.

BB17₂ Dahl, James. "A Faulkner Reminiscence: Conversations with
Mrs. Maud Falkner." *Journal of Modern Literature*, 3
(April 1974), 1026–30.
A visit in 1953.

— Blotner, Joseph. *Faulkner*. 2 vols. (A18₂; 1974).

BB18₂ Meriwether, James B. "Faulkner and the World War II
Monument in Oxford." In A21₂ (1974), pp. 105–06.

BB19₂ Meriwether, James B. "William Faulkner's Own Collection
of His Books in 1959." In A21₂ (1974), pp. 139–41.

BB20₂ Inge, M. Thomas. "The Virginia Face of Faulkner." *Virginia
Cavalcade*, Summer 1974, pp. 32–39.
Faulkner in Charlottesville.

BB21₂ Franklin, Malcolm A. "A Christmas in Columbus."
Mississippi Quarterly, 27 (Summer 1974), 319–22.
A trip with Faulkner around 1930.

BB22₂ Sanford, Robert. "Faulkner's Oxford Isn't So Dry Now." *St.
Louis Post-Dispatch*, February 16, 1975, p. K3.

BB23₂ Lopez, Guido. "Letters and Comments: 'Faulkner and the
Horses.'" Trans. Ruth Feldman. *Yale Review*, 64 (Spring
1975), 468–76.
Faulkner in Italy, 1955.

BB24₂   Wells, Dean Faulkner. "Dean Swift Faulkner: A Biography."
        M.A. Thesis, Univ. of Mississippi, 1975.
        Biography of her father, Faulkner's brother.

BB25₂   Wharton, Don. "William Faulkner: The Man Behind the
        Genius." *Reader's Digest*, June 1976, pp. 51–58.
        Comments by persons who knew Faulkner personally.

BB26₂   Sansing, David. "History of Northern Mississippi." In A33₂
        (1976), pp. 5–22.

BB27₂   Brown, Andrew H. *History of Tippah County, Mississippi:
        The First Century*. Ripley, Miss.: The Tippah County
        Historical and Genealogical Society, 1976. Reviewed by
        David Paul Ragan in *Mississippi Quarterly*, 31 (Summer
        1978), 482–86.

BB28₂   Dardis, Tom. "William Faulkner: 'They're Gonna Pay Me
        Saturday, They're Gonna Pay Me Saturday.'" *Some Time in
        the Sun: The Hollywood Years of Fitzgerald, Faulkner,
        Nathanael West, Aldous Huxley, and James Agee*. New
        York: Scribner's, 1976, pp. 78–149.

BB29₂   Sobotka, C. John. *A History of Lafayette County,
        Mississippi*. Oxford: Rebel Press, 1976. Reviewed by
        Thomas L. McHaney, *Mississippi Quarterly*, 32 (Summer
        1979), 523–26.
        For a more comprehensive history of Mississippi, see KK24₂.

—   Wilde, Meta Carpenter, and Orin Borsten. *A Loving
        Gentleman* (A37₂; 1976).

BB30₂   Silver, James W. "Faulkner's South." *Southern Humanities
        Review*, 10 (Fall 1976), 301–12.
        The impact of Faulkner's fiction and Faulkner the person on Silver.

BB31₂   Wells, Dean Faulkner, and Lawrence Wells. "The Trains
        Belonged to Everybody: Faulkner as Ghost Writer."
        Southern Review, 12 (October 1976), 864–71.
        Includes an anecdotal tale Faulkner wrote out for his brother's sister-in-
        law.

BB32₂   Davis, Sally. "The Secret Hollywood Romance of William
        Faulkner." *Los Angeles*, November 1976, pp. 131–34,
        206–07. Report in *New York Times*, October 30, 1976, p. 28.
        Includes interview with Meta Carpenter Wilde, and cartoons drawn by
        Faulkner.

BB33₂   McKelway, Bill. "Gentleman, 76, is 'Finally There.'"
        Richmond Times-Dispatch, January 6, 1977, pp. 1, 4.
        A butler's reminiscence.

BB34₂   Kotkin, Joel. "Faulkner's Hollywood Love." *Washington
        Post*, February 2, 1977, p. C4.
        Article on and interview with Meta Wilde.

—   Franklin, Malcolm. *Bitterweeds* (A42₂; 1977).

BB35₂   Cerf, Bennett. *At Random: The Reminiscences of Bennett
        Cerf.* New York: Random House, 1977, pp. 129–37.

BB36₂   Wilde, Meta Doherty. "An Unpublished Chapter from *A
        Loving Gentleman.*" *Mississippi Quarterly*, 30 (Summer
        1977), 449–60.
        Covers her background in Mississippi and its importance to her
        relationship with Faulkner.

BB37₂   Wasson, Ben. "William Faulkner's First Grand Opera."
        Delta Democrat-Times [Greenville, Miss.], July 31, 1977, p.
        33.
        Faulkner attending *Carmen*.

BB38₂   Black, Victoria, et al. "William Faulkner of Oxford: Panel
        Discussion." In A52₂ (1978), pp. 187–203.
        Questions answered by Black, Evans Harrington, Lucy Howorth, Mary
        McClain, Christine Drake, and Dean Faulkner Wells.

BB39₂   Duvall, Howard, et al. "Faulkner in Oxford: Panel
        Discussion." In A52₂ (1978), pp. 161–86.
        Questions answered by Duvall, Phil Mullen, Robert J. Farley, James W.
        Webb, William McNeil Reed, William Stone, and William Roane.

—   Cofield, Jack. *William Faulkner* (A50₂; 1978).

BB40₂   Commins, Dorothy. *What Is an Editor? Saxe Commins at
        Work.* Chicago: Univ. of Chicago Press, 1978, pp. 194–228.
        Chapters on "William Faulkner and the Nobel Prize" and "William
        Faulkner as Cultural Ambassador."

BB41₂   Walser, Richard. "On Faulkner's Putting Wolfe First."
        South Atlantic Quarterly, 78 (Spring 1979), 172–81.

—   Wittenberg, Judith B. *Faulkner* (A61₂; 1979).

BB42₂   Hamblin, Robert W. "Lucas Beauchamp, Ned Barnett, and
        William Faulkner's 1940 Will." *Studies in Bibliography*, 32
        (1979), 281–83.

BB43[2]   Kraft, Stephanie. "William Faulkner and Rowan Oak." *No Castles on Main Street: American Authors and Their Homes*. Chicago: Rand McNally, 1979, pp. 139–44.

BB44[2]   Martinez, Elsie. "By William Faulkner in Love." *New Orleans Times-Picayune*, October 21, 1979, Dixie, pp. 20–24.
           Hand-illustrated books for Helen Baird.

BB45[2]   Warren, Robert Penn. "William Faulkner: A Life on Paper." *TV Guide*, December 15, 1979, pp. 12–14.

BB46[2]   Minter, David. "On the Dating of a Faulkner Letter." *Notes on Mississippi Writers*, 12 (Winter 1980), 80.
           A 1944 letter to Malcolm Cowley.

BB47[2]   Blotner, Joseph. "Faulkner as seen by a friend." *Michigan Alumnus*, February 1980, pp. 4–8.

BB48[2]   Bosha, Francis J. "William Faulkner and the Eisenhower Administration." *Journal of Mississippi History*, 42 (February 1980), 49–54.

BB49[2]   Williams, Joan. "Twenty Will Not Come Again." *Atlantic Monthly*, May 1980, pp. 58–65.

—   Bezzerides, A. I. *William Faulkner, a Life on Paper* (A62[2]; 1980).

BB50[2]   Boozer, William. "William Faulkner: Transcending the Place Mississippi." In *Mississippi Heroes*. Ed. D. F. Wells and H. Cole. Jackson: Univ. Press of Mississippi, 1980, pp. 190–214.

BB51[2]   Baker, Carlos. "Faulkner: An Orientation, 1940." In A65[2] (1980), pp. 9–13.
           Personal reminiscence.

BB52[2]   Blotner, Joseph. "Did You See Him Plain?" In A64[2] (1980), pp. 3–22.
           Faulkner's personal image to others, including Blotner.

BB53[2]   Blotner, Joseph. "The Sources of Faulkner's Genius." In A64[2] (1980), pp. 248–70.
           Heredity, memory, and the drive to write.

—   Minter, David. *William Faulkner* (A66[2]; 1980).

BB54[2]   Campbell, Harry Modean. "Faulkner in the Classroom— 1947." In A63[2] (1980), pp. 1–6.
           Faulkner and Phil Stone at the University of Mississippi.

BB55$_2$ James, Susie. "Homage to William Faulkner's Homestead." *Washington Post*, August 13, 1980, p. B2.

BB56$_2$ Faulkner, Jim. "Memories of Brother Will." *Southern Review*, 16 (Fall 1980), 907–20.
            Faulkner in the 1930s.

BB57$_2$ Wells, Dean Faulkner, ed. *The Ghosts of Rowan Oak: William Faulkner's Ghost Stories for Children.* Oxford: Yoknapatawpha Press, 1980.
            Introduction by Willie Morris.

BB58$_2$ Morris, Willie. "Faulkner's Ghost Stories." *American Bookseller*, October 1980, pp. 40–41.
            On Faulkner's storytelling.

BB59$_2$ James, Susie. "The Ghosts of 'Pappy' Faulkner." *New Orleans Times-Picayune*, November 9, 1980, Dixie, pp. 30–31, 33.

BB60$_2$ Wells, Dean Faulkner. "A Christmas Remembered." *Parade*, December 21, 1980, pp. 4–5.

BB61$_2$ Boozer, William. "Fireside Thrillers: Heart-Pounding Moments with Faulkner's Ghosts." *Detroit News*, January 25, 1981, p. F2.

BB62$_2$ Mullener, Elizabeth. "Oxford: Shrine to Faulkner." *New Orleans Times-Picayune*, February 28, 1981, Sec. 4, pp. 1–2.
            An adjacent article by Mullener, "Another Mississippian Spins Yarns on Smaller Scale," includes comments on Faulkner by Oxford resident Bill Appleton.

BB63$_2$ Faulkner, Jim. "No Pistol Pocket." *Southern Review*, 17 (April 1981), 358–65.
            Continues BB56$_2$, memories of the 1930s.

BB64$_2$ Brown, Calvin S. "Faulkner's Rowan Oak Tales." *Mississippi Quarterly*, 34 (Summer 1981), 367–74.

—   Collins, Carvel. Introduction to *Helen: A Courtship* (X150$_2$; 1981).

BB65$_2$ Wells, Dean Faulkner. "The Werewolf." *Paris Review*, 79 (1981), 200–210.
            On a ghost story Faulkner once told.

BB66₂ Lamar, Thomas E. "Debits and Credits in Faulkner's Hand Found in Old Bank Ledgers." *Faulkner Newsletter*, July–September 1981, pp. 1, 3.

> On Faulkner's work in an Oxford bank. A news article appeared in the *New Orleans Times-Picayune*, September 7, 1981, p. 19.

BB67₂ Ewing, Jack. "Collector Finds Consolation Stone." *Faulkner Newsletter*, July–September 1981, p. 2.

> On a writing contest Faulkner entered in 1911.

BB68₂ Wells, Lawrence. "John Maxwell's 'Oh, Mr. Faulkner, Do You Write?' Inspires Renewed Awe of Subject." *Faulkner Newsletter*, October–December 1981, pp.1–2.

> On a traveling two-act show about Faulkner. A news article, "Ex-teacher thriving in one-man Faulkner show in Miss." by Ron Harrist, appeared in the *New Orleans Times-Picayune*, October 12, 1981, Sec. 2, p. 4.

BB69₂ Boozer, William. "Oxford Grows as Literary World Shrine." *Faulkner Newsletter*, October–December 1981, pp. 1, 3.

CC. Studies of Style, Structure, and Technique

CC1₂ James, Stuart. "Faulkner's Shadowed Land." *Denver Quarterly*, 6 (Autumn 1971), 45–61.

> Considers Faulkner's experiments with point of view.

CC2₂ Murray, Edward. "The Stream-of-Consciousness Novel and Film, III—William Faulkner." In *The Cinematic Imagination: Writers and the Motion Pictures*. New York: F. Ungar, 1972, pp. 154–67.

> Reviews cinematic devices in fiction, novels adapted for film, and Faulkner's screenwriting.

CC3₂ Swink, Helen. "The Novelist as Oral Narrator." *Georgia Review*, 26 (Summer 1972), 183–209.

> Considers the influence of the "Southern oral tradition" on Faulkner's prose style.

CC4₂ Gidley, M. "Elements of the Detective Story in William Faulkner's Fiction." *Journal of Popular Culture*, 7 (Summer 1973), 97–123.

> Included in *Dimensions of Detective Fiction* (See G13₂; 1976), pp. 228–46.

CC5₂ Kinney, Arthur F. "Faulkner's Fourteenth Image." *Paintbrush*, 2, No. 2 (Autumn 1974), 36–43.

Faulkner formulates "unfolding epistemologies" in his novels and explores cognitive structures.

CC6₂   Murray, D. M. "Faulkner, the Silent Comedies, and the Animated Cartoon." *Southern Humanities Review*, 9 (Summer 1975), 241–57.

Similarities between Faulkner's humor and the effects in film comedy or cartoon.

CC7₂   Subramanyam, N. S. "William Faulkner's Prose Style." *Calcutta Review*, 1 (April–June 1976), 41–53.

CC8₂   Kantak, V. Y. "Faulkner's Technique." In *Studies in American Literature: Essays in Honor of William Mulder*. Delhi: Oxford Univ. Press, 1976, pp. 77–96.

Time, point of view, moral vision in the major novels.

—   Guerard, Albert J. "Faulkner: Problems of Technique." In *The Triumph of the Novel* (A32₂; 1976), pp. 204–34.

Discusses "split structure and ironic counterpoint," "arts of modulation," and rhetorical devices. Makes comparisons with Conrad by discussing their "congenial and uncongenial" materials and techniques.

CC9₂   Maini, D. S. "The Rhetoric of William Faulkner." *Indian Journal of English Studies*, 16 (1976), 29–43.

CC10₂   Adams, Robert M. *Afterjoyce: Studies in Fiction After Joyce*. New York: Oxford Univ. Press, 1977, pp. 82–89.

On stream of consciousness and mythical "counterstructure."

CC11₂   Guerard, Albert J. "Faulkner the Innovator." In A53₂ (1978), pp. 71–88.

On Faulkner's complex use of stream of consciousness, and innovations in the novel form.

CC12₂   Watson, James G. "Faulkner: Short Story Structures and Reflexive Forms." *Mosaic*, 11, No. 4 (Summer 1978), 127–38.

Studies reflexive formal patterns in several novels: characters are both external figures and spokesmen for a point of view, thereby creating a mosaic of interlocking and mutually revealing patterns.

CC13₂   Müller, Christopher. "On William Faulkner's Manner of Narration." *Kwartalnik Neofilologiczny*, 25, No. 2 (1978), 201–12.

A study of Faulkner's manner of narration clarifies his view of reality.

CC14₂   Gidley, M. "William Faulkner and Willard Huntington
          Wright's *The Creative Will.*" *Canadian Review of American
          Studies*, 9 (Fall 1978), 169–77.
              Considers the influence of Wright's book on Faulkner.

CC15₂   Pearce, Richard. "Reeling through Faulkner: Pictures of
          Motion, Pictures in Motion." *Modern Fiction Studies*, 24
          (Winter 1978), 483–95.
              Considers such techniques as the hovering narrator and "passing" the
              story, as well as the function of motion in Faulkner's fiction.

CC16₂   Hoffer, Bates. "The Sociolinguistics of Literature: Faulkner's
          Styles and Dialects." In *Perspectives on Applied
          Sociolinguistics.* Ed. R. N. St. Clair. Lawrence, Kansas:
          Coronado, 1979, pp. 212–23.

CC17₂   Ono, Kiyoyuki. "'Life Is Motion': An Aspect of William
          Faulkner's Style." *William Faulkner: Materials, Studies, and
          Criticism*, 2, No. 2 (December 1979), 48–66.

CC18₂   Folks, Jeffrey J. "The Influence of Poetry in the Narrative
          Technique of Faulkner's Early Fiction." *Journal of Narrative
          Technique*, 9 (Fall 1979), 184–90.

CC19₂   Kawin, Bruce. "The Montage Element in Faulkner's
          Fiction." In A57₂ (1979), pp. 103–26.
              Reviews Faulkner's integral use of montage (counterpoint, rapid cutting
              and collisions, parallel associations) in such novels as *The Wild Palms*,
              The Sound and the Fury, and *Absalom, Absalom!*

CC20₂   Lind, Ilse Dusoir. "Faulkner's Uses of Poetic Drama." In
          A57₂ (1979), pp. 66–81.
              Considers the influence of expressionism, especially on *Marionettes* and
              Light in August.

CC21₂   Lind, Ilse Dusoir. "The Effect of Painting on Faulkner's
          Poetic Form." In A57₂ (1979), pp. 127–48.
              Studies relationships between Faulkner's fiction and visual arts in terms
              of influences (Beardsley, Cezanne, and others) and similarities.

CC22₂   Porter, Carolyn. "Faulkner and His Reader." In A63₂ (1980),
          pp. 231–58.
              Studies the visual mode in Faulkner's major novels, and the spatiality
              of the reader's experience.

CC23₂   Broughton, Panthea R. "The Cubist Novel: Toward Defining
          the Genre." In A71₂ (1981), pp. 36–58.

> The "arranging and patterning of narrative shapes which typifies the modern novel," such as *The Sound and the Fury*, can best be described as "cubist" and can be related to cubist painting.

CC24[2]   Broughton, Panthea R. "Faulkner's Cubist Novels." In A71[2] (1981), pp. 59–94.

> The major transformation in his work between 1925 and 1928 was due to a rejection of a "destructive romanticism" and a progression from realistic fiction toward modernist techniques, influenced by cubism, which unsettles the reader's preconceptions. These techniques can be seen in such novels as *The Sound and the Fury*, *As I Lay Dying*, and *The Wild Palms*.

CC25[2]   Bunselmeyer, J. E. "Faulkner's Narrative Styles." *American Literature*, 53 (November 1981), 424–42.

> Uses speech act theory and transformational grammar to analyze ways in which "narrative syntax creates tone and point of view." Compares, for example, the "comic and the contemplative styles." Uses several novels as examples.

EE.   The Nobel Prize

EE1[2]   Edwards, C. Hines, Jr. "A Hawthorne Echo in Faulkner's Nobel Prize Acceptance Speech." *Notes on Contemporary Literature*, 1, No. 2 (March 1971), 4–5.

EE2[2]   Barger, James. *William Faulkner, Modern American Novelist and Nobel Prize Winner*. Ed. D. Steve Rahmas. Outstanding Personalities Series, No. 63. Charlotteville, N.Y.: SamHar Press, 1973. Ricks No. 5638.

EE3[2]   Rothford, John. "The Concept of Time in Faulkner's Nobel Speech." *Notes on Mississippi Writers*, 11 (Winter 1979), 73–83.

EE4[2]   Grimwood, Michael. "The Self-Parodic Context of Faulkner's Nobel Prize Speech." *Southern Review*, 15 (April 1979), 366–75.

> A more ironic reading of the speech than is usual.

GG.   Checklists and Bibliographical Materials

GG1[2]   Straumann, Heinrich. "The Early Reputation of Faulkner's Work in Europe: A Tentative Appraisal." *English Studies Today*. 4th ser. Rome, 1966, pp. 443–59.

GG2₂   Leary, Lewis. *Articles on American Literature 1950–1967*. Durham: Duke Univ. Press, 1970, pp. 165–94.

GG3₂   Materassi, Mario. "Faulkner Criticism in Italy." *Italian Quarterly*, 15, No. 57 (Summer 1971), 47–85.
Historical survey from 1931 to the 1960s.

GG4₂   Lloyd, J. B. "An Annotated Bibliography of William Faulkner, 1967–1970." *University of Mississippi Studies in English*, 12 (1971), 1–57.

GG5₂   Crane, Joan St. C. "Rare or Seldom-Seen Dust Jackets of American First Editions: IV." *Serif*, 8 (1971), 21–23.
Reproduces four Faulkner dust jackets. Also see 7 (1970), 64–66.

GG6₂   Meriwether, James B. "A Proposal for a CEAA Edition of William Faulkner." In *Editing Twentieth Century Texts*. Ed. F. G. Halpenny. Toronto: Univ. of Toronto Press, 1972, pp. 12–27.

GG7₂   Proffer, Carl, ed. *Soviet Criticism of American Literature in the Sixties: An Anthology*. Ann Arbor: Ardis, 1972.
The introduction lists translations, and the book includes two articles on Faulkner.

GG8₂   Landor, Mikhail. "Faulkner in the Soviet Union." In GG7₂ (1972), pp. 173–80.

GG9₂   Millgate, Michael. "Faulkner." In *American Literary Scholarship: An Annual: 1970*. Ed. J. A. Robbins. Durham: Duke Univ. Press, 1972, pp. 116–31.

GG10₂   Adelman, Irving, and Rita Dworkin. *The Contemporary Novel*. Metuchen, N.J.: Scarecrow Press, 1972, pp. 134–96.
Checklist.

—   Bassett, John. *William Faulkner: An Annotated Checklist of Criticism* (A3₂; 1972).

GG11₂   Gribbin, Daniel V. "Stories and Articles by William Faulkner in the Rare Book Collection of the University of North Carolina Library." *Bookman*, September 1972, pp. 23–27.

GG12₂   Moore, Robert H., ed. *The Faulkner Concordance Newsletter*, No. 1 (December 1972).
Later issues are No. 2 (November 1973); No. 3 (May 1974); No. 4 (February 1975); and No. 5 (November 1976), edited by ʌ. H. Blair. The

Newsletter was then incorporated into the *Newsletter of the Society for the Study of Southern Literature.* Also see, on the use of manuscript material by the Concordance Project, "Book Note," *American Notes and Queries,* 11 (May 1973), 144.

GG13₂   Emerson, O. B. "Faulkner and His Bibliographers." *Bulletin of Bibliography,* 30 (April-June 1973), 90–92.

GG14₂   Brooks, Cleanth. "The British Reception of Faulkner's Work." In A17₂ (1973), pp. 41–55.
Explains Faulkner's unenthusiastic reception in Britain.

GG15₂   Cambon, Glauco. "My Faulkner: The Untranslatable Demon." In A17₂ (1973), pp. 77–93.
Covers interest in Faulkner among Italian writers, as well as Cambon's problems translating *Absalom, Absalom!* His 1954 preface to that novel is included.

GG16₂   Szladits, Lola L. *New in the Berg Collection, 1970–1972.* New York: New York Public Library, 1973.

GG17₂   Langford, Gerald. "Insights into the Creative Process: The Faulkner Collection at the University of Texas." In A17₂ (1973), pp. 115–33.
Also comments on Faulkner's revisions in several novels.

GG18₂   Pownall, David E. "William Faulkner." In *Articles on Twentieth Century Literature: An Annotated Bibliography, 1954–1970.* New York: Kraus-Thomson, 1973. Vol. II, pp. 885–1025.
Checklist based on annual lists in *Twentieth Century Literature.*

GG19₂   Millgate, Michael. "Faulkner." In *American Literary Scholarship: An Annual: 1971.* Ed. J. Woodress. Durham: Duke Univ. Press, 1973, pp. 104–19.

GG20₂   Meriwether, James B., ed. "Faulkner's Correspondence with *Scribner's Magazine*." *Proof,* 3 (1973), 253–82.
Prints letters, 1928–35.

GG21₂   Capps, Jack L. "Computer Program Revisions and the Preparation of a Concordance to *Go Down, Moses.*" *Faulkner Concordance Newsletter,* No. 2 (November 1973), pp. 2–5.

GG22₂   McHaney, Thomas L. "The Text of *Flags in the Dust.*" *Faulkner Concordance Newsletter,* No. 2 (November 1973), pp. 7–8.

Reply by Albert Erskine and further comments by McHaney are in No. 3 (May 1974), pp. 2–4.

GG23₂ Meriwether, James B. "William Faulkner." In *Sixteen Modern American Authors: A Survey of Research and Criticism.* Ed. J. R. Bryer. Durham: Duke Univ. Press, 1974, pp. 223–75.

An updating of GG85.

GG24₂ Millgate, Michael. "Faulkner." In *American Literary Scholarship: An Annual: 1972.* Ed. J. Woodress. Durham: Duke Univ. Press, 1974, pp. 114–30.

GG25₂ Woodress, James. *American Fiction, 1900–1950: A Guide to Information Sources.* Detroit: Gale, 1974, pp. 91–97.

GG26₂ Capps, Jack L., ed. *The William Faulkner Collection at West Point and the Faulkner Concordances.* West Point: United States Military Academy, 1974. Thirty-page pamphlet, with introduction by Capps, "William Faulkner and West Point," pp. 1–5.

GG27₂ Moore, Robert H. "The Faulkner Concordance and Some Implications for Textual and Linguistic Studies." In GG26₂ (1974), pp. 6–13.

GG28₂ Erskine, Albert. "Authors and Editors: William Faulkner at Random House." In GG26₂ (1974), pp. 14–19.

GG29₂ McIntosh, William A., and Walton D. Stallings. "A Selective Listing of the William Faulkner Collection at the United States Military Academy." In GG26₂ (1974), pp. 20–28.

GG30₂ McDonald, W. U., Jr. "Bassett's Checklist of Faulkner Criticism: Some 'Local' Addenda." *Bulletin of Bibliography,* 32 (April–June 1975), 76.

— Petersen, Carl. *Each in Its Ordered Place: A Faulkner Collector's Notebook* (A27₂; 1975).

GG31₂ Meriwether, James B. "Faulkner." In *American Literary Scholarship 1973.* Ed. J. Woodress. Durham: Duke Univ. Press, 1975, pp. 135–49.

— Bassett, John. *William Faulkner: The Critical Heritage* (A23₂; 1975).

GG32₂ Crane, Joan St. C., and Anne E. H. Freudenberg, eds. *Man Collecting: Manuscripts and Printed Works of William Faulkner in the University of Virginia Library.* Charlottesville: Univ. of Virginia Library, 1975.

> A 142-page catalogue printed for items "On Exhibition in the Rare Book and Manuscript Departments of the University of Virginia Library, Charlottesville, Virginia, 16 November 1975 – 31 January 1976."

GG33₂ Kelly, Brian. "William Faulkner—In One Long Sentence." *Washington Star*, November 16, 1975, p. D1.

> On the Virginia exhibit.

GG34₂ Lloyd, James B. "The Oxford *Eagle*, 1902–1962: A Census of Locations." *Mississippi Quarterly*, 29 (Summer 1976), 423–31.

> In 1977 the *Mississippi Quarterly* published Lloyd's 58-page listing, *The Oxford Eagle, 1900–1962: An Annotated Checklist of Material on William Faulkner and the History of Lafayette County.* The most complete listing of items on Faulkner in the Oxford newspaper, it is reviewed by Noel Polk in *Mississippi Quarterly*, 31 (Summer 1978), 486–87.

GG35₂ Zender, Karl F. "Faulkner." In *American Literary Scholarship 1974.* Ed. J. Woodress. Durham: Duke Univ. Press, 1976, pp. 123–38.

—   McHaney, Thomas L. *William Faulkner: A Reference Guide* (A36₂; 1976).

GG36₂ *William Faulkner: An Exhibit.* St. Louis: Washington Univ. Library, 1976.

> Brochure describing exhibit, August 23 to October 15, 1976.

GG37₂ *A Catalog for "The William Faulkner Collection" at the University of Toledo.* Toledo: The Friends of the Univ. of Toledo Libraries, 1977.

> Prepared at the William F. Carlson Library, this includes an introduction by W. U. McDonald, Jr.

GG38₂ Zender, Karl F. "Faulkner." In *American Literary Scholarship 1975.* Ed. J. Woodress. Durham: Duke Univ. Press, 1977, pp. 143–65.

GG39₂ Robbins, J. Albert, ed. *American Literary Manuscripts.* 2nd ed. Athens: Univ. of Georgia Press, 1977, p. 106.

> Lists the locations of manuscript materials.

GG40$_2$ Meriwether, James B. "The Books of William Faulkner: A
        Guide for Students and Scholars." *Mississippi Quarterly*, 30
        (Summer 1977), 417–28.

> A list of Faulkner's books, this updates the 1963 list in *Modern Fiction Studies*.

GG41$_2$ Meriwether, James B. "Faulkner's Correspondence with *The
        Saturday Evening Post*." *Mississippi Quarterly*, 30 (Summer
        1977), 461–75.

> Previously unpublished letters, 1927–31, to and from Faulkner, with annotations.

GG42$_2$ Kawin, Bruce. "A Faulkner Filmography." *Film Quarterly*,
        30, No. 4 (Summer 1977), 12–21.

GG43$_2$ Monteiro, George. "Fugitive Comments on Early Faulkner."
        Notes on Mississippi Writers, 10 (Winter 1977), 95–96.

> Three early notices in *McNaught's Monthly*.

GG44$_2$ Oberhelman, Harley D. "William Faulkner's Reception in
        Spanish America." *The American Hispanist*, 3, No. 26 (April
        1978), pp. 13–17.

GG45$_2$ Boozer, William. "Collecting Faulkner." In A52$_2$ (1978), pp.
        125–37.

GG46$_2$ Williams, Jerry T. *Southern Literature 1968–1975: A
        Checklist of Scholarship*. Boston: G. K. Hall, 1978, pp.
        113–47.

> Checklist based on annual lists in *Mississippi Quarterly*.

GG47$_2$ Harmon, Robert. *The First Editions of William Faulkner*.
        Los Altos, Calif.: Hermes Publications, 1978.

> An 18-page pamphlet.

GG48$_2$ Broughton, Panthea Reid. "Faulkner." In *American Literary
        Scholarship 1976*. Ed. J. A. Robbins. Durham: Duke Univ.
        Press, 1978, pp. 119–40.

GG49$_2$ Hayhoe, George F. "Faulkner in Hollywood: A Checklist of
        His Film Scripts at the University of Virginia." *Mississippi
        Quarterly*, 31 (Summer 1978), 407–19.

> Describes thirty-five items at Alderman Library, with cross-references to the list in Kawin's book.

GG50$_2$ Capps, Jack L. "The Faulkner Concordance." *Literary
        Research Newsletter*, 3 (Spring 1978), 72–73.

GG51₂   McHaney, Thomas L., et al. "Faulkner 1977: A Survey of Research and Criticism." *Mississippi Quarterly*, 31 (Summer 1978), 429–47.

GG52₂   Brooks, Diana. "Criticism on American Humor: An Annotated Checklist." *Studies in American Humor*, 6 (Spring 1979), 19–44.

GG53₂   Southern Studies Program. *The Making of William Faulkner's Books, 1929-1937: An Interview with Evelyn Harter Glick.* Columbia: Univ. of South Carolina, 1979.

> This pamphlet, an interview with a woman who designed eight of Faulkner's books, includes anecdotes and information on publication of the books.

GG54₂   Emerson, O. B., and Marion C. Michael. *Southern Literary Culture: A Bibliography of Masters' and Doctors' Theses.* Rev. and enl. ed. University: Univ. of Alabama Press, 1979, pp. 41–71.

> A supplement to this is Jack D. Wages and William D. Andrews, "Southern Literary Culture: 1969-1975," *Mississippi Quarterly*, 32 (Winter 1978-79), 49–70.

GG55₂   Petersen, Carl. *On the Track of the Dixie Limited: Further Notes of a Faulkner Collector.* La Grange, Ill.: Colophon Book Shop, 1979.

> Updates earlier list (A27₂).

GG56₂   Hayhoe, George F. "Faulkner in Hollywood: A Checklist of His Filmscripts at the University of Virginia: A Correction and Additions." *Mississippi Quarterly*, 32 (Summer 1979), 467–72.

GG57₂   McHaney, Thomas L., et al. "Faulkner 1978: A Survey of Research and Criticism." *Mississippi Quarterly*, 32 (Summer 1979), 497–518.

GG58₂   Broughton, Panthea Reid. "Faulkner." In *American Literary Scholarship 1977.* Ed. J. Woodress. Durham: Duke Univ. Press, 1979, pp. 135–61.

GG59₂   Brodsky, Louis D., and Robert W. Hamblin. *Selections from the William Faulkner Collection of Louis Daniel Brodsky: A Descriptive Catalogue.* Charlottesville: Univ. Press of Virginia, 1979.

Also see *William Faulkner: A Perspective from the Brodsky Collection* (Cape Girardeau: Southeast Missouri State Univ., 1979), which describes the exhibit; and Brodsky's speech on collecting Faulkner, *The Collector as Sleuthsayer* (Cape Girardeau: Southeast Missouri State Univ., 1979).

GG60$_2$ Bonner, Thomas, Jr. *William Faulkner. The William B. Wisdom Collection: A Descriptive Catalogue.* New Orleans: Tulane Univ. Libraries, 1980. A 90-page pamphlet, with introductory essays by Bonner, Cleanth Brooks, and Carvel Collins.

GG61$_2$ McHaney, Thomas L., et al. "Faulkner 1979: A Survey of Research and Criticism." *Mississippi Quarterly*, 33 (Summer 1980), 390–412.

GG62$_2$ Broughton, Panthea Reid. "Faulkner." In *American Literary Scholarship 1978*. Ed. J. A. Robbins. Durham: Duke Univ. Press, 1980, pp. 127–51.

GG63$_2$ Boozer, William. "Faulkner Sketch, Letter and Signed Editions Among Emerson Collection." *Faulkner Newsletter*, January–March 1981, pp. 1, 3.

On the Faulkner collection at Vanderbilt University. This is an article in the first issue of *The Faulkner Newsletter & Yoknapatawpha Review*, published four times during the year.

GG64$_2$ Babiiha, Thaddeo K. "The Faulkner Section in Leary's *Articles on American Literature, 1968–1975*." *Papers of the Bibliographical Society of America*, 75 (January–March 1981), 93–98.

On errors in the checklist.

GG65$_2$ Mullen, Phil. "Phil Knew Bill as Friend, Saved Only a Few Collectibles." *Faulkner Newsletter*, April–June 1981, pp. 1, 4.

On Phil Mullen's collection of letters and manuscripts.

—   Ricks, Beatrice. *William Faulkner: A Bibliography of Secondary Works* (A76$_2$; 1981).

GG66$_2$ Brodsky, Louis D. "The Collector as Sleuthsayer." In A71$_2$ (1981), pp. 125–48.

Tells the story of gathering his large Faulkner collection over many years.

GG67₂   Cox, Dianne L., et al. "Faulkner 1980: A Survey of
         Research and Criticism." *Mississippi Quarterly*, 34 (Summer
         1981), 343–66.

GG68₂   Broughton, Panthea R. "Faulkner." In *American Literarary
         Scholarship: An Annual/1979*. Ed. J. Woodress. Durham:
         Duke Univ. Press, 1981, pp. 133–54.

V. Other Materials

HH. Reviews of Books about Faulkner[1]

HH1$_2$ Everett, Walter K. Review. *Notes on Mississippi Writers*, 1 (Fall 1968), 72–77. (M. Falkner)

HH2$_2$ Everett, Walter K. Review. *Notes on Mississippi Writers*, 2 (Spring 1969), 35–40. (Adams)

HH3$_2$ Simpson, Hassell A. Review. *Notes on Mississippi Writers*, 2 (Fall 1969), 74–77. (Smart)

HH4$_2$ Simpson, Hassell A. Review. *Notes on Mississippi Writers*, 3 (Spring 1970), 43–47. (Kerr)

HH5$_2$ Early, James. "Faulkner Through French Eyes." *Southwest Review*, 56 (Summer 1971), 293–95. (Coindreau)

HH6$_2$ Blotner, Joseph. "The Achievement of Maurice Edgar Coindreau." *Southern Literary Journal*, 4, No. 1 (Fall 1971), 95–96. (Coindreau)

HH7$_2$ Carey, Glenn O. "Faulkner Scholarship: The Old and the New." *CEA Critic*, 34, No. 2 (January 1972), 32–33. (Meriwether, Seyppel)

HH8$_2$ Adams, Richard P. "Coindreau on Faulkner." *CEA Critic*, 34, No. 2 (January 1972), 34. (Coindreau)

HH9$_2$ James, Stuart. "The Importance of Maurice Coindreau's Faulkner." *University of Denver Quarterly*, Summer 1972, pp. 77–81. (Coindreau)

HH10$_2$ Polk, Noel. "The Manuscript of *Absalom, Absalom!*" *Mississippi Quarterly*, 25 (Summer 1972), 359–67. (Langford)

HH11$_2$ Ficken, Carl. Review. *Mississippi Quarterly*, 25 (Summer 1972), 368–77. (Inge, Minter, Bleikasten, Pitavy)

HH12$_2$ McHaney, Thomas L. Review. *Mississippi Quarterly*, 25 (Summer 1972), 377–78. (Seyppel)

HH13$_2$ Showett, H. K. Review. *Mississippi Quarterly*, 25 (Summer 1972), 378–80. (Mottram)

---

[1]Brief journalistic reviews are generally not included. The list is limited to reviews in scholarly and critical journals and long reviews in magazines and newspapers. The book or books reviewed are indicated by author's name in parentheses.

HH14₂   Boyle, Karen P. Review. *Mississippi Quarterly*, 25 (Summer 1972), 380–85. Reviews dissertations by Powell, Petesch, and Watson.

HH15₂   White, William. "Faulkner's 'Absalom!' A Study of the Ms." *The American Book Collector*, Summer 1972, p. 4. (Langford)

HH16₂   Samway, Patrick. Review. *America*, October 21, 1972, pp. 325–26. (Barth)

HH17₂   Wheeler, Otis B. Review. *American Literature*, 44 (November 1972), 513–14. Reviews Hans Bungert, *William Faulkner und die humoristische Tradition des amerikanischen Sudens.*

HH18₂   White, William. "Faulkner's 'Sanctuary' Galleys vs. Book." *The American Book Collector*, November-December 1972, p. 7. (Langford)

HH19₂   Van Cromphout, Gustaaf. "Faulkner: Myth and Motion." *English Studies*, 53 (December 1972), 572–74. (Adams)

HH20₂   Bradford, M. E. Review. *Georgia Review*, 36 (Winter 1972), 522–24. (Barth)

HH21₂   Bleikasten, André. Review. *Modern Fiction Studies*, 18 (Winter 1972), 605–06. (Coindreau)

HH22₂   Meriwether, James B. Review. *American Literature*, 44 (January 1973), 693–95. (Langford)

HH23₂   Hoffman, Arnold R. "The Word, the Flesh, and the Difference." *CEA Critic*, 35, No. 3 (March 1973), 40–41. (Watkins)

HH24₂   Fabre, Michel. "The Time of William Faulkner." *Comparative Literature*, 25 (Spring 1973), 189–90. (Coindreau)

HH25₂   Heller, Terry, and Carol Cyganowski. Review. *Arizona Quarterly*, 29 (Spring 1973), 78–79. (Early)

HH26₂   Taylor, Walter. Review. *American Literature*, 45 (May 1973), 310–11. (Page)

HH27₂   Hemenway, Robert. Review. *Modern Fiction Studies*, 19 (Summer 1973), 271–73. (Bedell, Barth, Early)

HH28₂   Cebik, L. B. Review. *Georgia Review*, 27 (Summer 1973), 286–91. (Bedell)

HH29₂   Ingram, Forrest L. Review. *New Orleans Review*, 3, No. 3 (1973), 304–05. (Langford)

HH30₂   Utterbach, Sylvia W. Review. *Mississippi Quarterly*, 26 (Summer 1973), 421–35. (Bedell)

HH31₂   Muhlenfeld, Elisabeth. Review. *Mississippi Quarterly*, 26 (Summer 1973), 435–50. (Page)

HH32₂   McHaney, Thomas L. Review. *Mississippi Quarterly*, 26 (Summer 1973), 451–54. (Bungert)

HH33₂   Ficken, Carl. Review. *Mississippi Quarterly*, 26 (Summer 1973), 454–58. (Barth)

HH34₂   Polk, Noel. Review. *Mississippi Quarterly*, 26 (Summer 1973), 458–65. (Langford)

HH35₂   Meats, Stephen E. Review. *Mississippi Quarterly*, 26 (Summer 1973), 465–66. (Jarrett-Kerr)

HH36₂   Showett, H. K. Review. *Mississippi Quarterly*, 26 (Summer 1973), 466–68. (Early)

HH37₂   Rigsby, Carol R. Review. *Mississippi Quarterly*, 26 (Summer 1973), 468–71. (Bassett)

HH38₂   Meriwether, James B. Review. *Mississippi Quarterly*, 26 (Summer 1973), 471–72 (Schmitter)

HH39₂   "Telling It." *Times Literary Supplement*, August 31, 1973, p. 1003. (Reed)

HH40₂   Brylowski, Walter. Review. *Michigan Academician*, 6 (Fall 1973), 251–52. (Wagner)

HH41₂   Gold, Joseph. Review. *Humanities Association Review*, 24 (Fall 1973), 335–37. (Barth)

HH42₂   Polk, Noel. Review. *Humanities Association Review*, 24 (Fall 1973), 338–39. (Bassett)

HH43₂   Capps, Jack L. "Three Faulkner Studies." *Southern Literary Journal*, 6, No. 1 (Fall 1973), 117–21. (Langford-two books, Early)

HH44₂   Player, Ralegh P. Review. *Southern Humanities Review*, 7
         (Fall 1973), 448–49. (Peavy)

HH45₂   Waggoner, Hyatt H. Review. *American Literature*, 45
         (November 1973), 471–72. (Reed)

HH46₂   Estess, Ted L. Review. *Theological Studies*, 34 (December
         1973), 767–68. (Barth)

HH47₂   Heller, Terry. Review. *Arizona Quarterly*, 29 (Winter 1973),
         365–66. (Langford)

HH48₂   Kerr, Elizabeth. Review. *Modern Fiction Studies*, 18 (Winter
         1973), 592–95. (Langford-two books, Smart)

HH49₂   Covici, Pascal, Jr. "Anatomy of a Novel." *Southwest
         Review*, 58 (Winter 1973), 87–91. (Early)

HH50₂   Ruoff, Gene W. Review. *Western Humanities Review*, 27
         (Winter 1973), 92–93. (Early)

HH51₂   Tuttleton, James W. "The American Novelist: His Time and
         Place." *Yale Review*, 62 (Winter 1973), 305–07. (Early)

HH52₂   Adams, Richard P. "Genetic Faulkner." *CEA Critic*, 36, No.
         2 (January 1974), 33–34. (Early)

HH53₂   Carothers, James B. "Faulkner Criticism: Footprints and
         Monuments." *CEA Critic*, 36, No. 2 (January 1974), 38–40.
         (Bassett, Bleikasten, Hunter, Pitavy)

HH54₂   Boyle, Robert, S.J. Review. *Thought*, 49 (March 1974),
         95–97. (Barth)

HH55₂   Price, Reynolds. "Intruder in the Dust." *Washington Post*,
         March 10, 1974, Book World, pp. 1, 4. (Blotner)

HH56₂   Yardley, Jonathan. Review. *New York Times Book Review*,
         March 17, 1974, pp. 1, 3. (Blotner)

HH57₂   Littlejohn, David. "How Not to Write a Biography." *New
         Republic*, March 23, 1974, pp. 25–27. (Blotner)

HH58₂   Boozer, William. "Everything About Faulkner, and Then
         Some." *Memphis Commercial Appeal*, March 24, 1974, Sec.
         6, p. 6. (Blotner)

HH59₂   Kirsch, Robert. "Illuminating the Elusive William Faulkner."
         Los Angeles Times, March 24, 1974, Calendar, pp. 54, 59.
         (Blotner)

HH60₂   Cowley, Malcolm. "The Overbrimming Life of a Man of
         Literary Genius." *Chicago Tribune*, March 24, 1974, Sec. 7,
         Book World, pp. 1–2. (Blotner)

HH61₂   Clemons, Walter. "Hunting for Faulkner." *Newsweek*,
         March 25, 1974, pp. 91–92. (Blotner)

HH62₂   Gray, Paul. "Footnotes to Genius." *Time*, March 25, 1974,
         pp. 86, 88. (Blotner)

HH63₂   Harrington, Evans. "An Exercise in Discrete Biography."
         Richmond Mercury, March 27, 1974, Book Review, p. 9.
         (Blotner)

HH64₂   Lehmann-Haupt, Christopher. "A Huge Portrait in
         Hiccups." *New York Times*, March 27, 1974, p. 41. (Blotner)

HH65₂   Inge, M. Thomas. "Meticulously Assembled Biography of
         Faulkner." *Richmond Times-Dispatch*, March 31, 1974, p.
         F7. (Blotner)

HH66₂   Thomas, Sidney. "Too Many Facts About Faulkner."
         Atlanta Journal and Constitution, March 31, 1974, p. C10.
         (Blotner)

HH67₂   Gresset, Michel. Review. *Resources for American Literary
         Study*, 4 (Spring 1974), 100–105. (Bassett)

HH68₂   Oldsey, Bernard. Review. *College Literature*, 1 (Spring
         1974), 145–46. (Bassett, Wagner, Schmitter)

HH69₂   Watson, James G. Review. *Novel*, 7 (Spring 1974), 285–87.
         (Early)

HH70₂   Wilcox, Earl. Review. *South Carolina Review*, 6, No. 2
         (April 1974), 80–81. (Reed)

HH71₂   Newman, Charles L. "An Exemplary Life." *Harper's
         Magazine*, April 1974, pp. 98–100. (Blotner)

HH72₂   Friddell, Guy. "Why He Likes Virginians." *Richmond News
         Leader*, April 1, 1974, p. 15. (Blotner)

HH73₂   Baker, John F. "Joseph Blotner." *Publisher's Weekly*,
         April 1, 1974, pp. 6–7. (Blotner)

HH74₂   Bell, Pearl K. "Facts—Fatal and Fertile." *New Leader*, April
         29, 1974, pp. 14–15. (Blotner)

HH75₂   Bradford, M. E. "Blotner's Faulkner." *Triumph*, May 1974, pp. 32–34. (Blotner)

HH76₂   Howes, Victor. "A Monument to William Faulkner." *Christian Science Monitor*, May 1, 1974, p. F6. (Blotner)

HH77₂   Haddican, James. "In Depth Treatment of Faulkner, His Writing." *New Orleans Times-Picayune*, May 12, 1974, Sec. 3, p. 8. (Blotner)

HH78₂   Gass, William H. "Mr. Blotner, Mr. Feaster, and Mr. Faulkner." *New York Review of Books*, June 27, 1974, pp. 3–5. (Blotner)

HH79₂   Sharma, P. P. Review. *Indian Journal of American Studies*, 4 (June-December 1974), 112–15. (Page)

HH80₂   Yoder, Edwin M., Jr. "Heroic Fidelity." *National Review*, July 5, 1974, pp. 767–69. (Blotner)

HH81₂   McHaney, Tom. Review. *Commonweal*, July 26, 1974, pp. 412–13. (Blotner)

HH82₂   Fuller, Edmund. "Majestic Portrait of Faulkner." *Wall Street Journal*, July 29, 1974, p. 9. (Blotner)

HH83₂   Larson, Charles R. "Faulkner Complete." *American Scholar*, 43 (Summer 1974), 513–16. (Blotner)

HH84₂   Ficken, Carl. Review. *Mississippi Quarterly*, 27 (Summer 1974), 339–47. (Pitavy)

HH85₂   Ruppersburg, Hugh. Review. *Mississippi Quarterly*, 27 (Summer 1974), 347–53. (Bleikasten)

HH86₂   Bleikasten, André. Review. *Mississippi Quarterly*, 27 (Summer 1974), 353–56. (Zindel)

HH87₂   Anderson, Dianne L. Review. *Mississippi Quarterly*, 27 (Summer 1974), 356–57. (Hunter)

HH88₂   Millgate, Michael. Review. *Mississippi Quarterly*, 27 (Summer 1974), 357–59. (Wagner)

HH89₂   Cox, Leland. Review. *Mississippi Quarterly*, 27 (Summer 1974), 359–64. (Peavy)

HH90₂   Polk, Noel. Review. *Mississippi Quarterly*, 27 (Summer 1974), 364–67. (Reed)

HH91₂   Watson, James G. Review. *Modern Fiction Studies*, 20 (Summer 1974), 281–84. (Page, Hunter, Reed, Bleikasten)

HH92₂   Baker, Carlos. "From Genesis to Revelation." *Virginia Quarterly Review*, 50 (Summer 1974), 438–40. (Blotner)

HH93₂   Early, James. "Faulkner's Red Mississippians." *Southwest Review*, 59 (Summer 1974), 326–27. (Dabney)

HH94₂   Watkins, Floyd. "Faulkner, Faulkner, Faulkner." *Sewanee Review*, 82 (Summer 1974), 518–27. (Blotner)

HH95₂   Broughton, Panthea Reid. Review. *Southern Humanities Review*, 8 (Summer 1974), 402–03. (Page)

HH96₂   Keith, Don Lee. "Picking Up Private Faulkner Pieces Isn't Easy." *New Orleans Times-Picayune*, August 22, 1974, Sec. 4, p. 4. (Blotner) With interview.

HH97₂   Harter, Carol C. "Recent Faulkner Scholarship: Five More Turns of the Screw." *Journal of Modern Literature*, 4 (September 1974), 139–45. (Bedell, Early, Page, Langford-two books)

HH98₂   Malley, Terence. "Thoughts, Hopes, Endeavors, Failures." *Markham Review*, 4 (October 1974), 78–80. (Blotner)

HH99₂   Toynbee, Philip. "Faulkner Entombed." *The Observer*, October 6, 1974, p. 30. (Blotner)

HH100₂   Mitchell, Julian. "God's Own Country." *New Statesman*, October 25, 1974, pp. 582–83. (Blotner)

HH101₂   Wagner, Linda W. Review. *College Literature*, 1 (Fall 1974), 236–37. (Blotner) A longer review appeared in *South Carolina Review*, 7, No. 1 (November 1974), 102–06.

HH102₂   Minter, David. "Faulkner and the Uses of Biography." *Georgia Review*, 28 (Fall 1974), 455–63. (Blotner)

HH103₂   Adams, Richard P. Review. *American Literature*, 46 (November 1974), 392–93. (Blotner)

HH104₂   Trimmer, Joseph. Review. *Journal of Modern Literature*, 4 (November 1974), 313–20. (Barth, Bleikasten, Hunter, Pitavy, Reed)

HH105₂   Heller, Terry. Review. *Arizona Quarterly*, 30 (Winter 1974), 355–57. (Blotner)

HH106₂ Cavanaugh, Hilayne. "A Public Faulkner." *Prairie Schooner*, 48 (Winter 1974), 363–65. (Blotner)

HH107₂ Turner, Arlin. "William Faulkner: The Growth and Survival of a Legend—A Review Essay." *Southern Humanities Review*, 9 (Winter 1975), 91–97. (Blotner)

HH108₂ Vance, William. "Faulkner: Life and Art." *Boston University Journal*, 23, No. 1 (Winter 1975), 65–72. (Blotner)

HH109₂ Milum, Richard A. Review. *American Literature*, 46 (January 1975), 598–99. (Dabney)

HH110₂ Anderson, William R. Review. *Resources for American Literary Study*, 5 (Spring 1975), 101–06. (Blotner)

HH111₂ Monaghan, David M. Review. *Dalhousie Review*, 55 (Spring 1975), 197–98. (Dabney)

HH112₂ Leary, Lewis. Review. *American Literature*, 47 (May 1975), 289–90. (Broughton)

HH113₂ Wolk, Gerhard. Review. *Notes and Queries*, 220 (May 1975), 236–37. (Reed)

HH114₂ Beaver, Harold "The Count of Mississippi." *Times Literary Supplement*, May 30, 1975, pp. 600–601. (Blotner)

HH115₂ Sealy, Douglas. "Southern Gothic." *Irish Times*, May 31, 1975, p. 10. (Bassett) Includes parody of Faulkner's style.

HH116₂ Van Cromphout, Gustaaf. Review. *English Studies* [Belgium], 56 (June 1975), 172–73. (Reed)

HH117₂ Wolfe, Peter. Review. *College Language Association Journal*, 18 (June 1975), 591–93. (Blotner)

HH118₂ Stafford, William T. Review. *Modern Fiction Studies*, 21 (Summer 1975), 300–301. (Bassett)

HH119₂ Early, James. "Exhaustive Study of Faulkner's Life." *Southwest Review*, 60 (Summer 1975), 306–07. (Blotner)

HH120₂ Broughton, Panthea Reid. "Faulkner as Carpenter." *Southern Review*, 11 (Summer 1975), 681–84. (Reed)

HH121₂ Meriwether, James B. "Blotner's Faulkner." *Mississippi Quarterly*, 28 (Summer 1975), 353–69. (Blotner)

HH122₂ Polk, Noel. Review. *Mississippi Quarterly* 28 (Summer 1975), 387–92. (Dabney) Also a dissertation by Nigliazzo.

HH123₂   Kibler, James. Review. *Mississippi Quarterly*, 28 (Summer 1975), 392–93. (Leary)

HH124₂   Meriwether, James B. Review. *Mississippi Quarterly*, 28 (Summer 1975), 393–95. (Boozer)

HH125₂   Bleikasten, André. Review. *Mississippi Quarterly*, 28 (Summer 1975), 395–98. (Meindl)

HH126₂   Cowley, Malcolm. "Faulkner's Early Critics." *Sewanee Review*, 83 (Fall 1975), cxii–cxiv. (Bassett)

HH127₂   Kerr, Elizabeth. Review. *Journal of Modern Literature*, 4, No. 5 (1975), 1029–37. (Blotner)

HH128₂   Beaver, Harold. "Yoknapatawpha Observed." *Times Literary Supplement*, December 12, 1975, p. 1479. (Bassett)

HH129₂   Lind, Ilse Dusoir. Review. *Modern Fiction Studies*, 20 (Winter 1975), 560–64. (Blotner)

HH130₂   Backman, Melvin. Review. *Modern Fiction Studies*, 20 (Winter 1975), 573–74. (Dabney)

HH131₂   Gaston, Georg M. A. Review. *Southern Humanities Review*, 10 (Winter 1976), 99–100. (Pitavy)

HH132₂   Rouse, Blair. Review. *Style*, 10 (Winter 1976), 102–06. (Bleikasten)

HH133₂   West, Anthony. "The Real and the Trivial." *Books and Bookmen*, January 1976, pp. 50–52. (Blotner)

HH134₂   Langford, Gerald. Review. *American Literature*, 47 (January 1976), 644–45. (Fadiman)

HH135₂   Carey, Glenn O. "The Faulkner Heritage, Mostly Pre-Nobel." *CEA Critic*, 38, No. 3 (March 1976), 41–42. (Bassett, Howe, McHaney)

HH136₂   Wyatt, David M. "The Revenge Against Time." *Virginia Quarterly Review*, 52 (Spring 1976), 322–26. (Irwin)

HH137₂   Martine, James J. Review. *Studies in American Fiction*, 4 (Spring 1976), 123. (Bassett)

HH138₂   Oldsey, Bernard. *College Literature*, 3 (Spring 1976), 146–48. (Beck, Wagner)

HH139₂   Cowley, Malcolm. Review. *New Republic*, May 1, 1976, pp. 23–24. (Beck)

HH140₂ Samway, Patrick. Review. *Commonweal*, May 21, 1976, p. 346. (Irwin)

HH141₂ Polk, Noel. "Blotner's Faulkner." *Costerus*, 4 (1976), 173–79. (Blotner)

HH142₂ Harding, B. R. Review. *Yearbook of English Studies*, 6 (1976), 331–33. (Reed, Bleikasten, Pitavy)

HH143₂ Ross, Stephen M. Review. *Modern Fiction Studies*, 22 (Summer 1976), 305–08. (Weisgerber, Fadiman, McHaney, Irwin)

HH144₂ McHaney, Thomas L. Review. *Mississippi Quarterly*, 29 (Summer 1976), 451–57. (Irwin)

HH145₂ Pitavy, François. Review. *Mississippi Quarterly*, 29 (Summer 1976), 457–66. (Fadiman)

HH146₂ Anderson, Dianne Luce. Review. *Mississippi Quarterly*, 29 (Summer 1976), 466–70. (Levins)

HH147₂ Amriqua, Ahmed. Review. *Mississippi Quarterly*, 29 (Summer 1976), 470–72. Reviews Viola Sachs, ed., *Le Blanc et le Noir Chez Melville et Faulkner.*

HH148₂ Morrison, Gail M. Review. *Mississippi Quarterly*, 29 (Summer 1976), 472–75. (Wagner)

HH149₂ Meriwether, James B. Review. *Mississippi Quarterly*, 29 (Summer 1976), 476–77. (Petersen)

HH150₂ Blotner, Joseph. "40 Years of Faulkner Watching." *Milwaukee Journal*, July 25, 1976, Pt. 5, p. 4. (Beck)

HH151₂ Wagner, Linda W. Review. *Studies in American Fiction*, 4 (Autumn 1976), 237–38. (Bassett)

HH152₂ Brown, Calvin S. Review. *Comparative Literature*, 28 (Fall 1976), 362–64. (Blotner)

HH153₂ Cox, James M. Review. *Modern Language Notes*, 91 (October 1976), 1120–31. (Irwin) Essay-review critical of Irwin's psychoanalytic approach.

HH154₂ Foster, Ruel E. Review. *American Literature*, 48 (November 1976), 406–07. (McHaney)

HH155₂ Adams, Richard P. Review. *American Literature*, 48 (November 1976), 407–08. (Irwin)

HH156₂   Boozer, William. "An Oxford Gentleman Goes to Hollywood." *Memphis Commercial Appeal*, November 21, 1976, p. G6. Another review by Boozer appeared in the *Nashville Banner*, December 25, 1976, p. 12. (Wilde)

HH157₂   Inge, M. Thomas. "Open Discussion By a Paramour." *Richmond Times-Dispatch*, November 28, 1976, p. F5. Another review by Inge is "Intruding on Faulkner." *Chronicle of Higher Education*, February 7, 1977, p. 14. (Wilde)

HH158₂   Wagner, Linda W. Review. *Journal of Modern Literature*, 5, No. 4 (1976), 690–93. (Fadiman, Broughton, Weisgerber)

HH159₂   Brivic, Sheldon. Review. *Journal of Modern Literature*, 5, No. 4 (1976), 693–98. (Irwin)

HH160₂   Kirsch, Robert. "William Faulkner's Underside." *Los Angeles Times*, December 10, 1976, Sec. 4, p. 12. (Wilde)

HH161₂   Sadler, Rick. "William Faulkner's Love Story in Hollywood." *Los Angeles Times*, December 12, 1976, Book Review, pp. 3, 25. (Wilde)

HH162₂   Cowley, Malcolm. Review. *New York Times Book Review*, December 19, 1976, p. 2. (Wilde)

HH163₂   Cohen, George. Review. *Chicago Tribune*, December 19, 1976, Sec. 7, Book World, pp. 1, 3. (Wilde)

HH164₂   Stafford, William T. Review. *Modern Fiction Studies*, 22 (Winter 1976), 629. (McHaney)

HH165₂   Scura, Dorothy. Review. *Southern Humanities Review*, 11 (Winter 1977), 87–88. (Dabney)

HH166₂   Wasiolek, Edward. "The Past Reconstituted." *Novel*, 10 (Winter 1977), 182–84. (Irwin)

HH167₂   King, Richard H. "Faulkner and Freud." *Salmagundi*, 36 (Winter 1977), 133–39. (Irwin)

HH168₂   Kinney, Arthur F. Review. *American Literature*, 48 (January 1977), 608–09. (Levins)

HH169₂   Broyard, Anatole. "Oratory Out of Solitude." *New York Times*, January 31, 1977, p. 19. (Blotner)

HH170₂   Aldridge, John W. "Mule Talk in Yoknapatawpha County." *Saturday Review*, February 5, 1977, pp. 24–26. (Blotner)

HH171₂ Welty, Eudora. Review. *New York Times Book Review*, February 6, 1977, pp. 1, 28–30. (Blotner)

HH172₂ Grumbach, Doris. "Faulkner's Letters Are Illuminating, Especially to an Accountant." *Chicago Tribune*, February 6, 1977, Sec. 7, Book World, p. 3. (Blotner)

HH173₂ Yardley, Jonathan. "Letters from Yoknapatawpha." *Washington Post*, February 6, 1977, Book World, p. F9. (Blotner)

HH174₂ Clemons, Walter. "A Master's Advice." *Newsweek*, February 7, 1977, pp. 74–75. (Wilde, Blotner)

HH175₂ Boozer, William. "After Receiving Your Letters...." *Memphis Commercial Appeal*, February 20, 1977, p. G6. Another review by Boozer appeared in the *Nashville Banner*, March 5, 1977, p. 5. (Blotner)

HH176₂ Kirsch, Robert. "William Faulkner: His Life Was a Closed Book." *Los Angeles Times*, February 27, 1977, Book Review, pp. 1, 4–5. (Blotner)

HH177₂ Casper, Leonard. Review. *Thought*, 52 (March 1977), 110–11. (McHaney)

HH178₂ Larson, Charles R. "The Faulkner Letters: How Select Is 'Selected'?" *National Observer*, March 5, 1977, p. 17. (Blotner, Wilde)

HH179₂ Foote, Shelby. "At Home with 'Pappy.'" *Memphis Commercial Appeal*, March 6, 1977, p. G6. (Franklin)

HH180₂ Cowley, Malcolm. Review. *New Republic*, March 12, 1977, pp. 30–31. (Blotner)

HH181₂ Deemer, Charles. "An Obsession with Privacy." *New Leader*, March 28, 1977, p. 19. (Blotner)

HH182₂ Cavanaugh, H. E. "Four on Faulkner." *Prairie Schooner*, 51 (Spring 1977), 102–04. (Jehlen, Wolfe, Brown, Beck)

HH183₂ Eder, Doris. Review. *Dalhousie Review*, 57 (Spring 1977), 152–57. Another review in *Studies in American Fiction*, 6 (Spring 1978), 115–20. (Irwin)

HH184₂ Bassett, John. Review. *Resources for American Literary Study*, 7 (Spring 1977), 85–89. (Blotner, Wilde)

HH185₂   Beall, Chandler B. Review. *Comparative Literature*, 29
         (Spring 1977), 178–79. (Brown)

HH186₂   Wagner, Linda W. Review. *Criticism*, 19 (Spring 1977),
         184–85. (Brown)

HH187₂   Wolfe, George H. "Letters of a Private Man." *Book Forum*,
         3, No. 2 (1977), 304–09. (Blotner)

HH188₂   Creighton, Joanne V. "Faulkner's Cosmos." *Book Forum*, 3,
         No. 2 (1977), 309–12. (Barth)

HH189₂   Reed, Nancy Gail. "Letters of Faulkner Raise Familiar
         Question of Privacy." *Christian Science Monitor*, April 6,
         1977, p. 27. (Blotner)

HH190₂   Goldgar, Harry. "Faulkner's Early Letters Marked by Poor
         Mouthing." *New Orleans Times-Picayune*, April 24, 1977,
         Sec. 3, p. 12. (Blotner)

HH191₂   Morrison, Gail M. Review. *Mississippi Quarterly*, 30
         (Summer 1977), 477–82. (Bleikasten)

HH192₂   Cox, Leland H., Jr. Review. *Mississippi Quarterly*, 30
         (Summer 1977), 483–89. (Brown)

HH193₂   Muhlenfeld, Elisabeth. Review. *Mississippi Quarterly*, 30
         (Summer 1977), 489–92. (Schoenberg)

HH194₂   Anderson, Dianne Luce. Review. *Mississippi Quarterly*, 30
         (Summer 1977), 492–97. (Jehlen)

HH195₂   Ruppersburg, Hugh M. Review. *Mississippi Quarterly*, 30
         (Summer 1977), 497–500. (Collins-McRobbie)

HH196₂   Strandberg, Victor. Review. *Modern Fiction Studies*, 23
         (Summer 1977), 270–74. (Wagner, Beck)

HH197₂   Watkins, Floyd C. "Through a Glass Darkly: Recent
         Faulkner Studies." *Sewanee Review*, 85 (Summer 1977),
         484–93. (Beck, Bleikasten, Brown, Irwin, Jehlen, Levins,
         McHaney, Wilde, Wolfe)

HH198₂   Polk, Noel. "Some Recent Books on Faulkner." *Studies in
         the Novel*, 9 (Summer 1977), 201–10. (Beck, Bleikasten,
         McHaney, Brown, Broughton, Levins, Jehlen)

HH199₂   Samway, Patrick. Review. *Commonweal*, August 5, 1977,
         pp. 507–09. (Bleikasten, Wilde, Franklin, Blotner)

HH200₂   Harder, Kelsie B. Review. *Names*, 25 (September 1977), 177–79. (Brown)

HH201₂   Morton, Bruce. Review. *American Notes and Queries*, 16 (October 1977), 28–32. (Beck, Wagner)

HH202₂   Capps, Jack L. "Auxiliary Faulkner: Six New Volumes 1976–1977." *Southern Literary Journal*, 10, No. 1 (Fall 1977), 106–14. (Franklin, Jehlen, Wolfe, Levins, Brown, Blotner)

HH203₂   Longley, John. Review. *Resources for American Literary Study*, 7 (Autumn 1977), 212–13. (Bassett)

HH204₂   Heller, Terry. Review. *Arizona Quarterly*, 33 (Autumn 1977), 277–78. (Howe)

HH205₂   Waggoner, Hyatt H. Review. *American Literature*, 49 (November 1977), 480–81. (Blotner)

HH206₂   Bradford, M. E. "The Yoknapatawpha Letters." *National Review*, November 25, 1977, pp. 1373–74. (Blotner)

HH207₂   Kerr, Elizabeth M. Review. *Journal of Modern Literature*, 6, No. 4 (1977), 602–11. (Beck, Bleikasten, Brown, Jehlen, Levins)

HH208₂   Godden, Richard. "So That's What Frightens Them Under the Tree?" *Journal of American Studies*, 11 (December 1977), 371–77. (Bleikasten)

HH209₂   Tallack, Douglas. Review. *Journal of American Studies*, 11 (December 1977), 408–09. (Levins, Irwin)

HH210₂   Beaver, Harold. "Telling a Good Story." *Times Literary Supplement*, December 23, 1977, p. 1500. (Kawin)

HH211₂   Minter, David. Review. *Georgia Review*, 31 (Winter 1977), 973–78. (Wilde)

HH212₂   Blotner, Joseph. Review. *Georgia Review*, 31 (Winter 1977), 937–45. (Brown, Levins, Bleikasten)

HH213₂   Broughton, Panthea Reid. Review. *Modern Fiction Studies*, 23 (Winter 1977), 656–60. (Jehlen, Levins, Bleikasten)

HH214₂   Stafford, William T. Review. *Modern Fiction Studies*, 23 (Winter 1977), 672. (Brown)

HH215₂   Flora, Joseph M. Review. *Studies in Short Fiction*, 15 (Winter 1978), 115. (Williams)

HH216₂   Rouse, Blair. Review. *Style*, 12 (Winter 1978), 77–81. (Reed)

HH217₂   Wittenberg, Judith. "Second Generation." *Novel*, 11 (Winter 1978), 186–88. (Levins, Jehlen)

HH218₂   Perkins, George. Review. *Michigan Academician*, 10 (Winter 1978), 361–62. (Creighton)

HH219₂   Milum, Richard A. Review. *American Literature*, 49 (January 1978), 671–72. (Bleikasten)

HH220₂   Burgess, Anthony. "A World of His Own." *The Observer*, January 1, 1978, p. 33. (Blotner)

HH221₂   Mason, Michael. "Feeding the Cornshucker." *New Statesman*, January 6, 1978, pp. 19–20. (Blotner)

HH222₂   Moore, Rayburn S. Review. *American Literature*, 50 (March 1978), 128–29. (Schoenberg)

HH223₂   Pearce, Richard. Review. *Studies in American Fiction*, 6 (Spring 1978), 114–15. (Jehlen)

HH224₂   Heller, Terry L. Review. *Arizona Quarterly*, 34 (Spring 1978), 89–92. (Wolfe, Levins)

HH225₂   Moss, William M. "Recent Ores and Tailings from the Faulkner Mine." *Southern Humanities Review*, 12 (Spring 1978), 149–59. (Broughton, Irwin, Bassett)

HH226₂   Carr, Virginia Spencer. Review. *South Carolina Review*, 10, No. 2 (April 1978), 103–05. (Levins)

HH227₂   Moore, Geoffrey. Review. *Journal of American Studies*, 12 (April 1978), 122–23. (Wagner)

HH228₂   Watkins, Floyd C. Review. *American Literature*, 50 (May 1978), 295–96. (Creighton)

HH229₂   Anderson, Quentin. "New Critic Back Down South." *New York Times Book Review*, May 21, 1978, pp. 7, 31–32. (Brooks)

HH230₂   Inge, M. Thomas. "Understanding Faulkner." *Chronicle of Higher Education*, May 30, 1978, p. 17. (Brooks)

HH231₂ Haddican, James. "Critic Describes Forces Influencing Faulkner." *New Orleans Times-Picayune*, June 18, 1978, Sec. 3, p. 11. (Brooks)

HH232₂ Ross, Stephen, M. Review. *Modern Fiction Studies*, 24 (Summer 1978), 275–78. (Blotner, Wilde, Wolfe, Schoenberg)

HH233₂ Bucco, Martin. Review. *Literature and Psychology*, 18, No. 2 (1978), 93–96. (Irwin)

HH234₂ Polk, Noel. Review. *Studies in Short Fiction*, 15 (Summer 1978), 331–32. (Creighton)

HH235₂ Carey, Glenn O. Review. *Studies in Short Fiction*, 15 (Summer 1978), 342–44. (Jehlen)

HH236₂ Hunt, John W. "Outside Yoknapatawpha County with Cleanth Brooks and William Faulkner." *Mississippi Quarterly*, 31 (Summer 1978), 465–76. (Brooks)

HH237₂ McHaney, Thomas L. Review. *Mississippi Quarterly*, 31 (Summer 1978), 477–79. (Franklin)

HH238₂ Muhlenfeld, Elisabeth. Review. *Mississippi Quarterly*, 31 (Summer 1978), 479–81. (Wilde)

HH239₂ Knight, Katherine L. Review. *Mississippi Quarterly*, 31 (Summer 1978), 487–94. (Fadiman, Kawin)

HH240₂ Amriqua, Ahmed. Review. *Mississippi Quarterly*, 31 (Summer 1978), 494–96. Review of Jean Harzic, *Faulkner* (Paris, 1973).

HH241₂ Martin, John Stephen. Review. *Ariel*, July 1978, pp. 101–04. (Brooks)

HH242₂ Yardley, Jonathan. "The Two Faulkners: Romantic vs. the Realist." *Los Angeles Times*, July 9, 1978, Book Review, p. 6. (Brooks)

HH243₂ Simmons, Mabel C. "Turning Over a New Leaf." *New Orleans Times-Picayune*, July 16, 1978, Sec. 3, p. 12. (Cofield)

HH244₂ Bradbury, Malcolm. "Dreaming Ego." *New Statesman*, July 21, 1978, pp. 90–91. (Brooks)

HH245₂ Boozer, William. "Faulkner on Camera." *Memphis Commercial Appeal*, July 23, 1978, p. G6. (Cofield)

HH246$_2$ Cowley, Malcolm. Review. *New Republic*, July 29, 1978, pp. 33–35. (Brooks)

HH247$_2$ Godden, R. L. Review. *Journal of American Studies*, 12 (August 1978), 248–50. (Beck, Jehlen)

HH248$_2$ Bradford, M. E. "A Triumph of Pre-Criticism." *National Review*, September 15, 1978, pp. 1156–57. (Brooks)

HH249$_2$ East, Charles. "The Faulkner Photographs." *Southern Review*, 14 (Autumn 1978), 852–55. (Cofield)

HH250$_2$ Drake, Robert. "In and Out of Yoknapatawpha." *Modern Age*, 22 (Fall 1978), 418–20. (Brooks)

HH251$_2$ Blotner, Joseph. "Beyond Yoknapatawpha." *Yale Review*, 68 (Autumn 1978), 145–48. (Brooks)

HH252$_2$ Plummer, William. "Three Versions of Faulkner." *Hudson Review*, 31 (Autumn 1978), 466–82. (Blotner, Wilde, Brooks)

HH253$_2$ Moore, Rayburn S. Review. *American Literature*, 50 (November 1978), 506–08. (Brooks)

HH254$_2$ Putzel, Max. Review. *American Literature*, 50 (November 1978), 508–09. (Williams)

HH255$_2$ Beaver, Harold. "The Spirit of the South." *Times Literary Supplement*, November 3, 1978, p 1275. (Brooks)

HH256$_2$ McSweeney, Kerry. "Faulkner's 'Amazing Gift.'" *Critical Quarterly*, 21 (Spring 1979), 71–80. (Irwin, Bleikasten, Blotner, Wilde)

HH257$_2$ Samway, Patrick, S.J. "Faulkner Country." *Virginia Quarterly Review*, 55 (Spring 1979), 350–57. (Brooks)

HH258$_2$ Gidley, M. Review. *Journal of American Studies*, 13 (April 1979), 147–50. (Harrington, Creighton, Williams, Schoenberg, Brooks)

HH259$_2$ Collins, Carvel. Review. *American Literature*, 51 (May 1979), 287–89. (Kinney)

HH260$_2$ Hogan, Patrick G., Jr. Review. *Studies in Short Fiction*, 16 (Summer 1979), 247–48. (Irwin)

HH261$_2$ Friedman, Alan W. Review. *Studies in the Novel*, 11 (Summer 1979), 236–37. (Brooks)

HH262₂   Ross, Stephen M. Review. *Modern Fiction Studies*, 25 (Summer 1979), 325–28. (Brooks, Harrington, Fadiman, Kinney)

HH263₂   Ragan, David P. Review. *Mississippi Quarterly*, 32 (Summer 1979), 519–23. (Cofield)

HH264₂   Cox, Dianne Luce. Review. *Mississippi Quarterly*, 32 (Summer 1979), 526–31. (Kinney)

HH265₂   Morrison, Gail M. Review. *Mississippi Quarterly*, 32 (Summer 1979), 531–38. (Creighton)

HH266₂   Ruppersburg, Hugh M. Review. *Mississippi Quarterly*, 32 (Summer 1979), 538–45. (Williams)

HH267₂   Raval, Suresh. Review. *Arizona Quarterly*, 35 (Summer 1979), 183–85. (Irwin)

HH268₂   Heller, Terry. Review. *Arizona Quarterly*, 35 (Summer 1979), 185–86. (Williams)

HH269₂   McHaney, Thomas. "Brooks on Faulkner." *Review*, 1 (1979), 29–45. (Brooks)

HH270₂   Bassett, John Earl. Review. *Criticism*, 21 (Fall 1979), 387–89. (Stonum, Kinney)

HH271₂   Wyatt, David. "A History of Arrests." *Virginia Quarterly Review*, 55 (Autumn 1979), 757–62. (Stonum)

HH272₂   Gallafent, Edward. Review. *Notes & Queries*, 224 (October 1979), 482–84. (Brooks)

HH273₂   McSweeney, Kerry. "Faulkner's 'Many Glancing Colours.'" *Canadian Review of American Studies*, 10 (Winter 1979), 355–62. (Kinney, Harrington)

HH274₂   Ross, Stephen M. Review. *Modern Fiction Studies*, 25 (Winter 1979), 736–37. (Kerr, Harrington)

HH275₂   Arnold, Edwin T. Review. *Notes on Mississippi Writers*, 12 (Winter 1980), 91–93. (Fadiman)

HH276₂   Muhlenfeld, Elisabeth. Review. *Notes on Mississippi Writers*, 12 (Winter 1980), 94–96. (Kinney)

HH277₂   Carothers, James B. Review. *Notes on Mississippi Writers*, 12 (Winter 1980), 97–99. (Stonum)

HH278₂ Polk, Noel. Review. *Notes on Mississippi Writers*, 12 (Winter 1980), 100. (Cofield)

HH279₂ Watkins, Floyd. Review. *South Atlantic Quarterly*, 79 (Winter 1980), 117–18. (Kinney)

HH280₂ Mitchell, O. S. "A Faulkner Double Feature." *Canadian Review of American Studies*, 11 (Spring 1980), 109–16. (Fadiman, Kawin)

HH281₂ Bassett, John Earl. Review. *Resources for American Literary Study*, 10 (Spring 1980), 109–13. (Capps)

HH282₂ Morrow, Patrick D. Review. *Southern Humanities Review*, 14 (Spring 1980), 179–83. (Stonum, Kerr, Wittenberg, Kartiganer)

HH283₂ Capps, Jack L. Review. *American Literature*, 52 (May 1980), 321–23. (Kerr)

HH284₂ Muhlenfeld, Elisabeth. Review. In A65₂ (1980), pp. 153–57. (Brooks)

HH285₂ Gilpin, George H. Review. In A65₂ (1980), pp. 158–60. (Irwin)

HH286₂ Endel, Peggy G. Review. In A65₂ (1980), pp. 161–67. (Bleikasten)

HH287₂ Kerr, Elizabeth M. Review. In A65₂ (1980), pp. 169–72. (Williams)

HH288₂ Creighton, Joanne V. Review. In A65₂ (1980), pp. 173–75. (Jehlen)

HH289₂ Skipp, Francis E. Review. In A65₂ (1980), pp. 175–78. (Levins)

HH290₂ Mortimer, Gail. Review. In A65₂ (1980), pp. 178–81. (Schoenberg)

HH291₂ Watson, James G. Review. In A65₂ (1980), pp. 182–83. (Creighton)

HH292₂ Lyday, Lance. Review. In A65₂ (1980), pp. 183–85. (Kawin, Dardis)

HH293₂ Wagner, Linda W. Review. In A65₂ (1980), pp. 185–86. (Guerard)

HH294₂   Hagopian, John V. Review. In A65₂ (1980), pp. 186–88.
(Beck)

HH295₂   Donovan, Laurence. In A65₂ (1980), pp. 188–89. (Cofield)

HH296₂   Millgate, Michael. Review. *Mississippi Quarterly*, 33
(Summer 1980), 413–15. (Stonum)

HH297₂   Meriwether, James B. Review. *Mississippi Quarterly*, 33
(Summer 1980), 415–16. (Harmon GG47₂)

HH298₂   Kinney, Arthur F. Review. *Modern Fiction Studies*, 26
(Summer 1980), 336–45. (Harrington, Stonum, Kartiganer)

HH299₂   Bleikasten, André. Review. *Modern Language Quarterly*, 41
(September 1980), 298–300. (Kartiganer)

HH300₂   Meriwether, James B. "Faulkner Book as Bad as Film." *The
State* [Columbia, S.C.], September 14, 1980, p. B12.
(Bezzerides)

HH301₂   Hogan, Patrick G., Jr. Review. *Studies in Short Fiction*, 17
(Fall 1980), 509–10. (Brooks)

HH302₂   Wyatt, David. "Faulkner's Self-Characters." *Virginia
Quarterly Review*, 56 (Autumn 1980), 753–58. (Wittenberg)

HH303₂   Brown, Calvin. "Faulkner, Criticism, and High Fashion."
Sewanee Review, 88 (Fall 1980), 631–41. (Brooks, Kinney,
Kartiganer, Stonum, Wittenberg)

HH304₂   Brown, Dee. "A Remarkable Exploration of the Faulkner
Cosmos." *Chicago Tribune*, October 26, 1980, Sec. 7, p. 1.
(Minter)

HH305₂   Blotner, Joseph. Review. *American Literature*, 52
(November 1980), 483–85. (Stonum)

HH306₂   Settle, Mary Lee. "The Count of Yoknapatawpha."
Washington Post, November 9, 1980, Books, p. 3. (Minter)

HH307₂   McHaney, Thomas L. Review. *Modern Fiction Studies*, 26
(Winter 1980), 654–57. (Wittenberg, Kaluza, Hamblin,
Petersen)

HH308₂   Colson, Theodore. "More Guides to Yoknapatawpha."
Canadian Review of American Studies, 11 (Winter 1980),
381–87. (Brooks, Kerr, Harrington)

HH309₂   Bohlke, H. Brent. "A Promise Fulfilled." *Prairie Schooner*, 53 (Winter 1980), 373–74. (Brooks)

HH310₂   Quammen, David. "Concise Look at Faulkner." *Christian Science Monitor*, March 9, 1981, p. B9. (Minter)

HH311₂   McKinsey, Elizabeth. Review. *Studies in American Fiction*, 9 (Spring 1981), 123–25. (Brooks)

HH312₂   Samway, Patrick, S.J. "A Psychological Interpretation of Faulkner's Novels." *Southern Literary Journal*, 13, No. 2 (Spring 1981), 99–104. (Wittenberg)

HH313₂   Inge, M. Thomas. "Minter Biography Is Double Mirror." *Faulkner Newsletter*, April-June 1981, p. 2. (Minter)

HH314₂   Lyra, F. Review. *American Literature*, 53 (May 1981), 334–35. (Powers)

HH315₂   Little, Matthew. Review. *Modern Philology*, 78 (May 1981), 453–58. (Kerr, Stonum)

HH316₂   Boozer, William. "Books." *Southern World*, May-June 1981, p. 93. (Minter)

HH317₂   Samway, Patrick, S.J. "Faulkner Under Starlight." *America*, May 16, 1981, pp. 410–12. (Minter)

HH318₂   Mackinnon, Lachlan. "The Colonel and the Dandy." *Times Literary Supplement*, May 29, 1981, p. 598. (Minter)

HH319₂   Bigsby, C. W. E. "The was which is." *Times Literary Supplement*, July 10, 1981, p. 795. (Jenkins)

HH320₂   Morrison, Gail M. Review. *Mississippi Quarterly*, 34 (Summer 1981), 375–79. (Kerr)

HH321₂   Heller, Terry. Review. *Arizona Quarterly*, 37 (Summer 1981), 173–78. (Stonum, also *Uncollected Stories*)

HH322₂   Gidley, M. "Faulkner's Lives." *Journal of American Studies*, 15 (August 1981), 239–47. (Stonum, Minter, Bezzerides, Wittenberg)

HH323₂   Wagner, Linda W. Review. *Novel*, 15 (Fall 1981), 90–94. (Wittenberg, Kerr, Kartiganer)

HH324₂   Polk, Noel. Review. *Studies in Short Fiction*, 18 (Fall 1981), 466. (Minter)

HH325$_2$ Hogan, Patrick G., Jr. Review. *Studies in Short Fiction*, 18 (Fall 1981), 464–65. (reissue of Meriwether & Millgate, *Lion in the Garden*)

HH326$_2$ Boozer, William. "Noel Polk on Faulkner." *Faulkner Newsletter*, October-December 1981, pp. 2, 4. (Polk)

II. Magazine and Journal Articles[1]

II1$_2$ Robinson, Cecil. "The Fall of the 'Big House' in the Literature of the Americas." *Arizona Quarterly*, 24 (Spring 1968), 23–41.

II2$_2$ Hauck, Richard B. "The Comic Christ and the Modern Reader." *College English*, 31 (February 1970), 498–506.

II3$_2$ Epstein, Seymour. "Politics and the Novelist." *Denver Quarterly*, 4 (Winter 1970), 1–18.

II4$_2$ Milton, John R. "Conversations with Distinguished Western American Novelists." *South Dakota Review*, 9 (Spring 1971), 16–57.

II5$_2$ Schero, Elliot M. *"Another Country* and the Sense of Self." *Black Academy Review*, 2 (Spring–Summer 1971), 91–100.

II6$_2$ "Faulkner Concordance." *PMLA*, 86 (May 1971), 492.
A related article is Frank Wells, "Know Any Good Southernisms?" *Atlanta Constitution*, November 11, 1971, p. B11. Plans for a concordance.

II7$_2$ Riche, James. "Pragmatism: A National Fascist Mode of Thought." *Literature and Ideology*, No. 9 (1971), pp. 37–44.

II8$_2$ Kulin, Katalin. "Reasons and Characteristics of Faulkner's Influence on Modern Latin-American Fiction." *Acta Litteraria Academiae Scientiarum Hungaricae*, 13 (1971), 349–63.

II9$_2$ Cowley, Malcolm. "A Letter from Malcolm Cowley." *Fitzgerald/Hemingway Annual 1971*, pp. 317–18.

[1]This section lists brief articles on Faulkner that are not specifically on individual works and that do not fit into any of the other categories. It also includes other articles with brief but significant discussion of Faulkner. Incidental references to Faulkner, found in many discussions of modern fiction, are not included.

II10₂   Shimura, Masao. "John Barth, *The End of the Road*, and the Tradition of American Literature." *Studies in English Literature* [Japan], 1971, pp. 73–87.

II11₂   Rhynsburger, Mark. "Student Views of William Faulkner I." *Modern Occasions*, 1 (Winter 1971), 264–69.

II12₂   Fischel, Anne. "Student Views of Faulkner II." *Modern Occasions*, 1 (Winter 1971), 270–74.

II13₂   McAlexander, Hubert, Jr. "William Faulkner—The Young Poet in Stark Young's *The Torches Flare*." *American Literature*, 43 (January 1972), 647–49.

II14₂   Heseltine, H. P. "Some Reflections on the Faulkner-Cowley File." In *Pacific Circle 2*. Queensland: Univ. of Queensland Press, 1972.
        Studies roles assumed in the letters by reticent writer and critic.

II15₂   Detweiler, Robert. "The Moment of Death in Modern Fiction." *Contemporary Literature*, 13 (Summer 1972), 269–94.

II16₂   McWilliams, Dean. "William Faulkner and Michel Butor's Novel of Awareness." *Kentucky Romance Quarterly*, 19, No. 3 (1972), 387–402.

II17₂   Chatterton, Wayne. "Textbook Uses of Hemingway and Faulkner." *College Composition and Communication*, 23 (October 1972), 292–96.

II18₂   Boring, Phyllis Z. "Usmaíl: The Puerto Rican Joe Christmas." *College Language Association Journal*, 16 (March 1973), 324–33.
        Influence on Pedro Juan Soto.

II19₂   McElroy, John. "The Hawthorne Style of American Fiction." *ESQ*, 71 (2nd Quarter, 1973), 117–23.

II20₂   Duncan, Alastair B. "Claude Simon and William Faulkner." *Forum for Modern Language Studies*, 9 (July 1973), 235–52.
        Common interests and techniques.

II21₂   Simpson, Lewis P. "The Southern Recovery of Memory and History." *Sewanee Review*, 82 (Winter 1974), 1–32.

II22₂   Beards, Richard. "Parody as Tribute: William Melvin Kelley's *A Different Drummer* and Faulkner." *Studies in Black Literature*, 5, No. 3 (Winter 1974), 25–28.

II23₂   O'Brien, Matthew C. "Faulkner, General Chalmers, and the Burning of Oxford." *American Notes and Queries*, 12 (February 1974), 87–88.
        An error in a 1947 letter to the *Oxford Eagle* from Faulkner.

II24₂   Cole, Hunter McKelva. "Elizabeth Spencer at Sycamore Fair." *Notes on Mississippi Writers*, 6 (Winter 1974), 81–86.
        Spencer comments on Faulkner.

II25₂   Chitragupta. "The World of Books: Multiple Focus on Faulkner." *Thought* [India], March 1974, pp. 15–16.
        Report on a seminar in Delhi.

II26₂   Emerson, O. B. "William Faulkner's Nemesis—Major Frederick Sullens." *Journal of Mississippi History*, 36 (May 1974), 161–64.
        Hostile editorials in the *Jackson News* around 1950.

II27₂   Ginsberg, Elaine. "The Female Initiation Theme in American Fiction." *Studies in American Fiction*, 3 (Spring 1975), 27–37.

II28₂   Edward, Sister Ann. "Three Views on Blacks: The Black Woman in American Literature." *CEA Critic*, 37, No. 4 (May 1975), 14–16.

II29₂   Anderson, Don. "Comic Modes in Modern American Fiction." *Southern Review* [Australia], 8 (June 1975), 152–65.

II30₂   Willingham, Calder. "True Myth-Maker of the Post-Bellum South." *Georgia Historical Quarterly*, 59 (Summer 1975), 243–47.
        Erskine Caldwell not Faulkner was a true myth-maker.

II31₂   Oates, Joyce Carol. Letter, included in Dale Boesky, "Correspondence with Miss Joyce Carol Oates." *International Review of Psychoanalysis*, 2 (1975), 485.

II32₂   Prescott, Herman. "Hemingway vs. Faulkner: An Intriguing Feud." *Lost Generation Journal*, 3 (Fall 1975), 18–19.

II33₂   Alter, Robert. "The New American Novel." *Commentary*, November 1975, pp. 44–51.
        Compares Styron and Capote with Faulkner.

II34₂   Oberhelman, Harley D. "Gabriel García Márquez and the
         American South." *Chasqui: Revista de Literature
         Latinoamericana*, 5, No. 1 (November 1975), 29–38.

II35₂   Woodward, C. Vann. "Why the Southern Renaissance?"
         Virginia Quarterly Review, 51 (Winter 1975), 222–39.

II36₂   Faulkner, Howard. "The Uses of Tradition: William Melvin
         Kelley's *A Different Drummer*." *Modern Fiction Studies*, 21
         (Winter 1975), 535–42.

II37₂   Kolodny, Annette. "'Stript, shorne and made deformed':
         Images on the Southern Landscape." *South Atlantic
         Quarterly*, 75 (Winter 1976), 57–73.
         On Faulkner's criticism of destruction of the land.

II38₂   Sullivan, Walter. "The Decline of Myth in Southern
         Fiction." *Southern Review*, 12 (Winter 1976), 16–31.

II39₂   Leonard, Diane R. "Simon's *L'Herbe*: Beyond Sound and
         Fury." *French-American Review*, 1 (Winter 1976), 13–30.

II40₂   Kazin, Alfred. "'The Giant Killer': Drink and the American
         Writer." *Commentary*, March 1976, pp. 44–50.

II41₂   Wagner, Linda W. "The Poetry in American Fiction."
         Prospects: Annual of American Cultural Studies, 2 (1976),
         513–26.
         Dos Passos, Faulkner, and Hemingway.

II42₂   Cook, Bruce. "New Faces in Faulkner Country." *Saturday
         Review*, September 4, 1976, pp. 39–41.

II43₂   Gray, Paul. "Yoknapatawpha Blues." *Time*, September 27,
         1976, pp. 92–93.

II44₂   Rovit, Earl. "Faulkner, Hemingway, and the American
         Family." *Mississippi Quarterly*, 29 (Fall 1976), 483–97.

II45₂   Clifford, Paula M. "The American Novel and the French
         Nouveau Roman: Some Linguistic and Stylistic
         Comparisons." *Comparative Literature Studies*, 13
         (December 1976), 348–58.

II46₂   Gross, Seymour, and Rosalie Murphy. "From Stephen
         Crane to William Faulkner: Some Remarks on the Religious
         Sense in American Literature." *Cithara*, 16 (May 1977),
         90–108.

II47₂   Boring, Phyllis Z. "Faulkner in Spain: The Case of Elena
         Quiroga." *Comparative Literature Studies*, 14 (June 1977),
         166–76.
             Influence of Faulkner on Quiroga.

II48₂   McDonald, Walter R. "The Experience of Fiction."
         Christianity and Literature, 26, No. 4 (Summer 1977), 13–19.

II49₂   Millichap, Joseph R. "Distorted Matter and Disjunctive
         Forms: The Grotesque as Modernist Genre." *Arizona
         Quarterly*, 33 (Winter 1977), 339–47.

II50₂   Davis, Thadious M. "Southern Literature: From Faulkner to
         Others." *CEA Critic*, 40, No. 3 (March 1978), 14–18.
             Faulkner is the best point of departure for studying other Southern
             writers.

II51₂   Hauck, Richard. " 'Let's Licker'—Yarnspinning as
         Community Ritual." *American Humor*, 5 (Spring 1978),
         5–10.

II52₂   Baker, James T. "Merton on the Move." *Commonweal*, 105
         (April 28, 1978), 269–72.

II53₂   Fabre, Michel. "Bayonne or the Yoknapatawpha of Ernest
         Gaines." Trans. M. Dixon and D. Malaquin. *Callaloo*, 1
         (May 1978), 110–24.
             Comparison with Gaines.

II54₂   Rowell, Charles H. " 'This Louisiana Thing That Drives Me':
         An Interview with Ernest J. Gaines." *Callaloo*, 1 (May
         1978), 39–51.

II55₂   Radway, Janice A. "Phenomenology, Linguistics, and
         Popular Culture." *Journal of Popular Culture*, 12 (Summer
         1978), 88–98.

II56₂   Langman, Fred. "Landscape and Identity in the American
         Novel." *American Studies International*, 16, No. 4 (Summer
         1978), 34–47.
             On the use of landscape in such works as *Go Down, Moses* and "Golden
             Land."

II57₂   Colson, Theodore. "The Theme of Home in the Fiction of
         Canada, the United States, and the West Indies." *English
         Studies in Canada*, 4 (Fall 1978), 351–61.

II58₂   Oberhelman, Harley D. "Faulknerian Techniques in Gabriel
        García Márquez's *Portrait of a Dictator.*" *Proceedings of the
        Comparative Literature Symposium* [Lubbock, Texas], 10
        (1978), 171–81.

II59₂   Buell, Lawrence. "Observer-Hero Narrative." *Texas Studies
        in Literature and Language,* 21 (Spring 1979), 93–111.

II60₂   Rickels, Patricia. "An Interview with Ernest J. Gaines."
        Southwestern Review [Univ. of Southwestern Louisiana], 4
        (1979), 33–50.

II61₂   Folks, Jeffrey J. "Anderson's Satiric Portrait of William
        Faulkner in *Dark Laughter.*" *Notes on Mississippi Writers,*
        12 (Summer 1979), 23–29.

II62₂   Lennox, Sara. "Yoknapatawpha to Jerichow: Uwe Johnson's
        Appropriation of Faulkner." *Arcadia,* 14 (1979), 160–76.

II63₂   Leggett, B. J. "Notes for a Revised History of the New
        Criticism: An Interview with Cleanth Brooks." *Tennessee
        Studies in Literature,* 24 (1979), 1–35.

II64₂   Shimura, Masao. "Faulkner, De Assis, Barth: Resemblances
        and Differences." *William Faulkner: Materials, Studies, and
        Criticism,* 2, No. 2 (December 1979), 67–79.

II65₂   Durczak, Joanna. "Norman Mailer's *Why Are We in
        Vietnam?* as an Epilogue to William Faulkner's Hunting
        Sequel of Big Bottom Woods." *Studia Anglica Posnaniensia,*
        11 (1979), 183–200.

II66₂   Heller, Terry. "Notes on Technique in Black Humor."
        Thalia, 2, No. 3 (1979), 15–21.

II67₂   Bosha, Francis J. "Faulkner, Pound and the P.P.P."
        Paideuma, 8 (Fall 1979), 249–56.
        The Ezra Pound Case.

II68₂   McHale, Brian. "Modernist Reading, Post-Modern Text:
        The Case of *Gravity's Rainbow.*" *Poetics Today,* 1 (Autumn
        1979), 85–110.
        Compares modernists, for example Faulkner, with Pynchon, a post-
        modernist.

II69₂   Davis, Mary E. "William Faulkner and Mario Vargas Llosa:
        The Election of Failure." *Comparative Literature Studies,* 16
        (December 1979), 332–43.

II70₂ → **II70₂** Montgomery, Marion. "Southern Letters in the Twentieth Century." *Modern Age*, 24 (Spring 1980), 121 33.

II71₂ Bennett, Lee Shaw. "Modern Civil War Novels: The Still Unwritten War?" *Southern Studies*, 19 (Summer 1980), 105–27.

II72₂ Leal, Luis. "A Spanish-American Perspective of Anglo-American Literature." *Revista Canadiense de Estudios Hispanicos*, 5 (Fall 1980), 61–73.

Fuentes comments on Faulkner.

II73₂ Vasquez, Mary S. "The Creative Task: Existential Self-Intervention in Benet's *Una meditacion*." *Selecta*, 1 (1980), 118–20.

II74₂ Benoit, Raymond. "Again with Fair Creation: Holy Places in American Literature." *Prospects*, 5 (1980), 315–30.

II75₂ Winslow, William. "Modernity and the Novel: Twain, Faulkner, and Percy." *Gypsy Scholar*, 8 (Winter 1981), 19–40.

Compares different functions of "the community" in their fiction.

II76₂ MacAdam, Alfred, and Charles Russ. "The Art of Fiction LXVIII." *Paris Review*, 82 (Winter 1981), 140–75.

An interview with Carlos Fuentes. Another interview appears in *Diacritics*, 10 (February 1980), 46–56.

II77₂ Moorhead, Michael. "Faulkner and Kesey: Without Heat." *University of Portland Review*, Spring 1981, pp. 13–15.

On Kesey's use of a Faulkner phrase.

II78₂ Gardner, John. "What Writers Do." *Antaeus*, Nos. 40–41 (Spring 1981), pp. 416–26.

II79₂ Adams, Michael. "'How Come Everybody Down Here Has Three Names?': Martin Ritt's Southern Films." *Southern Quarterly*, 19 (Spring-Summer 1981), 143–55.

Ritt directed movies based on Faulkner's novels.

II80₂ Tharpe, Jac. "Interview with Erskine Caldwell." *Southern Quarterly*, 20 (Fall 1981), 64–74.

JJ. Newspaper Articles

JJ1₂   Michael, Thomas E. "Yoknapatawpha County Today." *Memphis Commercial Appeal*, April 4, 1965, Mid-South Magazine, pp. 6–7, 16–17.

JJ2₂   "Old Home Yields Faulkner Papers." *Memphis Commercial Appeal*, January 8, 1972, p. B2.

JJ3₂   "Mississippi's Best Crop: Novelists, Historians, Poets." *New Orleans Times-Picayune*, October 22, 1972, Sec. 1, p. 32.

JJ4₂   "Ole Miss Buys Faulkner Home." *New York Times*, July 19, 1973, p. 29.

JJ5₂   Berry, Jason. "Reading Faulkner." *Richmond Mercury*, March 27, 1974, Book Review, pp. 11, 20.
> A personal article about first reading Faulkner while in Mississippi.

JJ6₂   Mitchell, Henry. "A Time and Place for the Magic of William Faulkner." *Washington Post*, August 11, 1974, pp. M1, M3.
> Faulkner conference in Oxford. These annual events are covered each year in the *Memphis Commercial Appeal* and *Oxford Eagle*.

JJ7₂   Boozer, William. "The Light of a Faulkner August." *Memphis Commercial Appeal*, August 18, 1974, Sec. 6, p. 6.
> On a Faulkner conference in Oxford. Another article, "A Faulkner Festival," appeared in the *Commercial Appeal* on July 28, 1974, Sec. 6, p. 6.

JJ8₂   Wells, Lawrence. "Faulkner Fan with a Purpose." *New Orleans Times-Picayune*, April 25, 1976, Dixie, pp. 22–24.
> On the Yoknapatawpha Press.

JJ9₂   Ray, David. "What Mr. Faulkner Meant Writing "Wump-Wump." *Kansas City Star*, October 17, 1976, p. D10.

JJ10₂   Williams, Joan. "William Faulkner." *New York Times Book Review*, February 27, 1977, pp. 33–34.
> Letter includes criticism of Meta Carpenter.

JJ11₂   Boozer, William. "Faulkner Rates No. 1." *Nashville Banner*, July 23, 1977, p. 5.

JJ12₂   Jackson, Lily. "The Restoration of Rowan Oak." *New Orleans Times-Picayune*, September 3, 1978, Sec. 4, p. 1.

JJ13₂   Boozer, William. "Fans, Serious Students Swamp Faulkner
           Symposia, Workshops." *Nashville Banner*, October 21, 1978,
           p. 5.
             Covers several symposia on Faulkner.

JJ14₂   Le Clair, Thomas. "Hawkes and Barth Talk About Fiction."
           New York Times Book Review, April 1, 1979, pp. 7, 31–33.

JJ15₂   Mitchell, Henry. "Faulkner on Film." *Washington Post*,
           December 4, 1979, pp. B1, B11.

JJ16₂   Boozer, William. "Celebrations of Genius." *Memphis
           Commercial Appeal*, December 16, 1979, p. G6.
             On the television show about Faulkner, as well as *Mississippi Poems.*

JJ17₂   Smith, Cecil. "Sound and Fury of Faulkner's Life." *Los
           Angeles Times*, December 17, 1979, Sec. 4, p. 38.

JJ18₂   Rose, Willard P. "Willie Morris Finds You Can Go Home
           Again." *Chicago Tribune*, April 19, 1980, pp. 15–16.

JJ19₂   Howard, Edwin. "Faulkner's Friend and Confidante Ready
           to Tell Her Story." *Memphis Press-Scimitar*, June 7, 1980,
           p. 6.
             On Joan Williams' decision to write about her relationship with
             Faulkner.

JJ20₂   Speer, David. "Family Faulkner Collection Given to Ole
           Miss Library." *New Orleans Times-Picayune*, Sept. 14, 1980,
           Sec. 3, p. 6.
             The Douglas Wynn collection.

JJ21₂   "U-Va. Gets Faulkner Letter Calling Virginians Snobs."
           Washington Post, March 15, 1981, p. B8.
             New acquisition of letters, photographs, and family documents by the
             University of Virginia.

JJ22₂   Mitgang, Herbert. "Found: A Long-Lost Faulkner MS."
           New York Times, May 14, 1981, p. C21.
             A manuscript of *Soldiers' Pay* and four early letters are acquired by the
             Berg Collection. Article also includes the story of the manuscript's
             background.

JJ23₂   McDowell, Edwin. "Faulkner Signature Fabricated." *New
           York Times*, August 5, 1981, p. C21.
             Letters from Faulkner for a 1956 USIA program were apparently signed
             by a machine. Also see Joan St. C. Crane, "A William Faulkner
             'Machine' Signature." *American Book Collector*, July-August 1981, pp.
             13–14.

JJ24₂   Boozer, William. "Faulkner Attracts Literary Greats."
           Nashville Banner, August 15, 1981, p. A5.
           On a Faulkner conference in Oxford.

JJ25₂   Martin, Alex. "Faulkner sonnets to N. O. woman printed,
           released." *New Orleans Times-Picayune*, September 26, 1981,
           p. 17.
           On the publishing of *Helen: A Courtship*.

JJ26₂   Mullener, Elizabeth. "Faulkner Pilgrims in Oxford." *New
           Orleans Times-Picayune*, October 4, 1981, Dixie, pp. 6–18.
           On a Faulkner conference in Oxford.

KK. Books[1]

KK1₂   Te Selle, Sallie M. *Literature and the Christian Life.* New
           Haven: Yale Univ. Press, 1966, pp. 181–85.

KK2₂   Harss, Luis, and Barbara Dohmann. *Into the Mainstream:
           Conversations with Latin-American Writers.* New York:
           Harper & Row, 1967.

KK3₂   Tindall, George B. *The Emergence of the New South,
           1913–1945.* Baton Rouge: Louisiana State Univ. Press, 1967,
           pp. 653–57, 669–71.

KK4₂   Core, George, ed. *Southern Fiction Today: Renascence and
           Beyond.* Athens: Univ. of Georgia Press, 1969.
           A symposium, with comments on Faulkner by several critics and
           scholars.

KK5₂   Pearce, Roy Harvey. *Historicism Once More: Problems and
           Occasions for the American Scholar.* Princeton: Princeton
           Univ. Press, 1969, pp. 133–36.

KK6₂   Zolla, Elémire. *The Writer and His Shaman.* Trans. R.
           Rosenthal. New York: Harcourt Brace Jovanovich, 1969, pp.
           200–202.

KK7₂   Borges, Jorge Luis. *An Introduction to American Literature.*
           Trans. and ed. L. C. Keating and R. O. Evans. Lexington:
           Univ. Press of Kentucky, 1971.

KK8₂   Gross, Theodore L. *The Heroic Ideal in American
           Literature.* New York: Free Press, 1971.

[1]These books have short sections on Faulkner, or include comments on Faulkner by
significant figures.

KK9$_2$ Hays, Peter. *The Limping Hero: Grotesques in Literature.* New York: New York Univ. Press, 1971, pp. 82–84, 163–66.

KK10$_2$ Piper, Henry D. "Social Criticism in the American Novel in the Nineteen Twenties." In *The American Novel and the Nineteen Twenties.* Ed. M. Bradbury and D. Palmer. London: E. Arnold, 1971, pp. 59–83.

KK11$_2$ Ditsky, John. *Steinbeck: The Man and His Work.* Corvallis: Oregon State Univ. Press, 1971, pp. 11–23. Also see "Steinbeck and William Faulkner." In *Steinbeck's Literary Dimension: A Guide to Comparative Studies.* Ed. T. Hayashi. Metuchen, N.J.: Scarecrow Press, 1973, pp. 28–45.

KK12$_2$ Hassan, Ihab. *The Dismemberment of Orpheus: Toward a Post-modern Literature.* New York: Oxford Univ. Press, 1971.

KK13$_2$ Millgate, Michael. *Thomas Hardy: His Career as a Novelist.* New York: Random House, 1971, pp. 345–51.

KK14$_2$ Aldridge, John W. *The Devil in the Fire.* New York: Harper's Magazine Press, 1972.

KK15$_2$ Carr, John. *Kite-Flying and Other Irrational Acts.* Baton Rouge: Louisiana State Univ. Press, 1972.
Interviews with modern Southern writers.

KK16$_2$ Holman, C. Hugh. *The Roots of Southern Writing.* Athens: Univ. of Georgia Press, 1972, pp. 87–95.

KK17$_2$ Crunden, Robert M. *From Self to Society, 1919–1941.* Englewood Cliffs, N.J.: Prentice-Hall, 1972, pp. 167–76.
On Faulkner's conservative values.

KK18$_2$ Jameson, Frederic. "Three Methods in Sartre's Literary Criticism." In *Modern French Criticism.* Ed. J. K. Simon. Chicago: Univ. of Chicago Press, 1972, pp. 195–99.

KK19$_2$ Godbald, E. Stanley, Jr. *Ellen Glasgow and the Woman Within.* Baton Rouge: Louisiana State Univ. Press, 1972.

KK20$_2$ Hubbell, Jay B. *Who Are the Major American Writers?* Durham: Duke Univ. Press, 1972.

KK21$_2$ Longstreet, Stephen. *We All Went to Paris: Americans in the City of Light, 1776–1971.* New York: Macmillan, 1972.

KK22₂   Robinson, Clayton. "Memphis in Fiction: Rural Values in an Urban Setting." In *Myths and Realities: Conflicting Values in America.* Ed. B. Kalin and C. Robinson. Memphis: Memphis State Univ. Press, 1972, pp. 29–38.

KK23₂   Davidson, Marshall B., et al. *The American Heritage History of the Writer's America.* New York: American Heritage, 1973, pp. 338–41.

KK24₂   McLemore, Richard Aubrey, ed. *A History of Mississippi.* 2 vols. Hattiesburg: Univ. Press of Mississippi, 1973. Includes article on "Literature 1890–1970" by Sarah A. Rouse, Vol. II, pp. 446–76.

KK25₂   Guibert, Rita. *Seven Voices: Seven Latin American Writers Talk to Rita Guibert.* Trans. F. Partridge. New York: Knopf, 1973. Comments by García Márquez and others.

KK26₂   Ludington, Townsend, ed. *The Fourteenth Chronicle: Letters and Diaries of John Dos Passos.* Boston: Gambit, 1973.

KK27₂   Collmer, Robert G. "When 'Word' Meets *Palabra*: Crossing the Border with Literature." In A17₂ (1973), pp. 153–64.
     Faulkner's reception in Latin America.

KK28₂   Pells, Richard H. *Radical Visions and American Dreams: Cultural and Social Thought in the Depression Years.* New York: Harper & Row, 1973, pp. 240–46.
     On Faulkner as a conservative thinker.

KK29₂   Hobson, Fred C., Jr. *Serpent in Eden: H. L. Mencken and the South.* Chapel Hill: Univ. of North Carolina Press, 1974.

KK30₂   Seltzer, Alvin J. *Chaos in the Novel—the Novel in Chaos.* New York: Schocken, 1974.

KK31₂   Hanak, Miroslav J. "Nietzsche, Dostoevsky, and Faulkner: Rebellion against Society in the Light of the New Left." In *Proceedings of the 6th Congress of the International Comparative Literature Association.* Stuttgart: Bieber, 1975, pp. 739–43.

KK32₂   Kenner, Hugh. *A Homemade World.* New York: Knopf, 1975.

KK33₂   Steinbeck, Elaine, and Robert Wallsten, eds. *Steinbeck: A Life in Letters.* New York: Viking, 1975.
     Steinbeck comments on Faulkner and quotes a letter from Faulkner.

KK34₂ Edminstin, Susan, and Linda D. Cirino. *Literary New York: A History and a Guide.* Boston: Houghton Mifflin, 1976.

KK35₂ Kiell, Norman. *Varieties of Sexual Experience: Psychosexuality in Literature.* New York: International Universities Press, 1976.

KK36₂ Aaron, Daniel. "The South in American History." In A43₂ (1977), pp. 3–21.

KK37₂ Coover, Robert. *The Public Burning.* New York: Viking, 1977, pp. 420–21.
Faulkner is a character in the novel.

KK38₂ Donaldson, Scott. *By Force of Will: The Life and Art of Ernest Hemingway.* New York: Viking, 1977.

KK39₂ Hart, Henry. *A Relevant Memoir: The Story of the Equinox Cooperative Press.* New York: Three Mountains Press, 1977, pp. 30–32.
Publication of poem, "This Earth," in 1932.

KK40₂ Holman, C. Hugh. *The Immoderate Past: The Southern Writer and History.* Athens: Univ. of Georgia Press, 1977, pp. 72–79.
History and consciousness in Faulkner's novels.

KK41₂ Kadir, Djelal. *Juan Carlos Onetti.* Boston: Twayne, 1977.
Faulkner's influence.

KK42₂ Wilson, Edmund. *Letters on Literature and Politics 1912–1972.* New York: Farrar, Straus & Giroux, 1977.

KK43₂ Garvin, Harry R., ed. *Makers of the Twentieth-Century Novel.* Lewisburg, Pa.: Bucknell Univ. Press, 1977.
Includes slightly revised versions of articles by Hagan (J127), Slabey (F53), and Mellard (V207).

KK44₂ Berg, A. Scott. *Max Perkins: Editor of Genius.* New York: Dutton, 1978.

KK45₂ Friedman, Melvin J. "The Symbolist Novel: Huysman to Malraux." In *Modernism, 1890–1930.* Ed. M. Bradbury and J. McFarlane. Atlantic Highlands, N.J.: Humanities Press, 1978, pp. 453–66.

KK46₂ Jackson, Blyden. "Two Mississippi Writers: Wright and Faulkner." In A52₂ (1978), pp. 49–59.

KK47₂   Banta, Martha. *Failure and Success in America: A Literary Debate*. Princeton: Princeton Univ. Press, 1978.

KK48₂   Austin, James C. *American Humor in France*. Ames: Iowa State Univ. Press, 1978.

KK49₂   Bruccoli, Matthew, ed. *Selected Letters of John O'Hara*. New York: Random House, 1978.

KK50₂   Gardner, John. *On Moral Fiction*. New York: Basic Books, 1978.

KK51₂   Holman, C. Hugh. "Detached Laughter in the South." In *Comic Relief: Humor in Contemporary American Literature*. Ed. S. B. Cohen. Urbana: Univ. of Illinois Press, 1978, pp. 87–104.

KK52₂   Millgate, Michael. *The Achievement of William Faulkner*. Lincoln: Univ. of Nebraska Press, 1978.
        Reissue of 1966 book with new preface.

KK53₂   Westbrook, Perry. *Free Will and Determinism in American Literature*. Cranbury, N.J.: Associated University Presses, 1979.

KK54₂   Steinberg, Edwin R., ed. *Stream of Consciousness Technique in the Modern Novel*. Port Washington, N.Y.: Kennikat, 1979.

KK55₂   Devlin, Albert J. "Eudora Welty's Mississippi." In *Eudora Welty: Critical Essays*. Ed. P. W. Prenshaw. Jackson: Univ. Press of Mississippi, 1979, pp. 157–78.

KK56₂   Grimshaw, James A., Jr., ed. *Cleanth Brooks at the United States Air Force Academy, April 11–12, 1978*. United States Air Force Academy, Colorado: Department of English, 1980.

KK57₂   Bruccoli, Matthew J., ed. *The Correspondence of F. Scott Fitzgerald*. New York: Random House, 1980.

KK58₂   Young, Thomas Daniel. "Religion, the Bible Belt, and the Modern South." *The American South* (see AA187₂; 1980), pp. 110–17.

KK59₂   Sullivan, Walter. "The Fading Memory of the Civil War." *The American South* (see AA187₂; 1980), pp. 245–53.

KK60[2]   Holder, Alan. *The Imagined Past: Portrayals of Our History in Modern America*. Lewisburg, Pa.: Bucknell Univ. Press, 1980.

KK61[2]   Spivey, Ted R. *The Journey Beyond Tragedy: A Study of Myth and Modern Fiction*. Orlando: Univ. Presses of Florida, 1980.

KK62[2]   Westbrook, Wayne W. *Wall Street in the American Novel*. New York: New York Univ. Press, 1980.

KK63[2]   Benedict, Stewart, ed. *The Literary Guide to the United States*. New York: Facts on File, 1981.

KK64[2]   Betts, Glynne Robinson. *Writers in Residence: American Authors at Home*. New York: Viking, 1981.

KK65[2]   Hall, Donald, ed. *The Oxford Book of American Literary Anecdotes*. New York: Oxford Univ. Press, 1981.

KK66[2]   Johnson, Dorris, and E. Leventhal, eds. *The Letters of Nunnally Johnson*. New York: Knopf, 1981.

KK67[2]   Payne, Ladell. *Black Novelists and the Southern Literary Tradition*. Athens: Univ. of Georgia Press, 1981.

KK68[2]   Schlueter, Paul. *Shirley Ann Grau*. Boston: Twayne, 1981.

KK69[2]   Widmer, Kingsley. *Edges of Extremity: Some Problems of Literary Modernism*. Tulsa: Univ. of Tulsa Monograph Series, No. 17, 1981.

LL.   Doctoral Dissertations

LL1[2]   Grove, James L. "Visions and Revisions: A Study of the Obtuse Narrator in American Fiction from Brockden Brown to Faulkner." Harvard 1968.

LL2[2]   Levit, Donald J. "William Faulkner's *The Hamlet*: Its Revisions and Structure." Chicago 1968.

LL3[2]   Ott, Friedrich P. "The Literature of the Air: Themes and Imagery in the Work of Faulkner, Saint-Exupéry, and Gaiser." Harvard 1968.

LL4[2]   Norris, Carolyn B. "The Image of the Physician in Modern American Literature." Maryland 1969.

LL5₂   Momberger, Philip. "A Critical Study of Faulkner's Early Sketches and *Collected Stories*." Johns Hopkins 1970. *DAI* 33:2386A.

LL6₂   Nadeau, Robert L. "Motion and Stasis: Time as Structuring Principle in the Art of William Faulkner." Florida 1970.

LL7₂   Nash, Christopher W. "A Modern Bestiary: Representative Animal Motifs in the Encounter between Nature and Culture in the English, American, French and Italian Novel, 1900–1950." New York Univ. 1970. *DAI* 31:6622A.

LL8₂   Rose, Alan H. "The Evolution of the Image of the Negro as Demon in Southern Literature." Indiana 1970. *DAI* 31:4732A.

LL9₂   Seltzer, Alvin J. "Chaos in the Novel—the Novel in Chaos." Penn State 1970. *DAI* 32:984A.

LL10₂   Sequeira, Isaac. "The Theme of Initiation in Modern American Fiction." Utah 1970. *DAI* 31:2354A.

LL11₂   Bricker, Emil S. "Duality in the Novels of William Faulkner and Fyodor Dostoevsky." Michigan 1971. *DAI* 32:6413A.

LL12₂   Broughton, Panthea Reid. "Abstraction and Insularity in the Fiction of William Faulkner." North Carolina 1971. *DAI* 32:5220A.

LL13₂   Corridori, Edward L. "The Quest for Sacred Space: Setting in the Novels of William Faulkner." Kent State 1971. *DAI* 32:5224A.

LL14₂   Griffin, Mary N. "Coming to Manhood in America: A Study of Significant Initiation Novels, 1797–1970." Vanderbilt 1971.

LL15₂   Hand, Nancy W. "The Anatomy of a Genre: The Modern Novelette in English." Kent State 1971.

LL16₂   Haseloff, Cynthia. "Formative Elements of Film: A Structural Comparison of Three Novels and Their Adaptations by Irving Ravetch and Harriet Frank, Jr." Missouri 1971. *DAI* 438A. Covers *The Reivers* and *The Sound and the Fury*.

LL17₂   Hughes, Charles W. "Man Against Nature: *Moby-Dick* and 'The Bear.'" Texas Tech 1971. *DAI* 32:5230A.

LL18$_2$ Lenson, David R. "Examples of Modern Tragedy." Princeton 1971. *DAI* 32:6433A.

LL19$_2$ Meyer, Norma Lee. "Syntactic Features of William Faulkner's Narrative Style." Nebraska 1971. *DAI* 32:6406A.

LL20$_2$ Norris, Nancy R. "William Faulkner's Trilogy." Pennsylvania 1971. *DAI* 32:6994A.

LL21$_2$ Pindell, Richard P. "The Ritual of Survival: Landscape in Conrad and Faulkner." Yale 1971. *DAI* 32:3324A.

LL22$_2$ Pomeroy, Charles W. "Soviet Russian Criticism 1960–1969 of Seven Twentieth Century American Novelists." Southern California 1971. *DAI* 32:449A.

LL23$_2$ Ramsey, William C. "Coordinate Structure in Four Faulkner Novels." North Carolina 1971. *DAI* 33:283A.

LL24$_2$ Shelton, Frank W. "The Family in the Novels of Wharton, Faulkner, Cather, Lewis and Dreiser." North Carolina 1971. *DAI* 32:5244A.

LL25$_2$ Sieben, John K. "The Presentation of the Negro Character in the Best-Selling Novels of the Postwar Period 1946 Through 1965 in the United States." New York Univ. 1971. *DAI* 32:2709A.

LL26$_2$ Weybright, Myron D. "A Study of Tensiveness in Selected Novels of William Faulkner." Northwestern 1971. *DAI* 32:5389A.

LL27$_2$ Yamada, Agnes A. "The Endless Jar: 'Contraries' in William Faulkner." Oregon 1971. *DAI* 32:5249A.

LL28$_2$ Berk, Lynn M. L. "The Barrier of Words: A Study of William Faulkner's Distrust of Language." Purdue 1972. *DAI* 33:5163A.

LL29$_2$ Clark, Edward D. "Six Grotesques in Three Faulkner Novels." Syracuse 1972. *DAI* 33:302A.

LL30$_2$ Culley, Margaret M. "Eschatological Thought in Faulkner's Yoknapatawpha Novels." Michigan 1972. *DAI* 33:5167A.

LL31$_2$ Degenfelder, E. Pauline. "Essays on Faulkner: Style, Use of History, Film Adaptations on His Fiction." Case Western Reserve 1972. *DAI* 33:5169A.

LL32₂   Ficken, Carl F. W. "A Critical and Textual Study of
        William Faulkner's *Light in August*." South Carolina 1972.
        DAI 33:4411A.

LL33₂   Flory, Joseph W. "The New Rhetoric of Faulkner's Heroes
        in His Later Work." Indiana Univ. of Pennsylvania 1972.

LL34₂   Hochstettler, David. "William Faulkner's *A Fable*: A
        Fragmented Christ." Syracuse 1972. *DAI* 33:5724A.

LL35₂   Lannon, John M. "William Faulkner: A Study in Spatial
        Form." Masschusetts 1972. *DAI* 33:5184A.

LL36₂   McClelland, Benjamin W. "Not Only to Survive But to
        Prevail: A Study of William Faulkner's Search for a
        Redeemer of Modern Man." Indiana 1972. *DAI* 32:6438A.

LL37₂   MacMillan, Duane J. "The Non-Yoknapatawpha Novels of
        William Faulkner: An Examination of *Soldiers' Pay*,
        Mosquitoes, *Pylon*, *The Wild Palms*, and *A Fable*."
        Wisconsin 1972. *DAI* 32:6986A.

LL38₂   MacMillan, Kenneth D. "The Bystander in Faulkner's
        Fiction." British Columbia 1972. *DAI* 34:783A.

LL39₂   Milum, Richard A. "The Cavalier Spirit in Faulkner's
        Fiction." Indiana 1972. *DAI* 33:5737A.

LL40₂   Moore, Robert H. "Perspectives on William Faulkner: The
        Author and His Work as Reflected in Surveys of American
        History, Works on Southern Life and History, and Works
        and Comments by Mississippians." Wisconsin 1972. *DAI*
        32:5798A.

LL41₂   Parr, Susan D. R. "'And By Bergson, Obviously.' Faulkner's
        The Sound and the Fury, *As I Lay Dying* and *Absalom,
        Absalom!* from a Bergsonian Perspective." Wisconsin 1972.
        DAI 32:6996A.

LL42₂   Patten, Catherine M. "A Study of William Faulkner's *As I
        Lay Dying* Based on the Manuscript and Text." New York
        Univ. 1972. *DAI* 34:331A.

LL43₂   Peabody, Henry W. "Faulkner's Initiation Stories: An
        Approach to the Major Works." Denver 1972. *DAI*
        33:3663A.

LL44₂ Pierce, Constance M. "Earth, Air, Fire, and Water: The Elements in Faulkner's Fiction." Penn State 1972. *DAI* 33:6927A.

LL45₂ Robinson, Frederick M. "The Comedy of Language: Studies in Modern Comic Literature." Washington 1972. Covers *As I Lay Dying*.

LL46₂ Rosenzweig, Paul J. "The Wilderness in American Fiction: A Psychoanalytic Study of a Central American Myth." Michigan 1972. *DAI* 33:5140A.

LL47₂ Ross, Stephen M. "A World of Voices: 'Talking' in the Novels of William Faulkner." Stanford 1972. *DAI* 32:7002A.

LL48₂ Savarese, Sister Paul C., C.S.J. "Cinematic Techniques in the Novels of William Faulkner." St. Louis Univ. 1972. *DAI* 33:1179A.

LL49₂ Scanlan, Margaret C. T. "William Faulkner and *The Search for Lost Time*: Three Aspects of Literary Deformation." Iowa 1972. *DAI* 33:1741A.

LL50₂ Shulman, Irving. "A Study of the Juvenile Delinquent as Depicted in the Twentieth-Century American Novel to 1950." UCLA 1972. *DAI* 33:329A.

LL51₂ Smith, James F., Jr. "From Symbol to Character: The Negro in American Fiction of the Twenties." Penn State 1972. *DAI* 33:3672A.

LL52₂ Sullivan, Ruth E. "Some Variations on the Oedipal Theme in Three Pieces of Fiction: 'A Rose for Emily,' *Three Hours After Marriage*, and 'Christabel.'" Tufts 1972. *DAI* 33:4366A.

LL53₂ Thomas, Frank H., III. "The Search for Identity of Faulkner's Black Characters." Pittsburgh 1972. *DAI* 33:6935A.

LL54₂ Thompson, David J. S. "Societal Definitions of Individualism and the Critique of Egotism as a Major Theme in American Fiction." Brown 1972. *DAI* 33:4435A.

LL55₂ Thompson, Evelyn J. "William Faulkner's Yoknapatawpha: The Land of Broken Dreams." Texas Tech 1972. *DAI* 33:4435A.

LL56₂ Webb, Gerald F. "Jeffersonian Agrarianism in Faulkner's Yoknapatawpha: The Evolution of Social and Economic Standard." Florida State. 1972. *DAI* 33:5754A.

LL57₂ Berrone, Louis C., Jr. "Faulkner's *Absalom, Absalom!* and Dickens: A Study of Time and Change Correspondences." Fordham 1973. *DAI* 34:5158A.

LL58₂ Bowlin, Karla J. "The Brother and Sister Theme in Post-Romantic Fiction." Auburn 1973. *DAI* 34:1232A.

LL59₂ Chung, Hae-Ja Kim. "Point of View as a Mode of Definition in Conrad and Faulkner." Michigan 1973. *DAI* 35:442A.

LL60₂ Clark, William B. "The Serpent of Lust in the Southern Garden: The Theme of Miscegenation in Cable, Twain, Faulkner, and Warren." Louisiana State 1973. *DAI* 34:5958A.

LL61₂ Crow, Peter G. "Faulkner's Vitalistic Vision: A Close Study of Eight Novels." Duke 1973. *DAI* 34:764A.

LL62₂ Dean, Sharon W. "Lost Ladies: The Isolated Heroine in the Fiction of Hawthorne, James, Fitzgerald, Hemingway, and Faulkner." New Hampshire 1973. *DAI* 34:2616A.

LL63₂ Elder, John C. "Towards a New Objectivity: Essays on the Body and Nature in Faulkner, Lawrence, and Mann." Yale 1973. *DAI* 34:7228A.

LL64₂ Fitzgerald, James R. "William Faulkner's Literary Reputation in Britain, with a Checklist of Criticism, 1929–1972." Georgia 1973. *DAI* 34:5965A.

LL65₂ Foran, Donald J., S.J. "William Faulkner's *Absalom, Absalom!*: An Exercise in Affirmation." Southern California 1973. *DAI* 34:4259A.

LL66₂ Ford, Daniel G. "Uses of Time in Four Novels by William Faulkner." Auburn 1973. *DAI* 35:1654A.

LL67₂ Friedling, Sheila. "Problems of Perception in the Modern Novel: The Representation of Consciousness in Works of Henry James, Gertrude Stein, and William Faulkner." Wisconsin 1973. *DAI* 34:3391A.

LL68₂ Gladstein, Mimi R. "The Indestructible Woman in the Works of Faulkner, Hemingway, and Steinbeck." New Mexico 1973. *DAI* 35:1655A.

LL69₂ Gribbin, Daniel V. "Men of Thought, Men of Action: A Pattern of Contrasts in Faulkner's Major Novels." North Carolina 1973. *DAI* 34:5969A.

LL70₂ Heller, Terry L. "William Faulkner's Uses of Elaboration and Multiple Story Lines." Chicago 1973.

LL71₂ Hulley, Kathleen. "Disintegration as Symbol of Community: A Study of *The Rainbow, Women in Love, Light in August, Prisoner of Grace, Except the Lord, Not Honour More,* and *Herzog.*" California-Davis 1973. *DAI* 34:6643A.

LL72₂ Jenkins, Lee Clinton. "Images of the Negro in the Novels of William Faulkner." Columbia 1973. *DAI* 34:3403A.

LL73₂ Josephs, Mary J. "The Hunting Metaphor in Hemingway and Faulkner." Michigan State 1973. *DAI* 34:1282A.

LL74₂ Layman, Lewis M. "Fourteen Ways of Looking at a Blackbird: Point of View in *The Sound and the Fury.*" British Columbia 1973. *DAI* 34:7763A.

LL75₂ Lennox, Sara J. "The Fiction of William Faulkner and Uwe Johnson: A Comparative Study." Wisconsin 1973. *DAI* 34:6647A.

LL76₂ Levins, Lynn G. "William Faulkner: The Heroic Design of Yoknapatawpha." North Carolina 1973. *DAI* 34:2635A.

LL77₂ Lincoln, Ruth T. "Ontological Implications in Faulkner's Major Novels." Indiana 1973. *DAI* 34:1286A.

LL78₂ Major, Sylvia B. "*Absalom, Absalom!*: A Study of Structure." North Texas State 1973. *DAI* 34:5188A.

LL79 McAlexander, Hubert H., Jr. "History as Perception, History as Obsession: Faulkner's Development of a Theme." Wisconsin 1973. *DAI* 34:6596A.

LL80₂ Memmott, Albert J. "The Theme of Revenge in the Fiction of William Faulkner." Minnesota 1973. *DAI* 34:4273A.

LL81₂ Nigliazzo, Marc A. "Faulkner's Indians." New Mexico 1973. *DAI* 34:6650A.

LL82₂   Porter, Carolyn J. "Form and Process in American
        Literature." Rice 1973. *DAI* 34:1291A.

LL83₂   Pryse, Marjorie L. "The Marked Character in American
        Fiction: Essays in Social and Metaphysical Isolation."
        California-Santa Cruz 1973. *DAI* 35:1119A.

LL84₂   Reynolds, Gordon D. "Psychological Rebirth in Selected
        Works by Nathaniel Hawthorne, Stephen Crane, Henry
        James, William Faulkner, and Ralph Ellison." California-
        Irvine 1973. *DAI* 34:7719A.

LL85₂   Rigsby, Carol R. "The Vanishing Community: Studies in
        Some Late Novels by William Faulkner." Toronto 1973.
        DAI 36:1509A.

LL86₂   Rose, Maxine S. "From Genesis to Revelation: The Grand
        Design of Faulkner's *Absalom, Absalom!*" Alabama 1973.
        DAI 34:6656A.

LL87₂   Routh, Michael P. "The Story of All Things: Faulkner's
        Yoknapatawpha County Cosmology by Way of *Light in
        August.*" Wisconsin 1973. *DAI* 34:6657A.

LL88₂   Schermbrucker, William G. "Strange Textures of Vision: A
        Study of the Significance of Mannered Fictional Techniques
        in Six Selected Novels of D. H. Lawrence, William
        Faulkner, and Patrick White, Together with a Theoretical
        Introduction on 'The Novel of Vision.'" British Columbia
        1973. *DAI* 35:473A.

LL89₂   Smith, Kearney I. "Some Romantic Elements in the Works
        of William Faulkner." Georgia 1973. *DAI* 34:4286A.

LL90₂   Stonum, Gary Lee. "William Faulkner: The Dynamics of
        Form." Johns Hopkins 1973. *DAI* 34:3433A.

LL91₂   Tumulty, Michael J., C.M. "Youth and Innocence in the
        Novels of William Faulkner." St. John's 1973. *DAI*
        34:4292A.

LL92₂   Vest, David C. "Perpetual Salvage: The Historical
        Consciousness in Modern Southern Literature." Vanderbilt
        1973. *DAI* 34:5209A.

LL93₂   Weeks, Willis E. "Faulkner's Young Males: From Futility to
        Responsibility." Arizona State 1973. *DAI* 34:2663A.

LL94₂   Williams, David L. "William Faulkner and the Mythology of Woman." Massachusetts 1973. *DAI* 34·6610A.

LL95₂   Williams, Mina G. "The Sense of Place in Southern Fiction." Louisiana State 1973. *DAI* 34:3440A.

LL96₂   Bailey, Dennis L. "The Modern Novel in the Presence of Myth." Purdue 1974. *DAI* 35:7292A.

LL97₂   Ballew, Stephen E. "Faulkner's Psychology of Individualism: A Fictional Principle and *Light in August*." Indiana 1974. *DAI* 35:6700A.

LL98₂   Beauchamp, Fay Elizabeth. "William Faulkner's Use of the Tragic Mulatto Myth." Pennsylvania 1974. *DAI* 36:297A.

LL99₂   Bond, Christopher J. "I. Sir James Frazer's 'Homeopathy' and 'Contagion' as Archetypal and Structural Principles in William Faulkner's *Go Down, Moses*." Rutgers 1974. *DAI* 35:3725A.

LL100₂   Burns, Mattie Ann. "The Development of Women Characters in the Works of William Faulkner." Auburn 1974. *DAI* 35:4502A.

LL101₂   Cantrill, Dante K. "Told by an Idiot: Toward an Understanding of Modern Fiction through an Analysis of the Works of William Faulkner." Washington 1974. *DAI* 35:4505A.

LL102₂   Fletcher, Mary Dell. "William Faulkner: The Calvinistic Sensibility." Louisiana State 1974. *DAI* 35:5400A.

LL103₂   Fowler, Doreen F. "Faulkner's Changing Vision: Narrative Progress toward Affirmation." Brown 1974. *DAI* 35:7302A.

LL104₂   Hiers, John T. "Traditional Death Customs in Modern Southern Fiction." Emory 1974. *DAI* 35:1103A.

LL105₂   Hinchey, John J. "Implausible Motion: Generation and Regeneration in the Novels of William Faulkner." Harvard 1974.

LL106₂   Hutcheon, Philip L. "Affirming the Void: Futilitarianism in the Fiction of Conrad and Faulkner." Rice 1974. *DAI* 35:2271A.

LL107₂   Ilacqua, Alma A. "Faulkner and the Concept of Excellence." Syracuse 1974. *DAI* 36:314A.

LL108$_2$ Jordan, Peter W. "Faulkner's Crime Fiction: His Use of the Detective Story and the Thriller." Connecticut 1974. *DAI* 34:2630A.

LL109$_2$ Labatt, Blair P., Jr. "Faulkner the Storyteller." Virginia 1974. *DAI* 34:7761A.

LL110$_2$ McColgan, Kristin P. "The World's Slow Stain: The Theme of Initiation in Selected American Novels." North Carolina 1974. *DAI* 36:279A.

LL111$_2$ Manley, Justine M. "The Function of Stock Humor and Grotesque Humor in Faulkner's Major Novels." Loyola 1974. *DAI* 35:1111A.

LL112$_2$ Matton, Collin G. "The Role of Women in Three of Faulkner's Families." Marquette 1974. *DAI* 35:2283A.

LL113$_2$ Murray, Trudy K. "Tricked by Words: Syntax and Style in Faulkner's *As I Lay Dying*." Washington 1974. *DAI* 36:3660A.

LL114$_2$ Perry, Thomas E. "Knowing in the Novels of William Faulkner." Rochester 1974. *DAI* 35:2289A.

LL115$_2$ Radomski, James L. "Faulkner's Style: A Syntactic Analysis." Kent State 1974. *DAI* 35:6154A.

LL116$_2$ Reirdon, Suzanne R. "An Application of Script Analysis to Four of William Faulkner's Women Characters." East Texas State 1974. *DAI* 35:4549A.

LL117$_2$ Roberts, Melvin R. "Faulkner's *Flags in the Dust* and *Sartoris*: A Comparative Study of the Typescript and the Originally Published Novel." Texas 1974. *DAI* 35:471A.

LL118$_2$ Rower, Ann D. "Work in Counterpoint: Faulkner's *The Wild Palms*." Columbia 1974. *DAI* 35:6731A.

LL119$_2$ Rudensky, Bernice J. "The Unalterable Doom: Horror as an Element of Tragedy in Four Novels by William Faulkner." Chicago 1974.

LL120$_2$ Samway, Patrick H., S.J. "A Textual and Critical Evaluation of the Manuscripts and Typescripts of William Faulkner's *Intruder in the Dust*." North Carolina 1974. *DAI* 36:328A.

LL121₂ Schlumpf, Otto N. "William Faulkner: Myth-Maker and Morals-Monger; Esthetics and Ethics in Yoknapatawpha County." California-Santa Barbara 1974. *DAI* 35:7327A.

LL122₂ Schoenberg, Estella. "Quentin Compson and the Fictive Process: A Four-Dimensional Study of *Absalom, Absalom!*" Tulsa 1974. *DAI* 35:6732A.

LL123₂ Serruya, Barbara B. "The Evolution of an Artist: A Genetic Study of William Faulkner's *The Hamlet*." UCLA 1974. *DAI* 35:2298A.

LL124₂ Siegel, Roslyn. "Faulkner's Black Characters: A Comparative Study." CUNY 1974. *DAI* 35:3009A.

LL125₂ Skenazy, Paul N. "Inarticulate Characters in Modern American Fiction: A Study of Fitzgerald, Hemingway, and Faulkner." Stanford 1974. *DAI* 34:7783A.

LL126₂ Slade, John H. "A Study of William Faulkner's *A Fable*." Stanford 1974. *DAI* 35:6160A.

LL127₂ Stephenson, Shelby D. "'You Smart Sheriffs and Such': The Function of Local Peace Officers in William Faulkner's *Light in August* and *Intruder in the Dust*." Wisconsin 1974. *DAI* 35:3012A.

LL128₂ Wee, Morris O. "Confronting the Ghost: Quentin Compson's Struggle with His Heritage in Faulkner's *Absalom, Absalom!*" Boston College 1974. *DAI* 35:6166A.

LL129₂ Whitaker, Charles F. "Psychological Approaches to the Narrative Personality in the Novels of William Faulkner." Purdue 1974. *DAI* 35:7276A.

LL130₂ Winkel, Carol A. "Faulkner's Style and Its Relation to Theme: A Stylistic Study of Two Stories from *Go Down, Moses*." Delaware 1974. *DAI* 35:3017A.

LL131₂ Wright, Ona R. "Though Myth Has Changed, Much Endures: Concepts of the Epic Hero in Selected Modern American Novels." Texas Woman's Univ. 1974. *DAI* 35:6738A.

LL132₂ Aiken, David H. "Joyce, Faulkner, O'Connor: Conceptual Approaches to Major Characters." SUNY-Stony Brook 1975. *DAI* 36:3680A.

LL133₂   Akin, Warren, IV. "Neither We from Them nor They from Us: An Interpretation of *Go Down, Moses.*" Bryn Mawr 1975. *DAI* 36:6094A.

LL134₂   Bellue, John V. "William Faulkner as Literary Naturalist." Wayne State 1975. *DAI* 36:7417A.

LL135₂   Blair, Arthur H. "Faulkner's Military World." North Carolina 1975. *DAI* 36:6679A.

LL136₂   Boyd, Gary M. "The Reflexive Novel: Fiction as Critique." Wisconsin 1975. *DAI* 37:293A.

LL137₂   Boyle, Anthony J. "Modernism, Radical Humanism, and the Contemporary Novel." SUNY-Buffalo 1975. *DAI* 36:1498A.

LL138₂   Brown, May Cameron. "Quentin Compson as Narrative Voice in the Works of William Faulkner." Georgia State 1975. *DAI* 36:5291A.

LL139₂   Burggraf, David L. "The Genesis and Unity of Faulkner's *Big Woods.*" Ohio Univ. 1975. *DAI* 36:6679A.

LL140₂   Clark, Anderson Aubrey. "Courtly Love in the Writings of William Faulkner." Vanderbilt 1975. *DAI* 36:4482A.

LL141₂   Dean, Charles W., Jr. "William Faulkner's Romantic Heritage: Beyond America." Massachusetts 1975. *DAI* 36:885A.

LL142₂   DeSpain, N. LaRene. "Stream of Consciousness Narration in Faulkner: A Redefinition." Connecticut 1975. *DAI* 37:306A.

LL143₂   Gernes, Sonia G. "The Relationship of Storyteller to Community in the Tales of the Southwest Humorists, Mark Twain and William Faulkner." Washington 1975. *DAI* 36:3685A.

LL144₂   Gill, Linda G. "Faulkner's Narrative Voices in *The Sound and the Fury.*" California-San Diego 1975. *DAI* 36:4489A.

LL145₂   Gregory, N. Eileen. "A Study of the Early Versions of Faulkner's *The Town* and *The Mansion.*" South Carolina 1975. *DAI* 36:3686A.

LL146₂   Hedin, Anne M. "The Self as History: Studies in Adams, Faulkner, Ellison, Belyj, Pasternak." Virginia 1975. *DAI* 36:6074A.

LL147₂   Kondravy, Connie R. "Faulkner's Study of Youth." Lehigh 1975. *DAI* 36:6100A.

LL148₂   Lisk, Thomas D. "Love, Law and the Nature of Character." Rice 1975. *DAI* 36:2198A.

LL149₂   Little, Matthew W. "Faulkner and American Humor: Traditions and Innovations." Chicago 1975.

LL150₂   Lloyd, James B. "Humorous Characterization and the Tradition of the Jonsonian Comedy of Manners in William Faulkner's Early Fiction: *New Orleans Sketches, Soldiers' Pay*, and *Mosquitoes*." Mississippi 1975. *DAI* 36:4493A.

LL151₂   Mallonee, Helen H. "Land-Character Relationships in Selected Works of Faulkner's Yoknapatawpha Saga." South Florida 1975. *DAI* 36:890A.

LL152₂   Moses, Edwin P. "Faulknerian Comedy." SUNY-Binghamton 1975. *DAI* 36:1507A.

LL153₂   Murphree, John W., Jr. "A Study of William Faulkner's Informal Dialect Theory and His Use of Dialect Markers in Eight Novels." Ball State 1975. *DAI* 36:2177A.

LL154₂   Newhall, Eric L. "Prisons and Prisoners in the Works of William Faulkner." UCLA 1975. *DAI* 36:5300A.

LL155₂   Randolph, Linda S. "A Question of Responsibility: The Villain in the Yoknapatawpha Fiction of William Faulkner." Mississippi 1975. *DAI* 36:7425A.

LL156₂   Rhode, Robert H. "William Faulkner and the Gods of Yoknapatawpha: An Essay in Comparative Mythopoesis." Syracuse 1975. *DAI* 36:6761A.

LL157₂   Solomon, Robert H. "Classical Myth in the Novels of William Faulkner." Penn State 1975. *DAI* 36:7428A.

LL158₂   Tololyan, Khachig. "The Cosmographic Strain in Narrative: From Homer to Faulkner, Joyce and Butor." Brown 1975. *DAI* 37:303A.

LL159₂   Trowbridge, William L. "Myth and Dream in the Novels of William Faulkner." Vanderbilt 1975. *DAI* 36:4498A.

LL160₂   Waters, Maureen A. "The Role of Women in Faulkner's Yoknapatawpha." Columbia 1975. *DAI* 36:332A.

LL161₂   Winn, Harlan H., III. "Short Story Cycles of Hemingway, Steinbeck, Faulkner, and O'Connor." Oregon 1975. *DAI* 36:4500A.

LL162₂   Yep, Laurence M. "Self-Communion: The Early Novels of William Faulkner." SUNY-Buffalo 1975. *DAI* 36:1513A.

LL163₂   Albert, Theodore G. "The Pastoral Argument of *The Sound and the Fury*." Rutgers 1976. *DAI* 37:3601A.

LL164₂   Alldredge, Betty J. "Levels of Consciousness: Women in the Stream of Consciousness Novels of Joyce, Woolf, and Faulkner." Oregon 1976. *DAI* 37:3610A.

LL165₂   Arthur, Christopher E. "Possibilities of Place: The Fiction of William Faulkner." Cornell 1976. *DAI* 38:1383A.

LL166₂   Barrett, Betty P. "The Tradition of the *Coincidentia Oppositorum* in Representative Modern Literary Works." Emory 1976. *DAI* 37:2856A.

LL167₂   Barricklow, Gary E. "Kenneth Burke's Structuralism: A Structural Description of Narrative and Technique in Faulkner's Fiction of the Southern Aristocracy." New Mexico 1976. *DAI* 37:2856A.

LL168₂   Barthelme, Helen M. "*Pylon*: The Doomed Quest. A Critical and Textual Study of William Faulkner's Neglected Allegory." Texas 1976. *DAI* 38:4163A.

LL169₂   Buck, Lynn D. "The Demonic Paradox: Studies in Faulkner's Imagery." SUNY-Stony Brook 1976. *DAI* 37:3620A.

LL170₂   Byrne, Mary Ellen. "An Exploration of the Literary Relationship between Sherwood Anderson and William Faulkner." Temple 1976. *DAI* 36:8055A.

LL171₂   Corwin, Ronald L. "The Development of Narrative Technique in the Apprenticeship Fiction of William Faulkner." Brandeis 1976. *DAI* 37:2869A.

LL172₂   Crigler, John P., III. "Faulkner's Early Short Story Career." Yale 1976. *DAI* 37:4352A.

LL173₂   Davis, Thadious M. "Faulkner's 'Negro': Art and the Southern Context, 1926–1936." Boston Univ. 1976.

LL174₂   Goodenberger, Mary Ellen. "William Faulkner's Compleat Woman." Nebraska 1976. *DAI* 38:4827A.

LL175₂   Grimwood, J. Michael. "Pastoral and Parody: The Making of Faulkner's Anthology Novels." Princeton 1976. *DAI* 37:5828A.

LL176₂   Hamblin, Bobby W. "William Faulkner's Theory of Fiction." Mississippi 1976. *DAI* 37:1546A.

LL177₂   Krefft, James H. "The Yoknapatawpha Indians: Fact and Fiction." Tulane 1976. *DAI* 37:1549A.

LL178₂   Lampl, Nancy W. "The Decomposing Form: Studies in Faulkner, Woolf and Beckett." Case Western Reserve 1976. *DAI* 37:7735A.

LL179₂   Matthews, John T. "Creative Responses to Time in the Novels of William Faulkner." Johns Hopkins 1976. *DAI* 37:6486A.

LL180₂   Mortimer, Gail L. "Rhetoric of Loss: An Analysis of Faulkner's Perceptual Style." SUNY-Buffalo 1976. *DAI* 37:971A.

LL181₂   Nochimson, Martha. "Against the Limitations of Rationalism: Undercurrents in the Works of William Faulkner." CUNY 1976. *DAI* 37:1551A.

LL182₂   Palumbo, Donald E. "Faith, Identity, and Perception: Three Existential Crises in Modern Fiction and Their Artistic Reconciliation: A Comparison of the Fiction of Dostoevsky, Joyce, Kafka, and Faulkner from the Perspective of the Works of Sartre and Camus." Michigan 1976. *DAI* 37:3616A.

LL183₂   Pearson, Theresa L. "*The Sound and the Fury*: An Archetypal Reading." New Mexico 1976. *DAI* 37:6487A.

LL184₂   Peters, Erskine A. "The Yoknapatawpha World and Black Being." Princeton 1976. *DAI* 37:5831A.

LL185₂   Pieper, Janet L. "Black Characters in Faulkner's Fiction." Nebraska 1976. *DAI* 37:2877A.

LL186₂   Pisani, Assunta S. "The Raging Impotence: Humor in the Novels of Dostoevsky, Faulkner and Beckett." Brown 1976. *DAI* 38:248A.

LL187₂   Robbins, Deborah L. "Characters in Crisis: Communication and the Idea of Self in Faulkner." Northwestern 1976. *DAI* 37:7132A.

LL188₂   Roth, Richard A. "From Gap to Gain: Outrage and Renewal in Faulkner and Mailer." Washington 1976. *DAI* 37:1554A.

LL189₂   Smith, Stella P. "The Evolution of Patterns of Characterization from Faulkner's *Soliders' Pay* (1926) through *Absalom, Absalom!* (1936)." Texas Tech 1976. *DAI* 37:2881A.

LL190₂   Spear, Karen I. "Will and Body: Dualism in *Light in August*." American Univ. 1976. *DAI* 37:1557A.

LL191₂   Thornton, Patricia E. "The Prison of Gender: Sexual Roles in Major American Novels of the 1920's." New Brunswick 1976. *DAI* 37:7133A.

LL192₂   Toles, George E., Jr. "The Darkening Window: Four Problematic American Novels." Virginia 1976. *DAI* 37:4378A.

LL193₂   Ziegfeld, Richard E. "A Methodology for the Study of Philosophy in Literature: Philosophy and Symbol in Selected Works of William Faulkner and Thomas Mann." Texas 1976. *DAI* 37:5105A.

LL194₂   Busby, Mark B. "Innocence, Suffering, and Release: The Merging Adam-Christ Figure in Contemporary American Fiction." Colorado 1977. *DAI* 38:4164A.

LL195₂   Butler, Rebecca R. "The Mad Preacher in Three Modern American Novels: *Miss Lonelyhearts*, *Wise Blood*, *Light in August*." Louisiana State 1977. *DAI* 38:4164A.

LL196₂   Castille, Philip D. "Faulkner's Early Heroines." Tulane 1977. *DAI* 38:2121A.

LL197₂   Cavanaugh, Hilayne E. "Faulkner, Stasis, and Keats's 'Ode on a Grecian Urn.'" Nebraska 1977. *DAI* 38:2783A.

LL198₂   Chavkin, Allan R. "The Secular Imagination: The Continuity of the Secular Romantic Tradition of Wordsworth and Keats in Stevens, Faulkner, Roethke, and Bellow." Illinois 1977. *DAI* 38:6129A.

LL199₂ Cox, Leland H., Jr. "Sinbad in New Orleans: Early Short Fiction by William Faulkner—An Annotated Edition." South Carolina 1977. *DAI* 38:2122A.

LL200₂ Dean, Elizabeth M. "The Contours of Eros: Landscape in Twentieth Century Art and Literature." Emory 1977. *DAI* 38:3455A.

LL201₂ Duffy, James T., Jr. "Two Alike: A Study of Twins in American Fiction." Penn State 1977. *DAI* 38:7331A.

LL202₂ Eaglin, Patrick G. "William Faulkner: The Search for Reality." Harvard 1977.

LL203₂ Folks, Jeffrey Jay. "Plot Materials and Narrative Form in Faulkner's Early Fiction." Indiana 1977. *DAI* 38:6724A.

LL204₂ Higgins, Johanna W. "Meta-Naturalism in Selected Twentieth Century American Novels." SUNY-Binghamton 1977. *DAI* 38:2126A.

LL205₂ Holden, Sarah H. "Changes in the Novel: A Structuralist Comparison of *Middlemarch*, *The Confidence Man*, and *Absalom, Absalom!*" Rice 1977. *DAI* 38:1409A.

LL206₂ Jaffe, Evelyn. "Endure and Prevail: Faulkner's Social Outcasts." Colorado 1977. *DAI* 38:2789A.

LL207₂ Keiser, Merle W. "Faulkner's *Sartoris*: A Comprehensive Study." New York Univ. 1977. *DAI* 38:7333A.

LL208₂ Kelly, Jimmy Lee. "The Artist in Shadow: Quentin Compson in William Faulkner's *The Sound and the Fury*." North Carolina 1977. *DAI* 39:279A.

LL209₂ Kolb, Deborah S. "The Theme of Community in Twentieth-Century Southern Novels." North Carolina 1977. *DAI* 38:3501A.

LL210₂ Komar, Kathleen L. "The Multilinear Novel: A Structural Analysis of Novels by Dos Passos, Doblin, Faulkner, and Koeppen." Princeton 1977. *DAI* 38:2101A.

LL211₂ Lyday, C. Lance. "Faulkner's *Commedia*: An Interpretation of *The Sound and the Fury*, *Sanctuary*, *As I Lay Dying*, and *Light in August*." Vanderbilt 1977. *DAI* 39:886A.

LL212₂ McDowell, Richard D. "Faulkner's Trilogy: A Revaluation." Tulane 1977. *DAI* 38:5481A.

LL213₂   Maguire, Robert E. "The Two Patrimonies of Isaac
         McCaslin: Responsibilities to Secular and Liminal Time in
         Faulkner's *Go Down, Moses*." Dallas 1977. *DAI* 39:3582A.

LL214₂   Marks, Margaret L. "Flannery O'Connor's American
         Models: Her Work in Relation to That of Hawthorne,
         James, Faulkner, and West." Duke 1977. *DAI* 38:4830A.

LL215₂   Miller, Bernice B. "William Faulkner's Thomas Sutpen,
         Quentin Compson, Joe Christmas: A Study of the Hero-
         Archetype." Florida 1977. *DAI* 38:6728A.

LL216₂   Millis, Ralph E. "Humanistic and Legal Values in Some
         Works of Faulkner." Iowa 1977. *DAI* 38:4170A.

LL217₂   Mumbach, Mary K. "'Remaining Must Remain': Patterns of
         Christian Comedy in Faulkner's *The Mansion*." Dallas 1977.
         DAI 42:1636A.

LL218₂   Orloff, Kossia. "Ring Composition: The Structural Unity of
         Go Down, Moses." Iowa 1977. *DAI* 38:4184A.

LL219₂   Rollyson, Carl E., Jr. "The Uses of the Past in the Novels of
         William Faulkner." Toronto 1977. *DAI* 37:6488A.

LL220₂   Ruppel, James R. "Narcissus Observed: The Pastoral Elegiac
         in Woolf, Faulkner, Fitzgerald, and Graeme Gibson."
         Toronto 1977. *DAI* 39:4249A.

LL221₂   Sederberg, Nancy B. "William Faulkner's World War I and
         Flying Short Fiction: An Imaginative Appropriation of
         History." South Carolina 1977. *DAI* 38:5484A.

LL222₂   Sengelli, Nazan Feride. "Literary Continuity Traced through
         the Progression in the Use of Time in Wordsworth,
         Faulkner, Virginia Woolf, T. S. Eliot and Yeats." George
         Peabody 1977. *DAI* 38:2766A.

LL223₂   Shaw, Joy F. "The South in Motley: A Study of the Fool
         Tradition in Selected Works by Faulkner, McCullers, and
         O'Connor." Virginia 1977. *DAI* 38:4162A.

LL224₂   Stock, Jerold H. "Suggestions of Death-Anxiety in the Life
         of William Faulkner." West Virginia 1977. *DAI* 38:2130A.

LL225₂   Tran, Phiet Qui. "The French and Faulkner: The Reception
         of William Faulkner's Writing in France and Its Influence
         on Modern French Literature." Texas 1977. *DAI* 38:4162A.

LL226[2]   Wilson, G. Jennifer. "The Uncreating Word: Creators of
            Fiction in William Faulkner's Major Novels." California-
            Santa Barbara 1977. *DAI* 38:6719A.

LL227[2]   Wittenberg, Judith B. "Faulkner: The Transfiguration of
            Biography." Brown 1977.

LL228[2]   Arnold, Edwin T., III. "William Faulkner's *Mosquitoes*: An
            Introduction and Annotations to the Novel." South Carolina
            1978. *DAI* 39:6125A.

LL229[2]   Bosha, Francis J. "The Textual History and Definitive
            Textual Apparatus for *Soldiers' Pay*: A Bibliographic Study
            of William Faulkner's First Novel." Marquette 1978. *DAI*
            39:5509A.

LL230[2]   Cain, Kathleen S. "Beyond the Meaning of History: The
            Quest for a Southern Myth in Faulkner's Characters."
            Marquette 1978. *DAI* 39:5509A.

LL231[2]   Campbell, Charles L. "The House and the Outsider: Eight
            Studies in a Narrative Landscape." Toronto 1978. *DAI*
            39:2284A. Covers *Light in August*.

LL232[2]   Conley, Timothy K. "Shakespeare and Faulkner: A Study in
            Influence." Penn State 1978. *DAI* 39:4945A.

LL233[2]   Cooper, Gerald H. "Furious Motion: Metamorphosis and
            Change in the Works of William Faulkner." Washington
            Univ. [St. Louis] 1978. *DAI* 39:4946A.

LL234[2]   Dale, Corinne H. "The Lost Cause: Myth, Symbol, and
            Stereotype in Southern Fiction." Michigan 1978. *DAI*
            39:881A.

LL235[2]   Davis, David G. "The Image of the Minister in American
            Fiction." Tulsa 1978. *DAI* 39:882A. Covers *Light in August*.

LL236[2]   Dodds, John L. "The Fatal Arc: The Evolution of Tragic
            Image and Idea in Three Novels by William Faulkner."
            Loyola 1978. *DAI* 38:6722A.

LL237[2]   Donohoe, Eileen M. "Psychic Transformation Through
            Memory-Work and Negation in William Faulkner's
            Absalom, Absalom!" Notre Dame 1978. *DAI* 39:1546A.

LL238₂   Egolf, Robert H. "Faulkner's Men and Women: A Critical
         Study of Male-Female Relationships in His Early
         Yoknapatawpha County Novels." Lehigh 1978. *DAI*
         39:4946A.

LL239₂   Golden, Kenneth L. "The Problem of Opposites in Five
         Fictional Narratives: Jungian Psychology and Comparative
         Mythology in Modern Literature." Southern Mississippi
         1978. *DAI* 39:5502A. Covers *Absalom, Absalom!*

LL240₂   Greene, Robert I. "Innocence and Experience in Selected
         Major Fiction of William Faulkner." Indiana 1978. *DAI*
         40:852A.

LL241₂   Hayes, Elizabeth T. "Comedy in Faulkner's Fiction."
         Syracuse 1978. *DAI* 40:256A.

LL242₂   Haynes, Michael A. "The Unity of *Collected Stories of
         William Faulkner*." Ball State 1978. *DAI* 39:2938A.

LL243₂   Hernandez, Joan L. "The Influence of William Faulkner in
         Four Latin American Novelists: Yañez, García Márquez,
         Cepeda Samudio, Donoso." Louisiana State 1978. *DAI*
         39:6756A.

LL244₂   Hlavsa, Virginia V. "*Light in August*: Biblical Form and
         Mythic Function." SUNY-Stony Brook 1978. *DAI*
         39:6130A.

LL245₂   Kauffman, Linda S. "Psychic Displacement and Adaptation
         in the Novels of Dickens and Faulkner." California-Santa
         Barbara 1978. *DAI* 39:3573A.

LL246₂   Knutsen, Marla T. "The Power of Mr. Compson in
         Absalom, Absalom!: Heroism/Homoeroticism/Approach-
         Avoidance Toward Women." Southern California 1978. *DAI*
         41:668A.

LL247₂   Marshall, Emma Jo. "Scenes from Yoknapatawpha: A Study
         of People and Places in the Real and Imaginary Worlds of
         William Faulkner." Alabama 1978. *DAI* 39:2276A.

LL248₂   Moore, Robert R. "Faulkner's *Sanctuary*: Radical Evil and
         Religious Vision." Virginia 1978.

LL249₂ Neidhardt, Frances E. "Verbal-Visual Simultaneity in Faulkner's *The Sound and the Fury*: A Literary Montage Filmscript for Quentin." East Texas State 1978. *DAI* 39:1165A.

LL250₂ Romig, Evelyn M. "Women as Victims in the Novels of Charles Dickens and William Faulkner." Rice 1978. *DAI* 39:1600A.

LL251₂ Ruppersburg, Hugh M. "Narrative Mode in the Novels of William Faulkner." South Carolina 1978. *DAI* 39:1576A.

LL252₂ Sherrill, John B., Jr. "The Humanistic Implications of General Systems Theory." Texas 1978. *DAI* 39:4224A. Discusses *Sanctuary*.

LL253₂ Snell, Susan. "Phil Stone of Yoknapatawpha." North Carolina 1978. *DAI* 40:259A.

LL254₂ Twigg, Carol Ann. "The Social Role of Faulkner's Women: A Materialist Interpretation." SUNY-Buffalo 1978. *DAI* 39:1578A.

LL255₂ Urie, Margaret Ann. "The Problem of Evil: The Myth of Man's Fall and Redemption in the Works of William Faulkner." Nevada-Reno 1978. *DAI* 39:4943A.

LL256₂ Washburn, Delores C. "The 'Feeder' Motif in Selected Fiction of William Faulkner and Flannery O'Connor." Texas Tech 1978. *DAI* 40:861A.

LL257₂ Webking, Robert H. "Faulkner's Sartoris Family and the Problem of Human Freedom." Virginia 1978. *DAI* 40:1062A.

LL258₂ Weisenburger, Steven C. "Accelerated Grimace: American Fiction in the Age of Speed." Washington 1978. *DAI* 39:2945A. Covers *Sartoris* and *Pylon*.

LL259₂ Whatley, John T. "A Topographical Study of Thomas Hardy and William Faulkner." Yale 1978. *DAI* 39:2266A.

LL260₂ Yun, Chung-Hei Kim. "A Fable of the Invincible Dust: Faulkner's Vision of Man in *A Fable*." Syracuse 1978. *DAI* 40:261A.

LL261₂ Christensen, Peter G. "The Trilogy as Experimental Form: Faulkner's *Snopes Trilogy*, Dos Passos' *U.S.A.*, and Sartre's *Les Chemins de la liberte*." SUNY-Binghamton 1979. *DAI* 40:2045A.

LL262₂ Cobley, Evelyn M. "Repetition and Structure: A Study of William Faulkner and Claude Simon." British Columbia 1979. *DAI* 40:5851A.

LL263₂ Dasher, Thomas E. "An Index to the Characters in the Published and Unpublished Fiction of William Faulkner." South Carolina 1979. *DAI* 40:1466A.

LL264₂ Hayhoe, George F. "A Critical and Textual Study of William Faulkner's *Flags in the Dust*." South Carolina 1979. *DAI* 40:4036A.

LL265₂ Kreiswirth, Martin L. "The Making of a Novelist: William Faulkner's Career to the Writing of *The Sound and the Fury*." Toronto 1979. *DAI* 40:6280A.

LL266₂ Leach, George B., Jr. "Faulkner's Comic Optimism: Structure, Form, and Theme in Four Novels." Indiana 1979. *DAI* 40:5443.

LL267₂ Lucente, Gregory L. "Realism and Myth in Modern Narrative: Verga, Lawrence, Faulkner, Pavese." Wisconsin-Madison 1979. *DAI* 40:5043A. Covers *The Hamlet*.

LL268₂ Ludwig, Alvin K. "Lyric Form in the Modern Novel." California-Berkeley 1979. *DAI* 40:4028A. Covers *The Sound and the Fury*.

LL269₂ Lundin, Roger W. "Present Past: Hawthorne, Faulkner, and the Problem of History." Connecticut 1979. *DAI* 40:1469A.

LL270₂ McDonald, William J. "The Image of Adolescence in William Faulkner's Yoknapatawpha Fiction." Oregon 1979. *DAI* 40:5050A.

LL271₂ Milloy, Sandra D. "The Development of the Black Character in the Fiction of William Faulkner." Michigan 1979. *DAI* 40:856A.

LL272₂ Nitsaisook, Malee. "An Analysis of Certain Stylistic Features of Selected Literary Works and Their Relationship to Readability." Southern Illinois 1979. *DAI* 40:4453A.

LL273₂ Patton, Oscar, Jr. "The Dynamistic Vision: An Examination of Faulkner's Sense of Motion." Florida State 1979. *DAI* 40:5058A.

LL274₂ Plummer, William H., Jr. "Faulkner's Early Writing: The Discomfort of the Text." Rutgers 1979. *DAI* 40:4029A.

LL275₂ Pruit, Thomas B. "The Economy of Memory in Faulkner's Yoknapatawpha." Dallas 1979. *DAI* 40:2647A.

LL276₂ Sisney, Mary F. "Black Fiction, to Discriminate or Not to Discriminate. A Comparative and Rhetorical Study of *Native Son, Invisible Man, The Man Who Cried I Am, Intruder in the Dust*, and *The Confessions of Nat Turner.*" Southern California 1979. *DAI* 40:4045A.

LL277₂ Wagstaff, Barbara O. "The Struggle with the Angel: Identity and Sympathy in Thomas Mann's *Doktor Faustus*, André Malraux's *Les Noyers de L'Altenburg*, and William Faulkner's *A Fable.*" California-Berkeley 1979. *DAI* 41:248A.

LL278₂ Young, Eugene O. "Keepers of the Faith: Sports from the Wilderness to the Space Age in Selected Modern American Novels." Tennessee 1979. *DAI* 40:6276A. Covers "The Bear."

LL279₂ Ait Daraou, Ahmed. "The German Reception of William Faulkner: Books and Dissertations, 1950–1979." South Carolina 1980. *DAI* 41:1050A.

LL280₂ Bryant, Sheril M. "The Theme of Invisibility in *The Scarlet Letter, The Adventures of Huckleberry Finn, Light in August*, and *Invisible Man.*" SUNY-Buffalo 1980. *DAI* 41:3577A.

LL281₂ Cox, Dianne L. "William Faulkner's *As I Lay Dying*: A Critical and Textual Study." South Carolina 1980. *DAI* 42:1148A.

LL282₂ Dardis, Thomas A. "Some Time in the Sun: The Hollywood Years of Fitzgerald, Faulkner, Nathanael West, Aldous Huxley, James Agee." Columbia 1980. *DAI* 41:4392A.

LL283₂ Dimino, Andrea. "Creating Human Time: Faulkner's Temporal Strategies in *The Hamlet, Absalom, Absalom!*, and *The Bear.*" Yale 1980. *DAI* 41:5100A.

LL284₂ Di Virgilio, Paul S. "Study of Voice in the Modern Novel." Toronto 1980. *DAI* 41:2592A. Covers *As I Lay Dying*.

LL285₂ Egan, Philip J. "Versions of the Dramatic Monologue in American Novels." Kansas 1980. *DAI* 41:5101A.

LL286₂ Hollowell, Dorothy M. "A Study of Conrad and Faulkner: Links to Imperialism." Tufts 1980. *DAI* 41:1054A.

LL287₂ Lee, William L. "Interpreting Insane Characters in *King Lear*, *The Duchess of Malfi*, *Rasselas*, *Maud*, and *As I Lay Dying*: Toward a Theory (Volumes I and II)." Yale 1980. *DAI* 41:2094A.

LL288₂ Morrison, Gail M. "William Faulkner's *The Sound and the Fury*: A Critical and Textual Study (Volumes I and II)." South Carolina 1980. *DAI* 41:3583A.

LL289₂ Paddock, Lisa O. "Contrapuntal Integration: A Study of Three Faulkner Short Story Volumes." Toronto 1980. *DAI* 41:674A.

LL290₂ Parker, Robert D. "Faulkner and the Novelistic Imagination." Yale 1980. *DAI* 42:698A.

LL291₂ Parks, Kae I. "Faulkner's Women: Archetype and Metaphor." Pennsylvania 1980. *DAI* 41:1054A.

LL292₂ Ramos-Escobar, Jose L. "From Yoknapatawpha to Macondo: A Comparative Study of William Faulkner and Gabriel García Márquez." Brown 1980. *DAI* 41:5092A.

LL293₂ Rifkin, Ellen R. "*Absalom, Absalom!* and the Curse of Inherited Fictions: Wherein a Student of Faulkner Reclaims Her Education and Requests Title to the Deed." California-Santa Cruz 1980. *DAI* 41:2113A.

LL294₂ Stroble, Woodrow L. "They Prevail: A Study of Faulkner's Passive Suicides." SUNY-Binghamton 1980. *DAI* 41:255A.

LL295₂ Thompson, Deborah Ann. "In Celebration of Outrage: William Faulkner and the Tragic Vision." Oregon 1980. *DAI* 41:3586A.

LL296₂ Turnbull, Patricia Ann. "Creating a Fictive Past." Columbia 1980. *DAI* 41:3111A.

LL297₂ Warne, Keith F. "Language in Faulkner's Trilogy: Truth and Fiction." Western Ontario 1980. *DAI* 41:5099A.

LL298₂   Bomze, Jo Ann W. "The Thematic and Structural Design of William Faulkner's *Collected Stories*." Pennsylvania 1981. *DAI* 42:4825A.

LL299₂   Burke, Maxine E. "James Joyce and His Influences: William Faulkner and Anthony Burgess." Drake 1981. *DAI* 42:4818A.

LL300₂   Corrick, James A., III. "Thematic Patterning as a Structural Device in William Faulkner's *Go Down, Moses*." Arizona 1981. *DAI* 42:1633A.

LL301₂   Dodson, Diane M. "A Theory of Tragedy." North Texas State 1981. *DAI* 42:1136A. Discusses *Absalom, Absalom!*

LL302₂   Douglass, Malcolm P., Jr. "In and Out of Time: Eliot, Faulkner, and the Legacy of Bergson." UCLA 1981. *DAI* 42:3599A.

LL303₂   Feldman, Leonard M. "A Matter of Money: Money and the World of the American Novel, 1893–1940." UCLA 1981. *DAI* 42:3599A. Discusses *The Hamlet*.

LL304₂   Foster, Thomas C. "What Will Suffice: Culture, History, and Form in Modern Literature." Michigan State 1981. *DAI* 42:2670A. Discusses *Go Down, Moses*.

LL305₂   Haselswerdt, Marjorie B. "On Their Hind Legs Casting Shadows: A Psychological Approach to Character in Faulkner." Michigan State 1981. *DAI* 42:1149A.

LL306₂   Hindin, Beverly N. "Death and the Imaginative Vision of Modern and Post-Modern American Fiction." Pennsylvania 1981. *DAI* 42:2676A. Discusses *The Sound and the Fury*.

LL307₂   Hutchinson, Kathryn L. "Companionship in William Faulkner's *A Fable*." Florida 1981. *DAI* 42:2132A.

LL308₂   Jones, Virginia M. "The Grotesque as Satiric Device in Modern and Contemporary Southern Literature." Georgia State 1981. *DAI* 42:3601A.

LL309₂   Kim, Wook-Dong. "The Edge of Nothing: An Existential Reading of William Faulkner." SUNY-Buffalo 1981. *DAI* 42:5117A.

LL310₂   Lowe, John W. "The Biblical Imagination and American Genius: Repetitive Patterns of Hebraic Myth in Faulkner's *Light in August*." Columbia 1981. *DAI* 42:4001A.

LL311₂   Magistrale, Anthony S. "The Quest for Identity in Modern
         Southern Fiction: Faulkner, Wright, O'Connor, Warren."
         Pittsburgh 1981. *DAI* 42:4001A.

LL312₂   Robinson, David B. "Creating the Past Anew: The Varieties
         of American Historical Fiction." Ohio State 1981. *DAI*
         42:4451A.

LL313₂   Smith, Gary. "William Faulkner and the Adamic Myth."
         Stanford 1981. *DAI* 42:3603A.

LL314₂   Trouard, Dawn. "A Morbidity of the Mind: A Study of
         Psychopathological Rhetoric in William Faulkner's Fiction."
         Rice 1981. *DAI* 42:707A.

LL315₂   Yonke, Jean M. "William Faulkner as a Moralist and
         Cultural Critic: A Comparison of His Views with Those of
         Historians and Social Scientists." Kansas 1981. *DAI*
         42:3160A.

MM.   British Theses and Dissertations[1]

MM1₂   Boecker, E. "William Faulkner's Later Novels in German: A
       Study in the Theory and Practice of Translation." Ph.D.
       Southampton 1971.

MM2₂   Baines, J. M. "The Critical Search for William Faulkner—A
       Study of Five Novels." M. A. Durham 1973.

MM3₂   Cox, R. A. "William Faulkner's Saga of Yoknapatawpha: A
       Cosmos in Miniature." Ph. D. Leeds 1973.

MM4₂   Quammen, D. "Structural Patterns in William Faulkner's
       Major Novels." B. Litt. Oxford 1973.

MM5₂   Healey, C. W. "Writers Against Society: Aspects of
       Modernism in Some Novels by Conrad, Lawrence and
       Faulkner." M. Litt. Stirling 1974.

MM6₂   Pikoulis, J. "The Waiting Past: A Critical Reassessment of
       William Faulkner." Ph. D. Wales-Cardiff 1974.

[1]Compiled from issues of Aslib. *Index to Theses Accepted for Higher Degrees in the Universities of Great Britain and Ireland.*

MM7$_2$ Gidley, M. "The Quality of William Faulkner's Intellectuality: Studies in His Extra-Literary Reading, Conceptual Thinking, and Relevant Critical Scholarship." D. Phil. Sussex 1975.

MM8$_2$ Tallack, D. "Fiction as Process: An Approach to William Faulkner's *Go Down, Moses* from the Reading Situation." M. A. Sussex 1975.

MM9$_2$ Jenkins, M. E. "The Role of the Negro in the Modern American Novel, with Special Reference to William Faulkner." M. A. Wales 1977.

Additional Items

This section includes criticism published in 1982 plus a few earlier items located after the main part of the typescript had been submitted. The 1982 listings, of course, are far from complete; one book missing is Tetsumaro Hayashi's *William Faulkner: Research Opportunities and Dissertation Abstracts* (Jefferson, N.C.: McFarland). In the first few months of 1983, moreover, several critical books on Faulkner have appeared—Eric Sundquist, *Faulkner: The House Divided* (Johns Hopkins Univ. Press); Walter Taylor, *Faulkner's Search for a South* (Univ. of Illinois Press); Hugh M. Ruppersburg, *Voice and Eye in Faulkner's Fiction* (Univ. of Georgia Press); Dirk Kuyk, Jr., *Threads Cable-Strong: William Faulkner's* Go Down, Moses (Bucknell Univ. Press); and Thadious M. Davis, *Faulkner's "Negro": Art and the Southern Context* (Louisiana State Univ. Press). UMI Research Press in Ann Arbor is publishing in 1983 four books, drawn from earlier dissertations—Keen Butterworth, *A Critical and Textual Study of Faulkner's* A Fable; Doreen Fowler, *Faulkner's Changing Vision: From Outrage to Affirmation*; Jessie A. Coffee, *Faulkner's Un-Christlike Christians: Biblical Allusions in the Novels*; and Jan M. Serafin, *Faulkner's Use of the Classics*. Garland Publishing is bringing out two new casebooks—Elizabeth Muhlenfeld, ed., *William Faulkner's* Absalom, Absalom!: *A Critical Casebook*; and Dianne L. Cox, ed., *William Faulkner's* As I Lay Dying: *A Critical Casebook*. Ben Wasson's memoir, *Count No' Count: Flashbacks to Faulkner* (Univ. Press of Mississippi), is also due; and by the end of 1983 at least a dozen books and scores of articles will have been added to the archives of Faulkner scholarship.

I. Books on Faulkner

A79₂   Bleikasten, André. *William Faulkner's* The Sound and the Fury: *A Critical Casebook*. New York: Garland, 1982.

> Collection of articles by Morrison (E114₂), Cecil (E154), Pitavy (E115₂), Ross (E38₂), Aswell (E131), Blanchard (E148), Chappell (E67₂), and Gross (E136), plus a collection of comments by Faulkner, a bibliography, and an introduction by Bleikasten.

A80₂   Bosha, Francis J. *Faulkner's* Soldiers' Pay: *A Bibliographic Study*. Troy, N.Y.: Whitston, 1982.

> Studies the textual history of the novel and the process of its composition, and tries to establish a definitive text.

A81$_2$ Brodsky, Louis D., and Robert W. Hamblin. *Faulkner: A Comprehensive Guide to the Brodsky Collection. Volume One: The Biobibliography.* Jackson: Univ. Press of Mississippi, 1982.

The Brodsky collection is catalogued to provide a chronological record of Faulkner's life and career.

A82$_2$ Cox, Leland H., ed. *William Faulkner: Biographical and Reference Guide.* Gale Author Handbook 1. Detroit: Gale Research, 1982.

Includes short critical introductions (not cross-listed below) to the novels and short stories, plus a 90-page biography.

A83$_2$ Cox, Leland H., ed. *William Faulkner: Critical Collection.* Gale Author Handbook 2. Detroit: Gale Research, 1982.

A collection of articles by Adams (BB61), Millgate (B2$_2$, from A44, AA152$_2$), Hayhoe (D25$_2$), Vickery (from A63), Bedient (F69), Pitavy (H145), Muhlenfeld (J162), McHaney (L4$_2$), Broughton (M93), Gold (M83), Arpad (U24), Thornton (N35$_2$), Polk (Q7$_2$), Hunt (from A28), Beck (AA29), Brooks (AA15$_2$), Flint (CC18), and Meriwether (GG75$_2$), plus a set of pieces by Faulkner ("Mississippi," "On Privacy," an interview, and several shorter statements) and a selective checklist of criticism.

A84$_2$ Fowler, Doreen, and Ann J. Abadie, eds. *Faulkner and the Southern Renaissance.* Jackson: Univ. Press of Mississippi, 1982.

Papers from the 1981 conference by King (AA225$_2$, AA231$_2$), Brooks (AA226$_2$, AA235$_2$), Watkins (AA227$_2$, AA229$_2$), Rubin (AA228$_2$), Spencer (AA230$_2$), Blackburn (AA232$_2$), Minter (AA233$_2$, AA234$_2$), and Samway (X162$_2$), with an introduction by Fowler.

A85$_2$ Kawin, Bruce, ed. *Faulkner's MGM Screenplays.* Knoxville: Univ. of Tennessee Press, 1982.

Includes an introduction to and commentaries on the screenplays Faulkner wrote for MGM in 1932-33.

A86$_2$ Kinney, Arthur F., ed. *Critical Essays on William Faulkner: The Compson Family.* Boston: G. K. Hall, 1982.

A research collection that includes an introduction by Kinney; comments by Faulkner on the Compsons plus early prose pieces that anticipate situations in the Compson story; reviews; selections from critical analyses; and several articles. The articles include studies by Coindreau (E37), Brooks (from A5), Absalom (E109), Millgate (from A44), Gresset (E113), Peavy (E111), Baum (E120), Hagopian (E121), Aswell (E131), Benson (E4$_2$), Geffen (E30$_2$), Dickerson (E37$_2$), Bleikasten (from A8$_2$), M. C. Brown (X63$_2$), Kinney (from A54$_2$), Young (J82$_2$), Cheuse (E99$_2$), Hunt (E116$_2$), Kartiganer (E117$_2$), Williams (E118$_2$), and Bassett (E102$_2$).

A87₂   Matthews, John T. *The Play of Faulkner's Language.*
         Ithaca, N.Y.: Cornell Univ. Press, 1982.

> Through detailed readings of four novels, Matthews analyzes Faulkner's
> preoccupation with problems of language and representation. Using
> Derrida's model of "différance" and "supplement," he explores the
> relationship between writing and loss, the ways in which language
> produces ideas and meaning, and Faulkner's attraction to the playfulness
> of writing in the space between the written and the written about.

A88₂   Pikoulis, John. *The Art of William Faulkner.* Totowa, N.J.:
         Barnes and Noble, 1982.

> Analyzes relationships between Faulkner's varied narrative techniques
> and his complex personal involvement with his own region. The novels
> show the influence of a strong tradition of rhetoric on a "private
> sensibility in acute but fertile disarray." Pikoulis rates *The Hamlet* and
> *The Unvanquished* highly, and neglects *As I Lay Dying* and *Light in
> August* as less than major works.

A89₂   Pitavy, François L. *William Faulkner's* Light in August*: A
         Critical Casebook.* New York: Garland, 1982.

> Collection of articles by Hirshleifer (H75), Benson (H83), Burroughs
> (H18₂), Collins (H22₂), Kartiganer (from A58₂), Abel (H86), Korenman
> (AA62₂), Jenkins (from A72₂), Morrison (H102), Pitavy (from A13₂),
> and Taylor (H66₂), "The Chronology of *Light in August*" by Stephen
> Meats, plus an introduction by Pitavy and a bibliography.

A90₂   Skei, Hans H. *William Faulkner: The Short Story Career.*
         Oslo: Universitetsforlaget, 1982.

> A chronological survey of Faulkner's stories in terms of marketing,
> themes, and re-use in novels.

II. Studies of Individual Novels

B. *Soldiers' Pay*

—   Bosha, Francis J. *Faulkner's* Soldiers' Pay*: A Bibliographic
         Study* (A80₂; 1982).

C. *Mosquitoes*

C7₂   Lind, Ilse Dusoir. "Faulkner's *Mosquitoes*: A New Reading."
         William Faulkner: Materials, Studies, and Criticism, 4, No.
         2 (July 1982), 1–18.

> The artistry of the novel can be understood only through its
> architectonics. Faulkner develops an "intricately interlocked, tripartite
> structural theme" around problems of time, perspective, and the artist.

— Matthews, John T. *The Play of Faulkner's Language* (A87$_2$; 1982), pp. 45–50.

— Pikoulis, John. *The Art of William Faulkner* (A88$_2$; 1982), pp. 11–16.

D. *Sartoris* and *Flags in the Dust*

— Matthews, John T. *The Play of Faulkner's Language* (A87$_2$; 1982), pp. 50–62.

— Pikoulis, John. *The Art of William Faulkner* (A88$_2$; 1982), pp. 1–10.

D45$_2$ Blair, Arthur H. "Bayard Sartoris: Suicidal or Foolhardy?" *Southern Literary Journal*, 15, No. 1 (Fall 1982), 55–60.
> An addition to the manuscript before publication made Bayard "more headstrong than suicidal."

E. *The Sound and the Fury*

E110$_2$ Morozova, Tatiana. "Faulkner Reads Dostoevsky." *Soviet Literature*, 1981, pp. 176–79.

E111$_2$ Buchanan, Harriette C. "Caddy Compson as the South in the 1920s." *Publications of the Missouri Philological Association*, 6 (1981), 10–13.

E112$_2$ Wagner, Linda W. "Language and Act: Caddy Compson." *Southern Literary Journal*, 14, No. 2 (Spring 1982), 49–61.
> Emphasizes Faulkner's technique in creating Caddy and her role as "language-creator and giver."

E113$_2$ Sasamoto, Seiji. "The First Section of *The Sound and the Fury*: Benjy and His Expressions." *William Faulkner: Materials, Studies, and Criticism*, 4, No. 2 (July 1982), 19–36.
> Closely studies the kinds of words Faulkner does and does not use in Benjy's section. For example, he does not use verbs that indicate thought processes or conjunctions that indicate reason, condition, or concession.

— Bleikasten, André. *William Faulkner's* The Sound and the Fury: *A Critical Casebook* (A79$_2$; 1982).

E114$_2$ Morrison, Gail M. "The Composition of *The Sound and the Fury*." In A79$_2$ (1982), pp. 33–64.

E115$_2$ Pitavy, François L. "Through the Poet's Eye: A View of Quentin Compson." In A79$_2$ (1982), pp. 79–100.

—   Kinney, Arthur F., ed. *Critical Essays on William Faulkner: The Compson Family* (A86$_2$; 1982).

E116$_2$ Hunt, John W. "The Disappearance of Quentin Compson." In A86$_2$ (1982), pp. 366–80.

> Studies the "pattern of Quentin's entrances into and exits from" Faulkner's fiction between 1928 and 1946, Faulkner's decisions to use him or to substitute another character for him.

E117$_2$ Kartiganer, Donald M. "Quentin Compson and Faulkner's Drama of the Generations." In A86$_2$ (1982), pp. 381–401.

> Analyzes generational relationships in Faulkner's fiction with special attention to the two novels about Quentin.

E118$_2$ Williams, Joan. "In Defense of Caroline Compson." In A86$_2$ (1982), pp. 402–07.

> Questions the validity of a totally negative view of Mrs. Compson.

—   Matthews, John T. "The Discovery of Loss in *The Sound and the Fury*." In *The Play of Faulkner's Language* (A87$_2$; 1982), pp. 63–114.

> In the novel loss is connected to writing and speech. Each narrator, in his own way, sees language and articulation as a means to "reappropriate what has been lost."

—   Pikoulis, John. "The Compson Devilment." In *The Art of William Faulkner* (A88$_2$; 1982), pp. 18–47.

> The novel displays a tension between its poetic resources (image) and novelistic resourcefulness (stories of characters); their interplay is the key to Faulkner's strength. Through metaphors of madness, death, bondage, and order the situations of the three brothers suggest Faulkner's complicated frame of mind in the late 1920s.

E119$_2$ Meriwether, James B. "The Old Roman and His Vase." *Faulkner Newsletter*, October–December 1982, pp. 2, 4.

> A possible allusion to *Quo Vadis*.

F.   *As I Lay Dying*

F58$_2$ McCarthy, Paul. "Several Words, Shapes and Attitudes in *As I Lay Dying*." *Notes on Mississippi Writers*, 14, No. 1 (1982), 27–38.

> The words "straight," "circles," and "angles" in the second paragraph of the novel indicate basic themes and attitudes important later in the book.

F59₂   Kloss, Robert J. "Faulkner's *As I Lay Dying.*" *American Imago,* 38 (Winter 1981), 429–44.

> A psychoanalytic study of Addie's sons, their obsession with their relationship to her and lack of interest in other women, and Addie's own incestuous fantasy.

F60₂   Pitavy, François L. "Through Darl's Eyes Darkly: The Vision of the Poet in *As I Lay Dying.*" *William Faulkner: Materials, Studies, and Criticism,* 4, No. 2 (July 1982), 37–62.

> Faulkner develops not a conventional interior monologue but a distinctive kind of "narrative monologue which gives the story its remarkable diegetic coherence." Darl is "a double of the author" who can establish a "narrative predominance" as "the great magician of the show." His searching insight and apocalyptic sense transcend the other narrative perspectives.

F61₂   Allen, William Rodney. "The Imagist and Symbolist Views of the Function of Language: Addie and Darl in *As I Lay Dying.*" *Studies in American Fiction,* 10 (Autumn 1982), 185–96.

> Through Addie and Darl respectively, Faulkner explores the differences between the Imagists' and the Symbolists' attitudes toward language.

G. *Sanctuary*

G33₂   Fletcher, John. "Faulkner, *Gulliver,* and the Problem of Evil." In *Orion Blinded: Essays on Claude Simon.* Ed. R. Birn et al. Lewisburg, Pa.: Bucknell Univ. Press, 1981, pp. 239–47.

G34₂   Ono, Kiyoyuki. "Sanctuary of the Heart—An Interpretation of *Sanctuary.*" *William Faulkner: Materials, Studies, and Criticism,* 4, No. 2 (July 1982), 63–78.

> Explores "the sanctuary of Horace's heart and the development of his feelings through three major revisions of the text ... to discover the reality of the Southern society in which Horace is deeply rooted."

G35₂   Lyday, Lance. "*Sanctuary*: Faulkner's *Inferno.*" *Mississippi Quarterly,* 35 (Summer 1982), 243–53.

> Studies influences on and parallels with Dante's *Inferno.*

—   Pikoulis, John. "That Time and That Wilderness." In *The Art of William Faulkner* (A88₂; 1982), pp. 58–65.

> Although a darkly personal book for Faulkner, it is also a parable of man's submission to the machine, of the final collapse of the Old South. Popeye and Temple are the thematic center, "answering extremes of the South's behavior."

H. *Light in August*

H76[2] Palumbo, Donald. "Coincidence in *Crime and Punishment* and *Light in August*: Evidence of Supernatural Agents at Work in the Novels of Dostoyevsky and Faulkner." *Lamar Journal of the Humanities*, 7, No. 1 (Spring 1982), 41–51.

— Pitavy, François L. *William Faulkner's* Light in August*: A Critical Casebook* (A89[2]; 1982).

H77[2] Halden, Judith. "Sexual Ambiguities in *Light in August*." *Studies in American Fiction*, 10 (Autumn 1982), 209–16.
Notes on imagery and theme in the affair between Joe and Joanna.

H78[2] Milum, Richard A. "Faulkner and the Comic Perspective of Frederick Burr Opper." *Journal of Popular Culture*, 16, No. 3 (Winter 1982), 139–50.
On the reference to Alphonse and Gaston in the final chapter.

J. *Absalom, Absalom!*

J117[2] Pearce, Richard. "Enter the Frame." In *Surfiction: Fiction Now ... and Tomorrow*. Ed. R. Federman. Chicago: Swallow, 1981, pp. 47–57.
Compares the narrative method with that in Beckett's *Molloy*.

J118[2] Landor, Mikhail. "*Absalom, Absalom!* in Russian." *Soviet Literature*, 1981, pp. 164–72.
On the Russian translation and its reception in the U.S.S.R.

J119[2] Schmidtberger, Loren F. "*Absalom, Absalom!*: What Clytie Knew." *Mississippi Quarterly*, 35 (Summer 1982), 255–63.
Analyzes what Clytie does and does not know: she knows Bon was Judith's half-brother, but she may not know of Bon's mixed racial background.

J120[2] LaRocque, Geraldine E. "*A Tale of Two Cities* and *Absalom, Absalom!*" *Mississippi Quarterly*, 35 (Summer 1982), 302–04.
Possible influence on several passages.

— Matthews, John T. "Marriages of Speaking and Hearing in *Absalom, Absalom!*" In *The Play of Faulkner's Language* (A87[2]; 1982), pp. 115–61.
An expanded version of J101[2] (1980), this analyzes the novel's concern with meaning as an infinite play of signifiers not the establishment of a single signified. Narration—speaking and hearing—is defined in terms of conjugal and sexual language, and loss. The desire for an absent beloved is related to the narrator's desire for the thing represented.

— Pikoulis, John. "Innocence and History." In *The Art of William Faulkner* (A88₂; 1982), pp. 66–111.

Relates the intricate narrative pattern to the conflict between innocence and history that characterizes Sutpen's story. Even though each narrator projects himself into his creation to achieve his own ends, the characters are used by the author in such ways as to blur their outlines as realistic individuals.

J121₂ Zamora, Lois Parkinson. "The End of Innocence: Myth and Narrative Structure in Faulkner's *Absalom, Absalom!* and García Márquez' *Cien Anos de Soledad*." *Hispanic Journal*, 4, No. 1 (Fall 1982), 23–40.

K. *The Unvanquished*

— Pikoulis, John. "The Sartoris War." In *The Art of William Faulkner* (A88₂; 1982), pp. 112–36.

Argues that the book is a "masterpiece of implication, . . . the nearest that Faulkner came to writing a novel of sustained and subtle moral inquiry."

L. *The Wild Palms*

L19₂ Merton, Thomas. "Faulkner Meditations: *The Wild Palms*." In *The Literary Essays of Thomas Merton*. Ed. Brother Patrick Hart. New York: New Directions, 1981, pp. 515–36.

L20₂ Fowler, Doreen A. "Measuring Faulkner's Tall Convict." *Studies in the Novel*, 14 (Fall 1982), 280–84.

The convict sacrifices freedom for order and responsibility, values set in opposition to the love and freedom in Charlotte's story.

M. *The Hamlet*

M25₂ Eddins, Dwight. "Metahumor in Faulkner's 'Spotted Horses.'" *Ariel*, 13, No. 1 (January 1982), 23–31.

Not only is humor a technique in the story, but its role in human life is a theme in the story.

— Matthews, John T. "*The Hamlet*: Rites of Play." In *The Play of Faulkner's Language* (A87₂; 1982), pp. 162–211.

Games and play, Faulkner indicates, arise from the absence of a clear center or authority or origin. Speaking and economic exchange are analogous systems of play. The novel suggests there are no intrinsic values before the development of a system of economic articulation to order values.

—   Pikoulis, John. "The Lost Domain." In *The Art of William Faulkner* (A88$_2$; 1982), pp. 137–91.

Through a highly expressive use of the tall tale and conventions of humor and romance, Faulkner profoundly explores incongruities between antebellum myths and the South's imminent future. Eula and Flem represent contrasting versions of the community's fate, and modes of humor indicated by Eula (celebratory) and Ratliff (temperate) govern the book's comic structure.

N.   *Go Down, Moses*

N78$_2$ Ford, Daniel G. "'The Bear': Faulkner's Tale of Two Worlds." *Publications of the Arkansas Philological Association*, 7, No. 1 (Spring 1981), 18–22.

N79$_2$ Scharr, John H. "Community or Contract? William Faulkner and the Dual Legacy." In *The Problem of Authority in America*. Philadelphia: Temple Univ. Press, 1981, pp. 93–111.

N80$_2$ Schleifer, Ronald. "Faulkner's Storied Novel: *Go Down, Moses* and the Translation of Time." *Modern Fiction Studies*, 28 (Spring 1982), 109–27.

Through discussion of the theme of fatherhood, the ritual of the hunt, and the function of time, this argues that the book is primarily concerned with man's possession of his past, "with time and events in time as objects of possession."

—   Matthews, John T. "The Ritual of Mourning in *Go Down, Moses*." In *The Play of Faulkner's Language* (A87$_2$; 1982), pp. 212–73.

The novel dwells on the process of loss, by relating loss of wives to the disappearance of the wilderness. A rhetoric of grief and related metaphors provide a problematic unity for the book, which also balances comic behavior in domestic spaces with solemn retreats into the wilderness.

—   Pikoulis, John. "The Keatsian Moment." *The Art of William Faulkner* (A88$_2$; 1982), pp. 192–226.

The novel revolves around the debate between nature and civilization in the South, the feasibility of restoring a balance, and the threat change and linear time pose for "the South."

R. *A Fable*

R17₂   Pladott, Dinnah. "Faulkner's *A Fable*: A Heresy or a
         Declaration of Faith?" *Journal of Narrative Technique*, 12
         (Spring 1982), 73–94.

> Connections between this novel and Faulkner's other fiction can best be
> traced by studying the paradigm of sacrifice. Faulkner suggests that
> sacrifice is regenerative "only in action of self-sacrificial nature."

U. *The Snopes Trilogy*

U23₂   Burelbach, Frederick M. "The Name of the Snake: A Family
         of Snopes." *Literary Onomastic Studies*, 8 (1981), 125–46.

U24₂   Renner, Charlotte. "Talking and Writing in Faulkner's
         Snopes Trilogy." *Southern Literary Journal*, 15, No. 1 (Fall
         1982), 61–73.

> Explains the function of narrative technique—particularly the choral
> narrator in *The Mansion* and the multiple voices in *The Town*—in
> relation to thematic patterns and Faulkner's sense of the relationship
> between history and fiction.

U25₂   Lindberg, Gary. "Diddling on a Large Scale: Robber
         Barons, Snopeses, and V. K. Ratliff." In *The Confidence
         Man in American Literature*. New York: Oxford Univ.
         Press, 1982, pp. 203–28.

> Connects Snopesism, Snopes watching, and Ratliff to patterns of
> collusion, duplicity, and social criticism in American culture; compares
> robber barons with Snopeses, muckraking and Huck Finn with Ratliff.

III. Studies of Short Stories, Poetry, and Miscellaneous Writings

X. *Critical Commentary*

"Barn Burning"

X155₂   Fowler, Virginia C. "Faulkner's 'Barn Burning': Sarty's
         Conflict Reconsidered." *College Language Association
         Journal*, 24 (June 1981), 513–21.

> Sarty's conflict is not simply between the values of his father and those
> of de Spain; his actions at the end grow out of "his own innate moral
> vision."

X156₂   Comprone, Joseph. "Literature and the Writing Process: A
         Pedagogical Reading of William Faulkner's 'Barn Burning.'"
         College Literature, 9, No. 2 (Winter 1982), 1–21.

"Golden Land"

X157₂   Winchell, Mark Royden. "William Faulkner's 'Golden Land':
Some Time in Hell." *Notes on Mississippi Writers*, 14, No. 1
(1981), 12–17.

> Faulkner's Hollywood is a "reverse Eden" that affords "no escape from
> itself."

"A Rose for Emily"

X158₂   Jacobs, John T. "Ironic Allusions in 'A Rose for Emily.'"
Notes on Mississippi Writers, 14, No. 2 (1982), 77–79.

> The name "Homer Barron" is suggestive.

X159₂   Littler, Frank A. "The Tangled Thread of Time: Faulkner's
'A Rose for Emily.'" *Notes on Mississippi Writers*, 14, No. 2
(1982), 80–86.

> Connects the title, the narrative method, and the theme of time.

X160₂   McLendon, Carmen Chaves. "A Rose for Rosalina: From
Yoknapatawpha to Ópera Dos Mortos." *Comparative
Literature Studies*, 19 (Winter 1982), 450–58.

> Compares Faulkner's story with a story by Autran Dourado.

General Commentary on Short Stories

—   Skei, Hans H. *William Faulkner: The Short Story Career*
(A90₂; 1982).

Commentary on Poetry and Miscellaneous Writings

X161₂   Champlin, Charles. "Faulkner: Poet of Love, Death." *Los
Angeles Times*, January 15, 1982, Part 5, p. 12.

> A review of *Helen: A Courtship* and *Mississippi Poems*.

X162₂   Samway, Patrick, S.J. "Faulkner's Poetic Vision." In A84₂
(1982), pp. 204–44.

> Surveys Faulkner's poetry—its sources, forms, and themes such as the
> returning soldier, the loss of the young woman, the acceptance of death.

X163₂   Dalgarno, Emily. "Faulkner's Pierrot." *Notes on Mississippi
Writers*, 14, No. 2 (1982), 73–76.

> Contrasts Faulkner's use of Pierrot with that by T. S. Eliot and others.

X164₂   Meriwether, James B., ed. "Pierrot, Sitting Beside the Body
of Colombine, Suddenly Sees Himself in a Mirror."
Mississippi Quarterly, 35 (Summer 1982), 305–08.

> A poem written around 1921 by Faulkner.

X165₂   Blotner, Joseph, ed. "Faulkner's Speech at Nagano, August
5, 1955." *Mississippi Quarterly*, 35 (Summer 1982), 309–11.

> A previously unpublished speech.

X166₂   Brodsky, Louis D. "William Faulkner: Poet at Large."
          Southern Review, 18 (October 1982), 767–75.
          Studies the genesis of *The Marble Faun* and other early poems, for
          example "Pregnancy," sent to Mrs. Homer Jones in 1924.

IV. Topical Studies

AA. General Studies

AA216₂   Brown, Calvin S. "Faulkner's Fist-Fights." *William
          Faulkner: Materials, Studies, and Criticism*, 2, No. 1 (July
          1979), 1–7.

AA217₂   Ohashi, Kenzaburo. "Creation Through Repetition or Self-
          Parody: Some Notes on Faulkner's Imaginative Process."
          William Faulkner: Materials, Studies, and Criticism, 2, No.
          2 (December 1979), 34–47.

AA218₂   Lubarsky, Jared. "The Highest Freedom: A Reconsideration
          of Faulkner on Race." *William Faulkner: Materials, Studies,
          and Criticism*, 3, No. 2 (April 1981), 9–17.

AA219₂   Watson, James G. "Literary Self-Criticism: Faulkner on
          Fiction." *Southern Quarterly*, 20, No. 1 (Fall 1981), 46–63.
          Emphasizes *Mayday* and *The Sound and the Fury.*

AA220₂   Hinkle, James. "What to Call Faulkner's Characters."
          William Faulkner: Materials, Studies, and Criticism, 3, No.
          2 (April 1981), 18–30.
          On the names of characters.

AA221₂   Izubuchi, Hiroshi. "Faulkner and Yeats: An Essay." *William
          Faulkner: Materials, Studies, and Criticism*, 4, No. 1
          (December 1981), 1–16.
          In Japanese, with an English summary.

AA222₂   Tanimura, Junjiro. "Yeoman Farmers and Their Role in
          Faulkner's Literature." *William Faulkner: Materials, Studies,
          and Criticism*, 4, No. 1 (December 1981), 17–33.
          In Japanese with an English summary.

AA223₂   Brown, Calvin S. "Supplemental Faulkner Glossary 2."
          William Faulkner: Materials, Studies, and Criticism, 4, No.
          1 (December 1981), 34–42.

AA224₂   Martin, Jay. "'The Whole Burden of Man's History of His
          Impossible Heart's Desire': The Early Life of William
          Faulkner." *American Literature*, 53 (January 1982), 607–29.
          A psychoanalytic study of Faulkner's early career revolving around his
          relationship with his mother, Estelle Oldham's departure, and Faulkner's
          creation of a public persona to divert attention from his private self.

AA225₂   King, Richard H. "Framework of a Renaissance." In A84₂
          (1982), pp. 3–21.
          Reconsiders the blossoming of Southern writing in the 1930s, the
          subsequent notion that this was a regional renaissance, and Faulkner's
          position within this development.

AA226₂   Brooks, Cleanth. "Faulkner and the Fugitive-Agrarians." In
          A84₂ (1982), pp. 22–39.
          Assesses parallels between Faulkner and the Nashville group, especially
          in relation to their treatment of the South, and documents the apprecia-
          tion of and insight into Faulkner's work by the Fugitive-Agrarians.

AA227₂   Watkins, Floyd C. "What Stand Did Faulkner Take?" In
          A84₂ (1982), pp. 40–62.
          Criticizes misguided interpretations of Faulkner; argues that although he
          took a stand for basic values, only in weaker novels did he become
          didactic; and suggests that his major themes are individualism, love,
          privacy, and man's desire for some kind of immortality or eternal
          identity.

AA228₂   Rubin, Louis D., Jr. "The Dixie Special: William Faulkner
          and the Southern Literary Renascence." In A84₂ (1982), pp.
          63–92.
          Connects Faulkner with his contemporaries in terms of their distrust of
          abstractions, their use of the dichotomy between thinking and feeling,
          and their ambivalent attitude toward their region.

AA229₂   Watkins, Floyd C. "The Hound Under the Wagon: Faulkner
          and the Southern Literati." In A84₂ (1982), pp. 93–119.
          Surveys Faulkner's personal relationships with Southern writers over his
          life, and shows that he was never part of a Southern literary circle.

AA230₂   Spencer, Elizabeth. "Emerging as a Writer in Faulkner's
          Mississippi." In A84₂ (1982), pp. 120–37.
          Discusses the impact of reading Faulkner in the 1940s, and raises
          questions about nihilism, women characters, and Snopeses in Faulkner's
          fiction.

AA231₂   King, Richard H. "Memory and Tradition." In A84₂ (1982),
          pp. 138–57.

Relates Faulkner to Freud and Nietzsche in terms of their "modernist" obsession with memory, historical consciousness, and cultural tradition; emphasizes Ike McCaslin's tragic dilemma in "The Bear"—his lack of any meaningful context for crucial action.

AA232₂   Blackburn, Alexander. "Faulkner and Continuance of the Southern Renaissance." In A84₂ (1982), pp. 158-81.

Ties Faulkner to a later generation of Southern writers, including Styron, and back to a long tradition of verse drama. The younger writers were influenced by but distanced from Faulkner.

AA233₂   Minter, David. "Family, Region, and Myth in Faulkner's Fiction." In A84₂ (1982), pp. 182-203.

Relates the interdependent themes of family, region, and self to patterns of talking, voices, and listening in Faulkner's fiction; discusses the function of "remembering" and "community" in Faulkner's fiction within a context of Hannah Arendt's ideas.

AA234₂   Minter, David. "'Truths More Intense Than Knowledge': Notes on Faulkner and Creativity." In A84₂ (1982), pp. 245-65.

Considers both the conservative—or preserving—and the radically inventive parts of Faulkner's creative imagination, and the importance of the irrational, of talking and listening, and of repetition to his writing.

AA235₂   Brooks, Cleanth. "Faulkner's Ultimate Values." In A84₂ (1982), pp. 266-81.

Explores such themes as courage and honor, pity and love, as they are presented in the novels.

AA236₂   Singal, Daniel Joseph. "William Faulkner and the Discovery of Southern Evil." In *The War Within: From Victorian to Modernist Thought in the South, 1919-1945*. Chapel Hill: Univ. of North Carolina Press, 1982, pp. 153-97.

Covering novels up through *The Unvanquished*, Singal explores Faulkner's ambivalent response to and analysis of nineteenth-century Southern mythology.

AA237₂   Werner, Craig H. "The Dangers of Domination: Joyce, Faulkner, Wright." In *Paradoxical Resolutions: American Fiction since James Joyce*. Urbana: Univ. of Illinois Press, 1982, pp. 9-32.

Studies Joycean influences, especially on *Go Down, Moses* and *As I Lay Dying*.

AA238₂   Oriard, Michael. "The Ludic Vision of William Faulkner." *Modern Fiction Studies*, 28 (Summer 1982), 169-87.

Faulkner makes use of comic and tragic games in his fiction. Games
suggest the possibility of some personal freedom within a general social
determinism.

BB. *Biographical Articles*

BB70$_2$ Bonner, Thomas J. "William Faulkner and New Orleans: A
Retrospective." *Xavier University Studies*, 1 (1980–81),
85–92.

BB71$_2$ Mullener, Elizabeth. "A Romance Remembered: Joan
Williams and William Faulkner." *New Orleans Times-
Picayune*, September 19, 1982, Dixie, pp. 8–18.

BB72$_2$ Broughton, Panthea Reid. "An Interview with Meta
Carpenter Wilde." *Southern Review*, 18 (October 1982),
776–801.

Wilde comments on both her personal relationship with Faulkner and
on her book about their relationship.

EE. The Nobel Prize

EE5$_2$ Herndon, Jerry A. "Faulkner's Nobel Prize Address: A
Reading." *South Atlantic Quarterly*, 81 (Winter 1982),
94–104.

Studies the speech as a "definition of man."

GG. *Checklists and Bibliographical Materials*

GG69$_2$ Ono, Kiyoyuki. "The Unpublished Stories of William
Faulkner: A Bibliography." *William Faulkner: Materials,
Studies, and Criticism*, 2, No. 1 (July 1979), 75–91.

GG70$_2$ Millgate, Michael. "Faulkner Studies in the Nineteen-
Eighties." *William Faulkner: Materials, Studies, and
Criticism*, 3, No. 2 (April 1981), 1–8.

GG71$_2$ Merton, Thomas. "Faulkner and His Critics." In *The
Literary Essays of Thomas Merton*. Ed. Brother Patrick
Hart. New York: New Directions, 1981, pp. 117–23.

The book also includes E18$_2$, L19$_2$, and AA217.

GG72$_2$ Liska, Christine and Robert Liska. "Carl Petersen's Faulkner
Collection Illuminates the Extraordinary Life, Work."
Faulkner Newsletter, April–June 1982, pp. 1, 3.

GG73[2]   Petersen, Carl. "Petersen's Reading of *As I Lay Dying* Sparked Collection." *Faulkner Newsletter*, April–June 1982, pp. 1, 4.

GG74[2]   Polk, Noel. "Six Novels Are Published; Five Others Planned." *Faulkner Newsletter*, April–June 1982, pp. 1, 4.
          On the concordances.

GG75[2]   Meriwether, James B. "The Books of William Faulkner: A Revised Guide for Students and Scholars." *Mississippi Quarterly*, 35 (Summer 1982), 265–81.
          A revision of GG40[2].

GG76[2]   Brodsky, Louis Daniel, and Thomas M. Verich. *Saxe and Bill: The Commins-Faulkner Archive from the Brodsky Collection.* Oxford, Miss.: John Davis Williams Library, 1982.
          A 20-page catalogue of an exhibit.

GG77[2]   Gallert, Petra M. "German-Language Translations of Faulkner." *Mississippi Quarterly*, 35 (Summer 1982), 283–300.
          A checklist of translations.

GG78[2]   Cox, Dianne L., et al. "Faulkner 1981: A Survey of Research and Criticism." *Mississippi Quarterly*, 35 (Summer 1982), 313–36.

—   Brodsky, Louis D., and Robert W. Hamblin. *Faulkner: A Comprehensive Guide to the Brodsky Collection. Volume One: The Biobibliography* (A81[2]; 1982).

GG79[2]   Hayashi, Fumiyo, and Shizue Uchida. "William Faulkner: An Annotated Checklist of Research and Criticism in Japan: VII." *William Faulkner: Materials, Studies, and Criticism*, 4, No. 2 (July 1982), 95–105.
          An annotated checklist of Japanese criticism, this is the seventh in a series of such lists. The others appeared in October 1978, June 1979, December 1979, July 1980, April 1981, and December 1981.

GG80[2]   Zender, Karl F. "Faulkner." In *American Literary Scholarship: An Annual/1980.* Ed. J. A. Robbins. Durham: Duke Univ. Press, 1982, pp. 143–72.

GG81[2]   Boozer, William. "Rowan Oak Papers Are Back Home." *Faulkner Newsletter*, October–December 1982, pp. 1–2.

GG82₂ Brodsky, Louis Daniel. "On Collecting William Faulkner: Snowball Effects." *Faulkner Newsletter*, October–December 1982, pp. 1–2, 4.

GG83₂ Hamblin, Robert W. "L. D. Brodsky Faulkner Collection Rich in Signed, Original Source Materials." *Faulkner Newsletter*, October–December 1982, pp. 1, 3–4.

V. Other Materials

HH. *Reviews of Books about Faulkner*

HH327₂ Fujihira, Ikuko. Review. *William Faulkner: Materials, Studies, and Criticism*, 2, No. 2 (December 1979), 84–91. (Kinney, Kerr, Stonum)

HH328₂ O'Faolain, Sean. "Hate, Greed, Lust and Doom." *London Review of Books*, April 16, 1981, pp. 16–17. (Minter)

HH329₂ Carothers, James B. Review. *Notes on Mississippi Writers*, 14, No. 1 (1982), 39–44. (Polk)

HH330₂ Broughton, Panthea R. Review. *American Literature*, 54 (March 1982), 131–34. (Minter)

HH331₂ Watkins, Floyd C. Review. *American Literature*, 54 (March 1982), 134–35. (Polk)

HH332₂ Hagopian, John V. Review. *American Literature*, 54 (March 1982), 135–37. (Jenkins)

HH333₂ Simpson, Lewis P. "Faulkner and the Comedy of History." *Michigan Quarterly Review*, 21 (Spring 1982), 365–73. (Powers, also *Uncollected Stories*)

HH334₂ Ragan, David Paul. Review. *Mississippi Quarterly*, 35 (Summer 1982), 337–42. (Carvel Collins' "Biographical Background for Faulkner's Helen" in *Helen: A Courtship*)

HH335₂ Ruppersburg, Hugh M. Review. *Mississippi Quarterly*, 35 (Summer 1982), 342–47. (Jenkins)

HH336₂ Ono, Kiyoyuki. Review. *William Faulkner: Materials, Studies, and Criticism*, 4, No. 2 (July 1982), 79–82. (Jenkins)

HH337₂ Koyama, Toshio. Review. *William Faulkner: Materials, Studies, and Criticism*, 4, No. 2 (July 1982), 83–94. (Polk)

HH338₂   Simpson, Lewis P. Review. *American Literature*, 54 (December 1982), 617–18. (Strandberg)

II. *Magazine and Journal Articles*

II81₂   Chaze, William L. "A Sentimental Journey to Faulkner Country." *U.S. News & World Report*, June 14, 1982, pp. 68–69.

JJ. *Newspaper Articles*

JJ27₂   Mulligan, Hugh A. "A Happy Boswell." *Houston Post*, January 31, 1982, p. AA15.
      On Joseph Blotner and Faulkner.

JJ28₂   Margolis, Jon. "Oxford Endured Despite the Changes, and Faulkner Would Be Pleased." *Chicago Tribune*, March 15, 1982, Sec. 3, p. 3.

JJ29₂   Keel, Pinckney. " 'Ole Bill' Faulkner revisited recaptures editor's memories." *Nashville Banner*, June 24, 1982, p. A19.
      Memory of a visit to Rowan Oak in 1951.

JJ30₂   Donahue, Michael. "The Day Faulkner Died." *Memphis Press-Scimitar*, July 13, 1982, pp. B1–B2.
      Recollections by Dean Faulkner Wells, William Styron, Shelby Foote, Joseph Blotner, and William McNeil Reed.

JJ31₂   Jaynes, Gregory. "Faithful pay—their homage to Faulkner." *New York Times*, August 14, 1982, pp. F1, F5.

JJ32₂   Blades, John. "FaulknerFest stirs up sound, fury and academic horsefeathers." *Chicago Tribune*, September 12, 1982, Bookworld, pp. 1–2.

KK. *Books*

KK70₂   Jones, Jon Griffin, ed. *Mississippi Writers Talking*. Jackson: Univ. Press of Mississippi, 1982.

KK71₂   Rubin, Louis D., Jr. *A Gallery of Southerners*. Baton Rouge: Louisiana State Univ. Press, 1982.
      Includes AA96₂ and other comments on Faulkner.

LL. *Doctoral Dissertations*

LL316₂   Anderson, Helen S. "The Isolated Intellectual in the Fiction of William Faulkner and Marcel Proust: An Analysis of Failure and Success in Transcendence of Time." Rice 1982. *DAI* 43:805A.

LL317₂   Belcamino, Gregory R. "Stylistic Decorum and Character in Faulkner's Snopes Trilogy." UCLA 1982. *DAI* 43:1970A.

LL318₂   Feldstein, Richard. "The Dispossession of Personae Non Gratae: A Study of Faulkner's Relation to the *Other*." SUNY-Buffalo 1982. *DAI* 43:1970A.

LL319₂   Foster, Dennis A. "Confession and Complicity in Narrative Structure: Hawthorne, Faulkner, and Beckett." California-Irvine 1982. *DAI* 43:808A.

LL320₂   Gissendanner, John M. "The 'Nether Channel': A Study of Faulkner's Black Characters." California-San Diego 1982. *DAI* 43:802A.

LL321₂   Henriques, Eunice R. "Elements of the Short Story Converging on Viewpoint: Katherine Mansfield, William Faulkner, Guimaraes Rosa and Clarence Lispector." North Carolina 1982. *DAI* 43:1561A.

LL322₂   Imbleau, Henry R. "Failed Manhood: Sexual Cowardice in William Faulkner." SUNY-Binghamton 1982. *DAI* 42:3600A.

LL323₂   Magee, Rosemary M. "'Ambassador of God': The Preacher in Twentieth-Century Southern Fiction." Emory 1982. *DAI* 43:1973A.

LL324₂   Rukas, Nijole M. "A Comparison of Faulkner's and Rulfo's Treatment of the Interplay Between Reality and Illusion in *Absalom, Absalom!* and *Pedro Paramo*." Arizona 1982. *DAI* 43:818A.

LL325₂   Singleton, Carl S. "Gavin Stevens: Faulkner's 'Good Man.'" Loyola 1982. *DAI* 43:804A.

LL326₂   Veisland, Jorgen S. "Kierkegaard and the Dialectics of Modernism." Washington 1982. *DAI* 42:5113. Discusses *As I Lay Dying*.

Commentary in Other Languages

1966

Bleikasten, André. "Faulkner et le nouveau roman." *Les Langues Modernes*, 60 (1966), 422–32.

Lyra, Franciszek. *William Faulkner*. Warsaw: Wiedza Powszechna, 1966.

Materassi, Mario. "Le prime prose narrative di William Faulkner." *Paragone*, 17, No. 196 (1966), pp. 74–92.

Peper, Jürgen. *Bewusstseinslagen des Erzählens und erzählte Wirklichkeiten*. Leiden: E. J. Brill, 1966.

A study of the nineteenth- and twentieth-century American novel, with special attention to Faulkner.

1967

Bleikasten, André. "L'espace dans *Lumière d'août*." *Bulletin de la Faculté des Lettres de Strasbourg*, 46 (1967), 406–20.

Materassi, Mario. "Il primo grande romanzo di Faulkner: *The Sound and the Fury*." *Convivium*, 35 (1967), 303–24.

Nagy, Péter. "William Faulkner." *Kritika* [Budapest], 5, No. 8 (1967), 10–18.

Wolpers, Theodor. "Formen mythisierenden Erzählens in der modernen Prosa: Joseph Conrad im Vergleich mit Joyce, Lawrence und Faulkner." In *Lebende Antike: Symposium für Rudolf Sühnel*. Ed. H. Meller and H.-J. Zimmermann. Berlin: E. Schmidt, 1967, pp. 397–422.

1968

Jäger, Dietrich. "Der 'verheimlichte Raum' in Faulkners 'A Rose for Emily' und Brittings 'Der Schneckenweg.'" *Literatur in Wissenschaft und Unterricht*, 1 (1968), 108–16.

Lanati, Barbara. "Il primo Faulkner: *As I Lay Dying*." *Sigma*, 19 (1968), 83–119.

Nicolaisen, Peter. "Hemingways 'My Old Man' und Faulkners 'Barn Burning': Ein Vergleich." In *Amerikanische Erzählungen von Hawthorne bis Salinger: Interpretationen*. Ed. P. G. Buchloh. *Kieler Beiträge zur Anglistik und Americanistik* [Neumünster], 6 (1968), 187–223.

Riese, Utz. "Das Dilemma eines dritten Weges: William Faulkners widersprüchlicher Humanismus." *Zeitschrift für Anglistik und Amerikanistik* [East Berlin], 16 (1968), 138–55, 257–73.

Skou-Hansen, Tage. "William Faulkner." In *Fremmede digtere i det 20 Århundrede.* Ed. S. M. Kristensen. Vol. II. Copenhagen: G. E. C. Gad, 1968, pp. 279–95.

Straumann, Heinrich. *William Faulkner.* Frankfurt am Main: Athenaum Verlag, 1968.

Szpotański, Zenon. "Slowacki a Faulkner." *Znak* [Krakow], 20, No. 4 (1968), 495–501.

Weisgerber, Jean. *Faulkner et Dostoievski: Confluences et Influences.* Brussels: Presses Universitaires de Bruxelles, 1968.

Yoshizaki, Yasuhiro. "The Unified Plot of *Light in August.*" *Maekawa Shunichi Kyōju Kanreki Kinen-ronbunshū.* Tokyo: Eihōsha, 1968, pp. 217–28. In Japanese.

1969

Akasofu, Tetsuji. *Kotoba to Fudo—"Shin-Hihyoka" no Faulkner ron o meguru Hihyo no Mondai.* Tokyo: Kaibunsha, 1969.

Alexandrescu, Sorin. *William Faulkner.* Bucharest: Editura Pentru Literatura Universală, 1969.

Kostjakov, V. *Trilogija Uil'jama Folknera.* Saratov: Saratovskogo universiteta, 1969.

1970

Anastas'ev, N. "Folkner: Put'k 'Derevuske.'" *Voprosy Literatury,* 14, No. 9 (1970), 122–41.

Backvis, Claude. "Faulkner versus Dostoevsky." *Revue de l'Université Libre de Bruxelles,* 1970–73, pp. 205–32.

Călinescu, Matei. "La o lectură a 'Cătunului' lui W. Faulkner." *Eseuri despre literatura modernă.* Bucharest: Editura Eminescu, 1970, pp. 314–20.

Coindreau, Maurice. "Faulkner, le moraliste." *Quinzaine Littèraire,* May 1, 1970, pp. 6–7.

Djankov, Krastan. "Zamislenijat genij ot Joknapatofa." *Uiljam Fornăr*. Plovdiv. H. G. Danov, 1970, pp. 7–29. "The meditative genius of Yoknapatawpha"—on the short stories. Ricks #6600.

Madeya, Ulrike. "Interpretationen zu William Faulkners 'The Bear': Das Bild des Helden und die Konstellation der Charaktere." *Literatur in Wissenschaft und Unterricht*, 3 (1970), 45–60.

Paliyevsky, Pyotr. *Uil'yam Folkner*. Moscow: Vysšhaya shkola, 1970.

1971

Akasofu, Tetsuji. "Faulkner *Hachigatsu no Hikari*." *Eigo Seinen*, 117 (1971), 306–07. On *Light in August*.

Bungert, Hans. *William Faulkner und die humoristische Tradition des amerikanischen Sudens*. Heidelberg: Carl Winter Universitäts Verlag, 1971.

Hanamoto, Kingo. *Faulkner Kenkyu: Shudai no Tsuikyu*. Vol. I. Tokyo: Manabu Shobo, 1971.

Landor, Mikhail. "Tvorčheskii metod Folknera v stanovlenii." *Voprosy Literatury*, 15, No. 10 (1971), 110–35. On the development of Faulkner's creative method.

Yoshida, Hiroshige. "Comments on *The Bear* and *The Old Man and the Sea*." *Hiroshima Studies in English Language and Literature*, 18 (1971), 69–77. In Japanese.

1972

Aínsa, Fernando. "En el santuario de William Faulkner." *Cuadernos Hispanoamericanos* [Madrid], 269 (1972), 232–43.

Alexandrescu, Sorin. "Unele aspecte ale relatiilor lui W. Faulkner cu literatura europeană." Diss. Univ. of Bucharest 1972. Faulkner's relationship to European literature.

Comsa, Ioan. "Faulkner: Un inovator al artei narative." *Revista Bibliotecilor*, 25, No. 9 (1972), 456–57.

Lopez, Guido. "Faulkner e i cavalli." In *I verdi i viola e gli arancioni*. Milan: Mondadori, 1972, pp. 181–92.

Ostendorf, Berndt. "Faulkner: *Absalom, Absalom!*" In *Der amerikanische Roman: Von den Anfängen bis zur Gegenwart*. Ed. H. Lang. Düsseldorf: August Bagel, 1972, pp. 249–75.

Ulich, Michaela. *Perspektive und Erzählstruktur in William Faulkners Romanen.* Heidelberg: Carl Winter, 1972.

Zindel, Edith. *William Faulkner in den deutschspraigen Ländern Europas: Untersuchungen zur Aufnahme seiner Werke nach 1945.* Hamburg: Hartmut Lüdke Verlag, 1972.

1973

Bleikasten, André. "Noces noires, noces blanches: Le jeu du désir et de la mort dans le monologue de Quentin Compson (*The Sound and the Fury*)." *Recherches Anglaises et Américaines*, 6 (1973), 142–69.

Chen, Yüan-yin. "Heng-ri yu Wei-erh-po-ssu chih Chien—Lun Hai-ming-wei yü Fu-ko-na." *Tamkang Journal* [Taiwan], 11 (1973), 217–24. Compares Faulkner with Hemingway.

Delay, Florence, and Jacqueline de Labriolle. "Márquez est-il le Faulkner colombien?" *Revue de Littérature Comparée*, 47 (1973), 88–123.

Egor, Gvozden. "Roman kao moralitet: Pasija po Foknerv." *Književnost* [Belgrade], 56 (1973), 342–51.

Fernández, Magali. "Análisis comparativo de las obras de Agustín Yáñez y William Faulkner (especialmente de sus novelas *Al filo del agua* y *As I Lay Dying*)." In *Homenaje a Agustín Yáñez: Variaciones en torno a su obra.* Ed. H. F. Giacoman. Long Island City: Anaya-Las Américas, 1973, pp. 295–320.

Günter, Bernd. "William Faulkners *Dry September*." *Die Neueren Sprachen*, 72 (1973), 607–16.

Harzic, Jean. *Faulkner.* Paris: Bordas, 1973.

Ohashi, Kenzaburo, ed. *Gendai Sakka Ron—William Faulkner.* Tokyo: Hayakawa Shobo, 1973.

Pavilionienė, Aušrinė. "Laikas ir V. Folknerio žmogus." *Pergalė*, 3 (1973), 132–37.

Pavilionienė, Marija-Aušrinė. "Apie amerikiečiu romantikų įtaką V. Folknerio kūrybai." *Literatūra*, 15, No. 3 (1973), 95–108.

Rouberol, Jean. "Les Indiens dans l'oeuvre de Faulkner." *Études Anglaises*, 26 (1973), 54–58.

Ruiz Ruiz, José M. "El sentido de la vida y de la muerte en *The Sound and the Fury*, de W. Faulkner." *Filología Moderna*, 13 (1973), 117–38.

Weisgerber, Jean. "Metamorphoses du réalisme: Dostoevskij et Faulkner." *Russian Literature*, 4 (1973), 37–50.

1974

Bernackaja, V. "Raspavšijsja projadok (O pisatel'skoj individual'nosti Folknera)." *Voprosy Literatury*, 18, No. 3 (1974), 85–100.

Brumm, Ursula. "Geschichte als Geschen und Erfahrung: Eine Analyse von William Faulkners *Absalom, Absalom!*" In *Der amerikanische Roman im 19. und 20. Jahrhundert*. Ed. E. Lohner. Berlin: Erich Schmidt, 1974, pp. 258–74.

Brunel, Elisabeth. "*Was*." In Sachs, *Le blanc* . . . (1974), pp. 135–42.

Caro-Radenez, Joëlle, and Philippe Radenez. "*The Sound and the Fury*." In Sachs, *Le blanc* . . . (1974), pp. 277–91.

Gruffaz-Besingue, Catherine, and Christine Le Du. "*The Old People*." In Sachs, *Le blanc* . . . (1974), pp. 167–81.

Lacroix, Annie. "*Delta Autumn*." In Sachs, *Le blanc* . . . (1974), pp. 199–210.

Laurent, Hélène. "*Pantaloon in Black*." In Sachs, *Le blanc* . . . (1974), pp. 157–66.

Laverdine, Joëlle. "*Go Down, Moses*." In Sachs, *Le blanc* . . . (1974), pp. 211–29.

Mathiex, Marie-Hélène. "Les négations et le problème racial dans *Go Down, Moses*." In Sachs, *Le blanc* . . . (1974), pp. 230–76.

Meindl, Dieter. *Bewusstsein als Schicksal: Zu Struktur und Entwicklung von Faulkners Generationenromanen*. Stuttgart: Metzler, 1974.

Pavilionienė, Marija-Aušrinė. "Malen'kij čelovek v tvorčestve V. Folknera." *Literatūra*, 16, No. 3 (1974), 75–88.

Peraile, Estaban and Lorenzo Peraile. "Una lectura de *Los invictos*." *Cuadernos Hispanoamericanos* [Madrid], 291 (1974), 692–701.

Roberts, Ann, with the assistance of Daliah Singer. "*The Bear*." In Sachs, *Le blanc* . . . (1974), pp. 182–98.

Robin, Régine. "*Absalom, Absalom!*" In Sachs, *Le blanc* . . . (1974), pp. 67–129.

Rougé, Robert. *L'Inquiétude religieuse dans le roman américain moderne.* Paris: Librairie C. Klincksieck, 1974.

Sachs, Viola, ed. *Le blanc et le noir chez Melville et Faulkner.* Paris: Mouton, 1974.

Suard, Jean-Marc, with the assistance of Zeynab Hafez. "*The Fire and the Hearth.*" In Sachs, *Le blanc* . . . (1974), pp. 143–56.

Vargas Saavedra, Luis. "La afinidad de Onetti a Faulkner." *Cuadernos Hispanoamericanos* [Madrid], 292–94 (1974), 257–65.

1975

Amette, Jacques-Pierre. "Le premier grand romancier de l'inconscient." *Sud*, 14 (1975), 7–11.

Kulin, Katalin. "Razones y características de la influencia de Faulkner en la ficción latinoamericana moderna." *Sin Nombre*, 6, No. 1 (1975), 20–36.

Ludmer, Josefina. "Onetti: 'La novia (carta) robada (a Faulkner).'" *Hispamerica*, 9 (1975), 3–19.

Magnan, Jean-Marie. "Inceste et mélange des sangs dans l'oeuvre de William Faulkner." *Sud*, 14 (1975), 150–84.

Pitavy, François. "Quentin Compson, ou le regard du poète." *Sud*, 14 (1975), 62–80.

Zmora, Zvi. "Hirhurim al-'Vered le-Emily.'" *Shdemot*, 56 (1975), 150–52.

1976

Anastas'ev, N. *Folkner.* Moscow: Xudozestvennaja, 1976.

Barrault, Jean-Louis. "Le Roman adapté au théâtre." *Cahiers de la Compagnie Madeleine Renaud-Jean Louis Barrault*, 91 (1976), 27–58.

Bleikasten, André. "Modernité de Faulkner." *Delta* [Montpellier], 3 (1976), 155–72.

Bleikasten, André. "Pylon, ou l'enfer des signes." *Études Anglaises*, 29, No. 3 (1976), 437–47.

Bleikasten, André. "*The Sound and the Fury*: Du Désir à l'Oeuvre." *Recherches Anglaises et Américaines*, 9 (1976), 18–34.

Brumm, Ursula. "William Faulkner, 'Was' (1942)." In *Die amerikanische Short Story der Gegenwart: Interpretationen*. Ed. P. Freese. Berlin: Schmidt, 1976, pp. 30–38.

Brushwood, John. "Importancia de Faulkner en la novela latino-americano." *Letras Nacionales*, 31 (August-September 1976), 7–14.

Eror, Gvozden. "Folkner u našoj kritici." *Uporedna istraživanja*. Ed. N. Stipčević. Vol. I. Belgrade: Inst. za književnost i umetnost, 1976, pp. 709–68.

Fabre, Michel. "Bayonne ou le Yoknapatawpha d'Ernest Gaines." *Recherches Anglaises et Américaines*, 9 (1976), 208–22.

Gresset, Michel. "Epithèse." *Delta* [Montpellier], 3 (1976), 173–91.

Gresset, Michel. "Faulkner, 1935." *Études Anglaises*, 29, No. 3 (1976), 448–55.

Gresset, Michel. "Homofaunie." *Delta* [Montpellier], 3 (1976), 85–93. On *The Hamlet*.

Gresset, Michel. "Théorème." *Recherches Anglaises et Américaines*, 9 (1976), 73–94. On *Pylon*.

Lang, Béatrice. "Comparison de *Requiem for a Nun* et *A Fable*." *Recherches Anglaises et Américaines*, 9 (1976), 57–72.

Ljubojević, Mirko. "Osciliranje perspektiva i foknerovska istina u *Buci i besu*." *Izraz*, 40, No. 5 (1976), 791–800. On *The Sound and the Fury*.

Müller, Christopher. "Zu William Faulkners Roman *The Reivers*." *Zeitschrift für Anglistik und Amerikanistik* [East Berlin], 24 (1976), 258–64.

Okaniwa, Noboru. *Faulkner: Tsurusareta Ningen no Yume*. Tokyo: Chikuma Shobo, 1976.

Orfali, Ingrid. "Silences de *Tandis que j'agonise*. *Delta* [Montpellier], 3 (1976), 19–21.

Pitavy, François L. "Faulkner poète." *Études Anglaises*, 29, No. 3 (1976), 456–67.

Pitavy, François L. "Le Reporter: Tentation et dérision de l'écriture." *Recherches Anglaises et Américaines*, 9 (1976), 95–108.

Pruvot, Monique. "Laverne." *Recherches Anglaises et Américaines*, 9 (1976), 108–23. On *Pylon*.

Pruvot, Monique. "Le Sacre de la vache." *Delta* [Montpellier], 3 (1976), 105–23.

Rouberol, Jean. "Faulkner et l'histoire." *Recherches Anglaises et Américaines*, 9 (1976), 7–17.

Savurenok, A. K. "Folkner i Oldos Xaksliik voprosu o kompoziaii romana Folknera Derevuška." In *Svavnitel'noe izučenie literatur: Sbornik statej k 80-letiju akademika M. P. Alekseeva*. Ed. E. A. Smirnova. Leningrad: Nauka, 1976, pp. 434–40.

Scherer, Olga. "La Contestation du jugement sur pièces chez Dostoievski et Faulkner." *Delta* [Montpellier], 3 (1976), 47–61.

Silhol, Robert. "Interrogation sur la constitution de *The Wild Palms*." *Recherches Anglaises et Américaines*, 9 (1976), 35–36.

Solery, Marc. "'Black Music' ou la métamorphose du regard." *Delta* [Montpellier], 3 (1976), 35–43.

Steinmetz-Schünemann, H. *Die Bedeutung der Zeit in den Romanen von Marguerite Duras: Unter besonderer Berücksichtigung des Einflusses von Faulkner und Hemingway*. Amsterdam: Rodopi, 1976.

Takigawa, Motoo. "The Relationship between God and Human Beings in American Literature." *Studies in English Literature*, 53 (1976), 59–73. In Japanese.

1977

Akasofu, Tetsuji. "Faulkner: Benjy no Chikaku." In *America Shosetsu no Tenkai*. Ed. K. Takamura and I. Iwamoto. Tokyo: Shohakusha, 1977, pp. 233–43.

Gribanov, B. "'Ja otkazyvajus' prinjat' konec čeloveka: Vil'jam Folkner o literature i o sebe." *Oktjabr'*, 3 (1977), 195–203.

Mathieu-Higginbotham, Corina. "Faulkner y Onetti: Una visión de la realidad a través de Jefferson y Santa María." *Hispanófila*, 61 (1977), 51–60.

Miyamoto, Yokichi. *America Shosetsu wo Yomy*. Tokyo: Shueisha, 1977.

Morita, Takashi. "Faulkner: 'Kuyashisa' Kokufuku no Kiseki." In *America Shosetsu no Tenkai*. Ed. K. Takamura and I. Iwamoto. Tokyo: Shohakusha, 1977, pp. 244–55.

Ohashi, Kenzaburo. *Faulkner Kenkyu li Shiteki Genso kara Shosetsuteki Genso e*. Tokyo: Nanundo, 1977. Faulkner: From Poetic Vision to Fictional Vision.

Pavilioniené, Aušriné. "Pervaja mirovaja vojna i drama folknerovskogo čeloveka." *Literatūra*, 19, No. 3 (1977), 93–104.

Rakić, Bogdan. "Rodenje Yoknapatawphe: Naličja Faulknerove prošlosti." *Izraz*, 42, No. 5 (1977), 589–97.

Schaller, H.-W. "Kompositionsformen im Erzählwerk William Faulkners: Entwicklungs züge von der Kurzprosazum Roman." *Dissertation Abstracts International*, 37 (1977), 3192C.

Scherer, Olga. "Faulkner et le fratricide pour une théorie des titres dans la littérature." *Études Anglaises*, 30 (1977), 329–36.

Stecenko, E. A. "Xudožestvennoe vremja v romanax U. Folknera." *Filologičeskie Nauki*, 19, No. 4 (1977), 36–46.

Zileger, Heide. *Existentielles Erleben und kurzes Erzählen: Das Komische, Tragische, Groteske un Muthische in William Faulkners Short Stories*. Stuttgart: J. B. Metzlersche, 1977.

1978

Gribanov, Boris. *Faulkner*. Bratislava: Obzor, 1978.

Labriolle, Jacqueline de. "Faulkner adapté ou trahi?" *Mélanges de littérature: Du moyen Age au XXe siècle*. Paris: Ecole Normale Supérieure de Jeunes Filles, 1978, pp. 823–33.

Materassi, Mario. "Le due 'fabulae' di 'A Rose for Emily' di Faulkner." *Spicilegio Moderno*, 9 (1978), 76–82.

Mickevič, Boris. Introduction, "Kogda nastalmoj čas." *Neman* [U.S.S.R.], 27 (1978), 70–75. Introduction to Russian translation of *As I Lay Dying*.

Ohashi, Kenzaburo, and K. Harakawa, eds. *William Faulkner: Shiryo, Kenkyu and hihyo*. Vol. I. Tokyo: Nan'undo, 1978. Faulkner materials, studies, and criticism—some articles in Japanese, some in English.

Skei, Hans H. "Kunstnerens vilkår og kunstens krav: En analyse av William Faulkners novelle 'Carcassonne.'" *Edda*, 1978, pp. 207–12.

Takada, Kunio. *William Faulkner no Sekai.* Eibei Bungaku Ser. 8. Tokyo: Hyoronsha, 1978.

Topuride, Eteri. "Strukturaufbau des Romans *Absalom, Absalom!* von William Faulkner." In *Erzählte Welt: Studien zur Epik des 20. Jahrhunderts.* Ed. H. Brandt and N. Kakabadse. Berlin: Aufbau, 1978, pp. 337–58, 453–55.

Zmora, Zvi. "Ein Miklat min ha-Ra." *Shdemot*, 65 (1978), 64–69. On *Sanctuary.*

1979

Anastas'ev, N. "Preodolenie ili razvitie? Folkner v svete klassičeskogo opyta." *Voprosy Literatury*, 9 (1979), 86–125.

Arild, Lars, and Poul Behrendt. "Fortolkning III." *Kritik*, 49 (1979), 44–62. On "A Rose for Emily."

Aytür, Necla. "Güneyli Hemseriler William Faulkner ile Yasar Kemal." *Bati Edebiyatlari Arastirma Dergisi* [Turkey], 2 (1979), 69–78.

Bleikasten, André. "Les Maîtres fantômes, paternité et filiation dans les romans de Faulkner." *Revue Française d'Etudes Américaines*, 8 (1979), 157–81.

Bleikasten, André. "Pan et Pierrot, ou les premiers masques de Faulkner." *Revue de Littérature Comparée*, 53 (1979), 299–310.

Imbert, Henri-François. "Une Technique de la fascination: Faulkner (*Absalom, Absalom!*), Giono (*Un Roi sans divertissement*)." *Revue de Littérature Comparée*, 53 (1979), 323–37.

Labriolle, Jacqueline de. "De Faulkner á Claude Simon." *Revue de Littérature Comparée*, 53 (1979), 358–88.

Lettau, Ernst Ulrik. *Faulkners* Intruder in the Dust*: Argumente für eine kritische Würdigung.* Trier Studien zur Lit. 2. Frankfurt: Lang, 1979.

Lundbye, Vagn. "Fortolkning II." *Kritik*, 49 (1979), 36–43. On "A Rose for Emily."

Madsen, Svend Åge. "Fortolkning I." *Kritik*, 49 (1979), 28–35. On "A Rose for Emily."

Niess, Robert. "Flaubert et Faulkner: Deux allégories de la chasse." *Essais sur Flaubert.* Ed. C. Carlut. Paris: A. G. Nizet, 1979, pp. 363–80.

Ohashi, Kenzaburo, K. Harakawa, and K. Ono, eds. *William Faulkner: Shiryo, kenkyu, and hihyo.* Vol. II. Tokyo: Nanundo, 1979. Faulkner materials, studies, and criticism—some articles in Japanese, some in English.

Ohashi, Kenzaburo, ed. *Faulkner Kenkyu 2.* Tokyo: Nanundo, 1979. See 1977 entry above.

Robles, Mercedes M. "La presencia de *The Wild Palms* de William Faulkner en *Punta de rieles* de Manuel Rojas." *Revista Iberoamericana,* 45 (1979), 563–71.

Scherer, Olga. "Rosie Coldfield et Vanka Karamazov: Le Diminutif au service de l'ambivalence." *Revue de Littérature Comparée,* 53 (1979), 311–22.

Schütze, Ute. "Metatest und innerliterarische Übersetzung: Fallstudie an Faulkner und Hemingway." *Semiotische Versuche zu literarischen Strukturen (Studien zu Philologie und Semiotik II).* Studia Semiotica 4. Hildesheim: Olms, 1979, pp. 365–426.

Shapiro, Joël. "'Une histoire contée par un idiot . . .': (W. Faulkner et J. Rulfo)." *Revue de Littérature Comparée,* 53 (1979), 338–47.

Yoshida, Michiku. "Chinmoku no uchu no naka de: Faulkner's *As I Lay Dying* ni kansuru ichi kosatsu." *Oberon,* 18, No. 1 (1979), 68–83.

1980

Akiba, Yuji. "'Wash' Kara *Absalom, Absalom!* e: Quentin no Katari ni tsuite." In *Bungaku to America.* Ed. K. Ohashi et al. Tokyo: Nanundo, 1980, Vol. I, pp. 185–97.

Bleikasten, André. "L'Education de Temple Drake." *Recherches Anglaises et Américaines,* 13 (1980), 76–89.

Gresset, Michel. "Genèse et avatars de *Requiem for a Nun.*" *Recherches Anglaises et Américaines,* 13 (1980), 5–37.

Haraguchi, Ryo. "Norsi to Miburi: Moshikuwa *Hachigatsu no Hikari* no Joe Christmas ni tsuite." In *Bungaku to America.* Ed. K. Ohashi et al. Tokyo: Nanundo, 1980, Vol. II, pp. 266–82.

Harakawa, Kyoichi. "Josoho Kako Kanryokei no Sekai: Faulkner Kanken." In *Bungaku to America*. Ed. K. Ohashi et al. Tokyo: Nanundo, 1980, Vol. III, pp. 378–89.

Hayashi, Fumiyo. "Yasei no Shuro Shiron." In *Bungaku to America*. Ed. K. Ohashi et al. Tokyo: Nanundo, 1980, Vol. II, pp. 298–314. On *The Wild Palms*.

Honma, Taketoshi. "Shi no Toko ni Yokotawarite: Addi Bundren no 'Fukushu' no Imo o Megutte." In *Bungaku to America*. Ed. K. Ohashi et al. Tokyo: Nanundo, 1980, Vol. II, pp. 243–53.

Ishida, Toshiyuki. "Shi no Toko ni Yokotawarite Ron." In *Bungaku to America*. Ed. K. Ohashi et al. Tokyo: Nanundo, 1980, Vol. II, pp. 254–65.

Kajima, Shozo. "Kakuju ni yoru Heiko: Faulkner no Sosaku no Shisei ni tsuite." In *Bungaku to America*. Ed. K. Ohashi et al. Tokyo: Nanundo, 1980, Vol. III, pp. 352–77.

Kanashiki, Tsutomu. "Bin no Kubi to Heso no o to: *Absalom, Absalom!* no Jikan." In *Bungaku to America*. Ed. K. Ohashi et al. Tokyo: Nanundo, 1980, Vol. II, pp. 283–97.

Karatani, Masako. "Dark Lady no Yokue: Fitzgerald ni tsuite no Ichikosatsu." In *Bungaku to America*. Ed. K. Ohashi et al. Tokyo: Nanundo, 1980, Vol. II, pp. 198–212.

Morita, Mitsuru. "Shinka no tenkai-ten: *The Town*: Snopes sanbusaku-ron kara." *Eigo Seinen*, 126 (1980), 322–26.

Ogami, Masaji. "*Hibiki to Ikari* to T. S. Eliot: 'Quentin Section' no Imagery Chushin ni." In *Bungaku to America*. Ed. K. Ohashi et al. Tokyo: Nanundo, 1980, Vol. III, pp. 329–51.

Ohashi, Kenzaburo. "Saishu Kogi: Faulkner no Hoho." In *Bungaku to America*. Ed. K. Ohashi et al. Tokyo: Nanundo, 1980, Vol. I, pp. 266–80.

Ono, Kiyoyuki. "Kokoro to Yu Seiiki." In *Suga Yasuo, Ogoshi Kazugo: Ryokyoju Taikan Kinen Ronbunshu*. Kyoto: Apollonsha, 1980, pp. 915–28.

Pothier, Jacques. "Naissance d'un sujet collectif: Jefferson." *Recherches Anglaises et Américaines*, 13 (1980), 48–63. On *Requiem for a Nun*.

Pruvot, Monique. "La Prison de Jefferson et Cecilia, musicienne du silence dans *Requiem for a Nun* de Faulkner." *Études Anglaises*, 33 (1980), 414–30.

Rouberol, Jean. "Le Sud dans les prologues de *Requiem for a Nun*: La vision et la voix." *Recherches Anglaises et Américaines*, 13 (1980), 38–47.

Saeki, Yasuki. "Fukuzaisuru Nendaiki: *Hibiki to Ikari* Dokusho no Kokoromi." In *Bungaku to America*. Ed. K. Ohashi et al. Tokyo: Nanundo, 1980, Vol. I, pp. 144–59. On *The Sound and the Fury*.

Takaya, Keiichiro. "Faulkner no 'Kuma' Dai 5 Sho no Imisru Mono." In *Suga Yasuo, Ogoshi Kazugo: Ryokyoju Taikan Kinen Ronbonshu*. Kyoto: Apollonsha, 1980, pp. 903–14. On "The Bear."

Terasawa, Mizuho. "Shuen to Fumetsu." In *Bungaku to America*. Ed. K. Ohashi et al. Tokyo: Nanundo, 1980, Vol. I, pp. 170–84.

Uchida, Shizue. "Benjy no Chihei." In *Bungaku to America*. Ed. K. Ohashi et al. Tokyo: Nanundo, 1980, Vol. I, pp.160–69.

Zlobin, G. "Osvoenie Folknera." *Novyj Mir*, 8 (1980), 243–47.

1981

Murakami, Yosuke. "Kenkyu no Genkyo to Kadai: Faulkner." *Eigo Seinen*, 127 (1981), 479–80.

Nakajima, Tokiya, and Jiro Eda. *William Faulkner to znin no Onna*. Tokyo: Oshisha, 1981.

Nicolaisen, Peter. *William Faulkner in Selbstzeugnissen und Bilddokumenten*. Hamburg: Rowohlt, 1981.

Ohashi, Kenzaburo. "Faulkner to Nippon no Shosetsu." *Eigo Seinen*, 127 (1981), 75–77 ff.

1982

Gresset, Michel. *Faulkner ou la Fascination: I. Poetique du Regard*. Paris: Editions Klincksieck, 1982. First half of a two-volume study.

Errata in 1972 Checklist

These errata in *William Faulkner: An Annotated Checklist of Criticism* have been brought to my attention. Doubtless there are others. A number of omitted reviews and journalistic items have also been sent to me, but are not included here.

vii (5)   two] two hundred

11 (A24.3)   Univ.] College

12 (A28.2)   1964] 1965

12 (A33.1)   Jeliffe] Jelliffe

13 (A40.1)   Meriwether, James B., ed.] Meriwether, James B.

13 (A43.2)   1961. Revised, 1966.] 1961.

14 (A46.1)   Minter, David L.] Minter, David L., ed.

14 (A47.1)   Mottram, Eric] Mottram, Eric, ed.

14 (A48.5)   figures.] figures. Originally published in 1962 (see AA165).

16 (A63.3)   1964] revised and expanded, 1964

42 (E86.2)   February] March

44 (Hunt.1)   1964] 1965

47 (E119.1)   in] in Faulkner:

49 (E141)   The original review is untitled. The reprinted review (in A41) carries the indicated title.

55 (F34.1)   "The Hero] "Hero

58 (F54.1)   *The Waste Land:*] 'The Waste Land'—

69 (G78.2)   *Review*] *A Review*

70 (G84.1)   or] or,

70 (G85.1)   Frazer's] Frazier's

80 (H98.1)   Christmas:] Christmas,

81 (H101.2)   *Washington State College Studies*] *Wisconsin Studies in Contemporary Literature*

110 (J122.1)   'Waste Land':] 'Waste Land'

111 (J132.1)   "A Skeletal Outline of] "An Index to

112 (Hunt.1)   1964] 1965

114 (J149.2)   *Conrad*] *Conrad,*

148 (M88.1)   Section:] Section—

156 (N69.1)   William Faulkner's] Faulkner's

159 (N101.2)   1965] 1963

161 (Hunt.1)   1964] 1965

165 (N137.1)   Legacy] Legacy,

166 (N151.1)   Expiration] Expiation

181 (O151.1)   DeCillier] DeVillier

189 (P98.2)   Gambit.'"] Gambit' and Gavin Stevens."

244 (S207.1)   "Faulkner's Town: Mythology as History."] "Snopes
                  Revisited."

318 (X13.2)   Summer] Winter

318 (X16.2)   Spring] Winter

326 (X96.1)   'Female Principle':] 'Female' Principle:

336 (AA39.2)   June] September

363 (BB61.2–3)   113–156; included in *Faulkner* (1968), pp. 16–56.]
                  113–156.

372 (CC38.1)   Faulkner's Comedy] Faulkner: Comedy

375 (CC66.1)   Boswell, G. W.] Boswell, George W.

375 (CC66.1)   Music] Musical

375 (CC66.3)   30] 31

377 (CC81.2)   Works] Work

378 (DD2.2)   1931] 1951

378 (DD9.1)   Michael] Michel

393 (FF129.1)   Hobley] Hobby

394 (FF149.3)   alcoholic] alcoholic hospital

399 (GG36.2)   136–158.] 136–158. Revised and published as a pamphlet, *William Faulkner: A Check List*. Princeton: Princeton University Library, 1957.

498 (LL169.1)   Millner] Milliner

499 (LL193.1)   Raymond] Raymonde

512   Butterworth, Abner Keen, Jr., LL115]
                Butterworth, Abner Keen, Jr., LL155

516   DeCillier] DeVillier

526   Hyde, Monique Nathan] Hyde, Monique Raymonde

527   Jeliffe] Jelliffe

534   Millner] Milliner

Index to Critics

The subscript 2 has been deleted from code numbers in the index. Items in the "Additional Items" section are designated by the letter "a," as in AA216a. Items in the "Commentary in Other Languages" section are not indexed.